DAVID WATKINS: AN AUTOBIOGRAPHY

David Watkins
an autobiography

David Watkins
Edited by David Parry-Jones

CASSELL
LONDON

CASSELL LTD.
35 Red Lion Square, London WC1R 4SG
and at Sydney, Auckland, Toronto, Johannesburg,
an affiliate of
Macmillan Publishing Co., Inc.,
New York.

First published 1980

ISBN 0 304 30692 4

Typeset by Inforum Ltd, Portsmouth
Printed in Great Britain by
Richard Clay (The Chaucer Press) Ltd.
Bungay, Suffolk

Contents

Illustrations

Following page 122

CHAPTER 1

Watkins Country

On the side of a valley a few miles north of Merthyr Tydfil, where I now work, there is a small, peaceful graveyard. It is dominated by a huge slate slab on which are carved the words, 'God forgive me'.

Beneath it are the remains of Robert Crawshay, one of the best known of that ruthless group of men who turned what we call the 'heads of the valleys' area of Gwent and Glamorgan into a nineteenth-century industrial metropolis by the exploitation of its mineral wealth. Coal and iron were in great demand, and poured out of townships like Merthyr itself, Dowlais, Ebbw Vale, Rhymney, Blaenavon and Nantyglo.

I can remember being taught at school about tycoons like Crawshay, Guest, Homfray and the others. In this part of Wales you can still see the magnificent homes that they built for themselves, where they lived like lords. They dined splendidly, they dressed their womenfolk in silks and satins, they amassed costly works of art. And they also kept bands of strong-arm men to protect them from the anger and frustration of those who sweated in their mines and at their furnaces.

For while they made their money these men were also responsible for what Alexander Cordell has called the 'rape of the fair country.' They exploited its people. They threw up row upon row of humble, dreary cottages for the immigrant workers. And they dirtied the landscape with slag heaps which are only today being cleared away.

The full extent of Crawshay's oppression may not be known until the year 2000. I hope I am still around then, when a great black coffer stuffed with archive documents is due to be opened at Cyfarthfa Castle, his former family seat. But his epitaph was surely well chosen.

As one born and bred in north Monmouthshire, or Gwent as it is called today, I must consider myself a product of the system operated by such men, and of that period in Welsh history. Yet when I look back on my own career it often strikes me that the wheel of fortune has turned quite a few times for a man whose immediate forebears were simple colliers.

The only exploitation of which I have been guilty is to cash in on folks' eagerness to see me display sporting skill. Yet, as I now put my days of playing rugby football behind me, I consider that my life-style is one which gives me at least as much pleasure and delight as any ironmaster or coal king could have taken in his.

My property outside Newport is no Cyfarthfa Castle, yet it combines functional qualities with a quiet taste and graciousness that owes much to the influence of my wife, Jane. It is our own, all paid for. We can afford to lay out £1000 a year on school fees for our small son, Nicholas, who has thus received a fine educational grounding since the age of four; and we intend, too, that our young daughter, Victoria, will benefit from the same experience.

We have chosen furniture that is comfortable and elegant, and pictures to please the eye. Our dining table is laid with good china and cutlery — and nowadays I know how to use it, whereas when I first attended a post-match banquet at seventeen I had to watch my elders out of the corner of my eye to see which knife I should use for cutting what! If Jane does not feel like cooking there is no need to wonder if we can afford to eat out. Off we go to a restaurant in one of our two cars. I take professional pride, too, from my executive position with Forward Trust, the Midland Bank's lending arm.

Then there is my wardrobe: suits, shirts, dinner jackets, yes, but more important the sports kit, the trademark and tools of my other profession as a paid rugby player. At the height of my career I possessed enough pairs of boots to have lasted me another decade in the game! Like my Salford team-mates I used to receive two or three pairs a season from the Adidas and Patrick firms, each worth around £25, while on tour the commercial patronage was even more lavish: I remember being given no fewer than seven pairs by different companies when Great Britain played in Australia during 1974. Track suits came my way too, and in 1978 I counted eight of them tucked away in various parts of the house — only eight, because each year I gave away two or three to youngsters whom I considered to be deserving cases either through skill or special need. The many sports bags given by firms like Adidas, Bukta and Patricks could have contained the kit for a whole Salford XIII travelling to an away match.

Before you accuse me of blowing a rather loud personal trumpet, let me say that I list these details to establish the total contrast between my lot today and my childhood three decades ago. At the age of eight, a single jersey in Aston Villa colours, which I expect my mother had picked up cheaply at some bazaar or other, had to last me two or three years. A pair of boots, fashioned of stiff, poor quality leather with toe-caps like solid rock, had to survive at least two seasons, and it was a tragedy when they finally became too small. Friends who owned a ball were the Brian Cloughs of the neighbourhood, and their word was law on the rules of our knock-about soccer games — or even on the final score. If you crossed them in an argument they simply tucked the ball under their arm and went home. But looking back, these boys — Brian Edmonds, Norman Ball, and Alan Ball who serves on the committee for Blaina RFC — were good pals.

Blaina was home for me until my mid-twenties, a typical Welsh mining village, with its colliery, shops, schools, houses, roads and railway line all crammed into the space along the valley floor. Looming above our small lives were high, forbidding hills, disfigured here and there with tips. For the young David Watkins this was a natural habitat; but I recall how astonished the members of a Salford team I brought to nearby Abertillery in later years were to see the angular contours and dizzy slopes where their club-mate had grown up.

I was equally shocked when, in the late sixties, I first saw for myself the poverty-stricken environment of central Manchester, old Salford and Rochdale. However, I kept my own counsel, preferring not to judge from impressions, for the humble, cramped terraces of Britain's older industrial areas often disguise interiors that glitter like palaces. And when you see little old ladies scrubbing their front door-steps and the pavement beyond, you must bear in mind the pride that motivates folk who live in the most humble circumstances.

The house in which I was brought up fell into this modest category. It was a two-up, two-down terraced cottage, where my parents Doreen and Jack raised their three sons: myself, the eldest, born on 5 March 1942, Brian and Martin. I must declare straightaway what a remarkable woman my mother is, and was. The brains of the family, she dealt with any necessary correspondence and made our money stretch. She took the important decisions, and organized our summer outings and Christmas festivities. There was always a welcome for little friends my brothers and I took home.

My father did not loom large as an influence upon my early life, and I now realize that his sole preoccupation in those days was to make enough money to keep us alive. Not content with working long, exhausting hours in the nearby pit during the week, he spent much of Sunday on a newspaper round which earned him ten shillings and allowed him to provide a few small luxuries for the family.

Dad's premature retirement from mining was forced upon him by a succession of injuries and illnesses which sapped his energies, culminating in a serious blood disorder. However, the gravity of his mishaps was occasionally overestimated by his young offspring: once, on our return from school there was an ambulance outside the house and neighbours explained that our father had broken his arm in a pit accident. I feared that he would be without the broken half for the rest of his life!

Today I am appalled that a father should have been driven to such lengths to sustain his dependants, and that the coal industry at large should have shown so little concern for his health and well-being. But it all goes back to those early industrialists and their cavalier disregard for the labourers who hewed their coal and stoked their furnaces. Near our street, Club Row (in which had stood the Institute) there were Clock Row, where workers had to check in on time lest their wages should be docked, and Shop Row, once the location of the notorious company shops, monopolistic establishments where tokens issued in pay packets were exchanged for goods — at extortionate prices. History, had I but known it, was all around us — and reflected in the face of Jack Watkins.

My father was skilled with his hands, and in the shed to the rear of our home were fashioned many a toy garage, truck, or farmyard complete with trees and animals to delight us on a Christmas morning. But Christmas Day was usually one when as a family we went up to Moriah Cottage for turkey and plum pudding, a place which seemed to us like a stately home, boasting as it did a front and back garden. This was the residence of my grandfather Semi — short for Sempronius — Bridgeman, who had played first-class rugby as a wing for Newbridge. Because of my father's ceaseless round of work, he was the adult who above all influenced my boyhood days.

Injured in a colliery accident, 'Bampa', as we called him, became steward of the local Working Men's Institute, to which it was frequently my job to take him a cooked lunch prepared by my grandmother. I had to run at top speed so that the food would not get cold under its protective layer of greaseproof paper, but the plate had to be held steady so that the gravy would not spill over. 'You'll be a great sportsman one day,' Bampa would declare when his mid-day meal was delivered perfectly and at oven temperature.

In this way a link was formed between the old gentleman and his small grandson. Soon, for in old age he would rather watch soccer than rugby, he began taking me to big football matches down on the coast. We would go to Somerton Park to cheer Newport stars like Len Weare and Ray Wilcox in action or, better still, a bit further afield to watch Cardiff City, then a Division One side, in action at Ninian Park. Trevor Ford, Gerry Hitchens and Alf Sherwood became my heroes, and it was thrilling to see visiting stars like Jesse Pye, Bert Williams and Billy Wright of Wolves, or Leslie Compton and Welshmen Jack Kelsey and Derek Tapscott in Arsenal colours.

My grandfather had no compunction in packing me off to the terraces to watch while he socialized with friends in the grandstand. Soccer was a safe game to support in those far off days before the vandals took over. Not long ago I used to believe that, since soccer is essentially a non-contact game, fans could be excused for ridding themselves of a certain amount of tension and physical frustration on the terraces, while the better behaviour of rugby supporters stemmed from being able to observe violence on the pitch, thus getting it out of their system. Now, however, things seem to have gone beyond simple theories like that. The excesses of the football crowds puts one in mind of the jungle, and rugby men have caught the disease — I have seen the coaches of visiting teams stoned by Rugby League fans, and I have seen arrests after International Rugby Union games at Cardiff Arms Park.

Alcohol seems to me to deserve much blame, but when tame sociologists, and youngsters themselves, cite the boredom felt by the rising generation these days I have no sympathy at all. Especially when I recall how the kids of Club Row and its neighbourhood applied themselves to the business of devising entertainment and keeping themselves amused and out of trouble.

Close to my home there was a triangular piece of ground known as Joe's *twmp*, possibly the only available bit of flat land in the district. This became our soccer pitch for all seasons, on which the Club Row boys would play needle matches against neighbouring sides which drew, believe it or not, small groups of spectators, who would often include my grandfather. We marked it out scrupulously with sawdust filched from a nearby mill, and took the field up a steep flight of steps which allowed us to imagine that we were star professional sportsmen darting into the sunlight from luxurious underground dressing rooms. Joe's *twmp* was our Wembley Stadium.

Sometimes today the bubbling energy of small boys and their insatiable appetite for kicking a ball around an area of turf amazes me, until I recall the seven-days-a-week schedule of us Blaina nippers. Matches were endless, and bizarre results like 74–70 were frequently recorded. Our curiously-shaped arena compelled attackers and defenders alike to indulge in some odd manoeuvres, but I am certain that in my own case there was laid the foundation of that geographic awareness of distances, gaps and boundaries that the crack footballer in any code needs. It was primitive, but it was fun — and afterwards my mother provided hot water in tin baths for the troupe of scruffy small boys who would descend exhausted but still reluctant from the hill-side dusk.

This, then, was my small but happy world, bounded on the north by the vast, airy uplands of the Brecon Beacons, and to the south by veritable conurbations like Cardiff and Newport, which actually had three-storey buildings. Youngsters these days go to the ends of the earth for holidays or to play competitive sport. For me, a week at Porthcawl with a bucket and spade was like a journey to outer space. But Blaina was, and is, a close-knit community with virtues of loyalty and compassion which I now acknowledge and applaud. A few adventurous souls leave there as year succeeds year but, for every ten who go, a hundred stay steadfastly with the thick loam which holds their roots.

You will have noticed that rugby football has yet to take a bow in my story. Soccer, indeed, was still my whole life, rugby a mere distraction played once a week at West Side Junior Mixed School between teams of up to thirty bewildered small boys. Came the time, though, when after puzzling and disappointing my parents by failing the 11-plus examination I became a pupil at Glanyrafon Secondary Modern School.

Here I was to fall under the spell of a man called Russell Cooper. He was to introduce me to another code. And another world.

CHAPTER 2

Making the Grade

Picture, if you can, a day at Nantyglo Comprehensive School during the splendid summer of 1976. Carefully dressed in a sober, dark suit I am seated on stage in the assembly hall occupying the place of honour reserved for the principal guest at the annual prize-giving — and I am nearly as apprehensive as one becomes in front of a Wembley cup final crowd.

For besides the 800 pairs of eyes trying to peer at the man behind the tall piles of books and wondering what pearls of wisdom I will utter, there are around me local dignitaries, their shoulders drooping under heavy gold chains of office, serious-faced school governors, and members of staff who two decades earlier could frighten the life out of me with a snap of the fingers. Giants from my schoolboy past.

Reassurance comes only gradually, as it dawns on me that today there is genuine respect in the faces of men to whom I looked up as a youngster. My own achievements in life, such as they are, clearly command their esteem, and even the stern science master, George James, who regularly and accurately predicted that I would never win a Nobel Prize for physics, seems now to have become something of a fan.

Often, though, during the ceremony my mind drifts back to a day in 1956 when the then outstanding stand-off half of the day, Cliff Morgan, came up the valley to perform the task I am now undertaking. That event took place at Salem Chapel, for no hall worthy of the name was possessed by Glanyrafon Secondary Modern School, now enveloped by Nantyglo as a result of the introduction of comprehensive schooling. I remember having chosen for my prize a rugby book by someone called Haydn Tanner, whose name meant but little to me, imagining that this would please the great Mr Morgan. But afterwards I could not recall whether he had shown approval or not — all my powers of concentration were bent on making sure that my left hand was used to accept the prize, leaving the other one free to be shaken by our chief guest.

And I think my knees would have folded under me had anyone suggested that one day I should stand in Cliff's place. That afternoon he was a demi-god, a creature from a remote world peopled by heroes like R.H. Williams, Jeff Butterfield and Tom Reid, who had just drawn a Test series against the mighty South Africans.

He, in other words, was supreme in his chosen sport, while in 1956 I was just getting to grips with the business of playing at stand-off half. However, looking back I must applaud my early perseverance, for my introduction to rugby football had been accompanied by the most painful experience imaginable.

Educational facilities are so magnificent nowadays that it will be hard for younger readers to believe that my first properly organized game of rugby, a school trial, took place on an asphalt pitch, namely the playground at Glanyrafon, a bare 35 yards across. To prevent cramping the backs, forwards were not allowed to take part in support play — which was just as well, for anything remotely like a ruck would have necessitated a few skin grafts.

I was on a wing that day, and practically the first time I received the ball and set off for the line a violent tackle crashed me heavily to the ground, banging my head against the iron fencing surrounding the yard. In a daze I was helped away to the nearby clinic for several stitches, where I ruefully decided that this handling game was definitely not for me.

In a crisis a boy is lucky if he can look to someone for the restoring of nerve and an injection of fresh confidence. My mentor was a tall, powerfully built former flanker from London Welsh called Russell Cooper, and after the pain of my bump had receded a little it was he who lifted my sagging morale and warned against throwing in the towel after one setback.

'You've got the agility and the speed,' he told me, pointing out that the previous summer I had been *victor ludorum* in the school sports for my age-group. 'Ability like that must not be wasted. I need you in the school team.'

I admired Russell and was keen to win his praise. Here was a man of distinction whose advice and judgment must be soundly-based — after all, had he not once marked the great Cliff Morgan? So, telling myself that if he thought me promising that was OK by me, I made the decision that was to dictate the shape of my career and my whole life: I would give rugby another chance. Russell was delighted, before long moving his small protégé to scrum half, a position which he promised would give more opportunities of running with the ball.

Russell Cooper and I have kept in touch. He regularly sent telegrams to mark milestones in my progress such as a first Welsh cap, selection for the British Lions, an appearance in the Rugby League Cup Final and my elevation to the Great Britain side. I was glad to be able to return the compliment when he eventually got his headmastership at a big Gwent secondary school. But his main importance to the young David Watkins was as a builder of character. He bestowed on me the beginnings of that scale of values that every youngster needs, and helped me to surmount the first of all the many obstacles that confront one in life. I owe him a lot.

There were other heroes besides Russell, many of them known only through the radio and the vivid International match commentaries of the great 'Jeevers,' G.V. Wynne Jones. Bryn Meredith, Rex Willis, and Ken Jones were names that came alive in my imagination, as did those of Englishmen like Cannell and W.P.C. Davies and — especially — strange-sounding Irish ones such as Cecil Pedlow and Tony O'Reilly. My interest, too, was moving away from soccer, probably because of the terrific enthusiasm for rugby in our part of the world, where the Abertillery back row of Alun Pask, Haydn Morgan and John Lewis were celebrated like the Pontypool front row of a later decade. Once, a Newport and Wales back row forward, Geoff Whitson, came to Blaina for his wedding to a local girl, and I was among an excited bunch of small admirers who waited for hours outside the chapel in the fond but vain expectation that the groom and any International team-mates in the congregation would be dispensing autographs en route to the reception. What a hope!

In its modest way, however, my own career was beginning to pick up momentum. Before I was yet thirteen my speed and agility were compensating for a slight frame, enabling me to claim a regular place in the school XV, where I played with boys as much as three years my senior. This meant performing on a real pitch, that is to say a flattened tip near the school, roughly marked out for rugby and soccer. Its blades of grass were few, and on a wet day its surface was streaked with the black, porridge-like substance that we call slurry in South Wales. But at least it was spacious, and certainly not as hard to fall on as that flinty playground.

Anxious not to be dropped, I put everything into these games, which were often attended by a crowd of schoolmates including the girls, ever wildly enthusiastic. One day I stole away from a scrummage, accelerated past the opposing back row and raced diagonally for a really good solo try near the corner-flag. The cheers were deafening, and I savoured a first, very gratifying taste of glory. But far more important was the effect on Russell Cooper: 'Fly half is where you clearly belong,' he told me. The switch was made, and so I arrived in the position where I was to begin carving a reputation for myself.

Believe me, I stood tall! Small boys are so impressionable, and even from today's vantage point few things in retrospect have thrilled me quite as much as the feel of the soft school rugby jersey that I used to take home for airing on the night before a match. It felt like £100 clutched in the fist, and for the journey to the changing hut was wrapped carefully inside a towel tied with a piece of string, lovingly folded along with socks and shorts. Surreptitiously, too, I eyed the illuminated photographs of previous school teams that hung in the corridor outside our classrooms, looking forward with a glow of pride to the day when David Watkins's face would be up there with the rest.

It may seem a blindingly obvious thing to say at this point, but in their early teens the main thing determining whether boys will take to a game is the degree of enjoyment they get out of it — I underline this because both in Wales and New Zealand I have seen ten-year-olds put through coaching sessions which would have taxed and exhausted the patience and energies of a group of senior players. Russell Cooper certainly appreciated the danger of such an intensive approach, preferring to keep his charges on a loose rein. This probably made all of us even more receptive to the advice he had to give on the improvement of our skills. At his prompting, for instance, I strove to master the art of passing to my right, always a difficult direction for a right-handed person. He taught me the 'cross-over' movement of the feet at the moment of delivering a pass, designed to straighten a back-line and partially block would-be coverers in the other team.

Russell insisted, too, that I learned to kick with the left foot as well as the right. So I developed a method of practising on my own, consisting of kicking a rugby ball left-footed up the side of a steep tip not far from our house. The ball would bounce and wobble its way back down the slope, so that the manoeuvre could be repeated endlessly. Youngsters today watching the polished, effortless-looking skill of their heroes need to realize how much it owes to hours of single-minded, often solitary, practice.

Such application is quite consistent with enjoyment, for the higher their degree of accomplishment, the greater the pleasure sportsmen will obtain from their game. However, fun and enjoyment do not necessarily mean a totally carefree approach. In the Glanyrafon XV I rapidly reached a conclusion which I still hold today, namely that sport is all about victory. I see no point in not playing to win. A competitor is, by definition, out to prove himself the best, and to do so is the consummation. Afterwards celebration and relaxation can be indulged in with a clear conscience. It is even possible for an individual to play badly in a team that wins and yet enjoy the overall experience since the other players are happy at the outcome.

By the end of my schooldays, then, rugby football had

acquired a firm hold on me. In a way, as I have hinted, my career is the result of circumstances, since talented youngsters in my village — with respect to Blaina West Side AFC and their strong following — were sucked inexorably into the oval ball scene. This is only natural, and in places like Liverpool and Manchester the younger generation would as soon embrace Rugby Union football as tiddley-winks. Equally, in Wigan the kids all want to be Eric Ashtons, and thirteen-a-side football rules the roost.

I had made a mark outside school, too, with a few games for the district schoolboys' XV in which Arthur Lewis, later a captain of Wales, was a leading back. My first appearance followed a minor scandal which caused Russell Cooper to play hell. Chosen as a reserve scrum half (Arthur held the stand-off half spot), I ought to have moved into the team when the first-choice player unexpectedly withdrew. The berth, however, was given to a boy from the local grammar school. Russell's protests so embarrassed the selectors that they picked me for all the subsequent matches!

The experience was a lesson to me. From it I learned that selectors at all levels are prone to play politics; and also that there were two distinct levels in society: grammar school products and the rest. I suspect that, happily, comprehensive schools may have ironed this out by today, but twenty years ago my only way of climbing onto equal terms with successful 11-plus boys was to excel at rugby. The game is a tremendous leveller, and once you pull on a jersey you can stand shoulder-to-shoulder with anyone.

To my private chagrin, Abertillery Grammar School also defeated Glanyrafon under my captaincy in the final of the district cup in my last year. But although I never obtained the hoped-for upgrading from my secondary modern, when I put away my satchel for the last time I did not find myself too greatly disadvantaged. Some school mates, inevitably, were taken on at the pit — not for her David, declared my mother emphatically. Others became clerks, but I proved just bright enough to gain a production traineeship with the Richard Thomas and Baldwins steelworks, as it was then, in the next valley at Ebbw Vale. My pay was £2 10s a week, while my job, involving scrutiny of supply and demand, was interesting and responsible. A mistake made by a junior like myself could interfere drastically with the smooth functioning of production lines. I was to remain in the post for three years.

At rugby I now had to push ahead without the reassuring presence of Russell Cooper. His final words of advice, however, which I heeded, were to join the nearby Cwmcelyn Youth side. Their headquarters building was a green Nissen hut, where most evenings members could dance, do physical jerks or play table-tennis.

Cwmcelyn's star stand-off half, Evan Davies had just graduated into senior rugby. Hence my two new coaches, schoolmasters Len Jones and Rumsey James, greeted the new arrival with open arms, drafting me immediately into their first team. 'Frankly, you're picked because there's no-one else,' they told me, 'but we think you'll make the grade.' And I did, reaping the reward of further wise and enlightened coaching by these two expert men. The time they put into their voluntary work was endless, and I would like to think that there are still people around with their dedication and commitment. To them the youth of Wales is hugely indebted.

At the age of sixteen, therefore, I had made an important step forward. Soon I became a regular member of Cwmcelyn's XV and a key part in its pattern of play. Our squad of twenty produced some fine form, and I picked up a lot from boys somewhat older than myself like Gwyn Weller, Mike Cayford and Fred Howells, whom I had previously viewed as superstars.

And indeed, there was beginning to be evidence that I might have star quality myself. For my age, my speed over the 20 or 25 yards that you need for a defence-splitting break was exceptional. An each-way side-step made me a slippery customer for opposing back rows, and that constant lone practice had given me the ability to hit long touch-finders or diagonal punts with each foot. A sure kicker was a great boon in those old days when elderly leather balls were often balloon-shaped and swiftly became heavy and unmanageable in the wet.

With encouragement from Rowland Hill, then our representative on the Welsh Youth Rugby Union, I progressed shortly into the Monmouthshire youth side and, wonder of wonders, began to see my name in print. Reports of our matches occupied a mere half a dozen lines in the *Football Argus* or *South Wales Echo*, but if you scored, as I was now doing consistently, your name appeared in capital letters. This was heady stuff, comparable with the applause that rippled out from crowds of 300 or 400 if you crossed for a good try.

The momentum was kept up with a trial for the Welsh Youth at Llanharan in mid-Glamorgan. My chief memory of the occasion concerns the half-time invasion of the pitch by my grandfather Semi, a little in the background these days but still a keen follower of my fortunes. I had been getting poor service from the lads in front, which subjected me to pressure from the opposing back row — until Semi penetrated our team huddle at the interval to demand better protection for 'the promising kid at fly half'. Inwardly I cringed, praying that the selectors would not know who he was.

Bampa's intervention was forgiven, and I was duly called up to play in the final trial. It took place at Bridgend, where other members of the family turned up to cheer for me, this time from the safe distance of the grandstand. Three uncles from the Rhondda plus my father kept Semi company. Afterwards they joined me in the tea-room, doing their best to rebuild my morale after the unimpressive game I feared I had played.

So, after what seemed an eternity of waiting while the selectors called out the names of their chosen full back and three quarters, it came as a staggering but unforgettable surprise when my name was announced. I was to play at stand-off half in our forthcoming clash with the Welsh Secondary Schools. Family congratulations came first, Rowland Hill clasped my hand next, and within twenty-four hours there followed telegrams from the Glanyrafon school staff, from my friends at work, and even from the local council. Highly delighted, too, were Cwmcelyn, who had produced a number of triallists in previous years but only one cap, a lad called Alan Silk.

That season and the next I played six matches for the Welsh Youth. They were all enjoyable save the meeting with France at Tulle, where we went down by 36–3, a margin which I fear is still a melancholy record for the series. I was so ashamed that on my return to Blaina I tried to pretend that the Press had misprinted the result and that we had only lost by 6–3.

While secretly thrilled with the distinction the rugby game was beginning to confer upon me I tried hard to remain level-headed. But it was so difficult! I recall wearing my blazer with its gorgeous three-feathered badge to every function I could, hoping that it would focus all eyes upon the wearer. Not everyone was impressed. Once Allan Lewis, a scrum half partner who toured with me in later years as a British Lion, accompanied me to a post-match reception after the 1960 Springboks had played a combined Cross Keys–Pontypool XV. So keen were we to be recognised by the tourists as up-and-coming prospects that we sat on the bar so that our badges could scarcely be missed. Alas, the Springboks took not a blind bit of notice!

Some of the older generation, though, let us share their limelight. There was one week when Blaina won the Ben Francis cup and I captained Cwmcelyn to victory in the Monmouthshire junior cup final. My team was allowed to take part in the senior club's triumphant procession down the main street of the village, and even tasted a first sip of champagne! Such gestures leave an indelible impression on youngsters, and cement their allegiance to a sport.

I have certain reservations about youth and school rugby in Wales. Several gifted teenagers with whom I played were somehow allowed to slip through the net and their talents were lost to the game. I also considered that an unfair share of caps went to youths from west Wales, since the bulk of the officials seemed to be based there, and it seems to me that this situation has changed scarcely at all.

Over-adulation and personality cults may also have a bad effect on boys prone to conceit, and the Press have a tremendous responsibility not to shower promising players with too much praise. At the same time they dare not dampen youngsters' ardour by curt dismissals of their potential. Bleddyn Williams is a writer whom I have always respected for getting the balance right.

However, on the whole the system works well, sifting out the kids who are likely to be successful at the highest level and bringing their names to the notice of big clubs. Mine was evidently on the lips of many committees, and it gradually dawned on me as I reached the age of eighteen that I was being wooed from all directions. Ebbw Vale had me along to their annual dinner, at which I was presented with a clock to mark my caps, plus a hint that should I join the Vale's ranks, RTB could be persuaded to adjust my shift-work to allow lots of free time for rugby.

Blaina presented me with a sports bag and the advice that I should definitely spend a year or two with them before venturing onto the first-class circuit. A similar gift came from Abertillery, accompanied by a warning that if I turned my back on them my future in the Welsh game would be slim indeed. Pontypool promised me Benny Jones's team place the moment he retired; but it is said that Benny got to hear of this, and was not at all amused.

Ultimately the next stage of my career was determined in the simplest possible way. Our local policeman was R.T. 'Bob' Evans, a famed and feared Newport wing forward of the post-war period who was capped by Wales and toured with the British Lions. One day he casually suggested that I might like a trial with his club, and that he would personally deliver a letter written by me to Newport's secretary, the late Bill Everson.

Join Newport! The idea seemed as realistic as applying to Real Madrid. On reflection, however, I decided to do as the man had said.

Newport wasted no time and a reply came by return. My application had been accepted and I would appear at fly half in their pre-season trials. The club were even going to bring the wily veteran Billy Watkins out of retirement to partner the new recruit.

So it was up to me. If I could only reproduce my normal form and avoid being overawed by the occasion, membership of the Black and Ambers lay within reach. I was about to come of age in rugby football.

CHAPTER 3

Black and Amber

Those who know little about rugby football can only guess at it; older and retired players may have forgotten it; but I am sure that my younger readers will apreciate exactly what I mean when I recall the incomparable thrill and excitement of knocking on the door of senior rugby. And if there is someone at hand ready to lift the latch, so much the better.

There is the challenge, and the business of rising to it. There are the hopes and expectations. There is the glamour. And there is the considerable mental and physical adjustment an eighteen-year-old must make. Especially if, like me, he has lorded it for a couple of seasons in youth rugby.

Determination is the prime ingredient needed, and I had plenty of that when I turned up at Rodney Parade for a first trial in August 1961. Since the first approach to me by Bob Evans I had thought of little else, and despite renewed overtures from the Blaina committee, who feared that I might be overplaying my hand, had decided that I wanted to be part of the Newport set-up. It seemed a tremendous compliment that the premier side in Gwent — and, to my way of thinking, in the whole world — had actually invited me for scrutiny. I was determined that their faith in me should be rewarded.

So, on that important evening, I played as thoughtful a game as I could, keeping my running instinct on a short leash for fear of being judged selfish, and had the satisfaction of being asked to attend a second, final run-out a few days later. At half-time chairman Bryn Williams and his committee switched me from the Possibles into a black and amber jersey, and when I — so reluctantly! — removed it in the changing room I formed the impression from officials and senior players that there might be a few games for Newport's second XV, the United, in the offing for me. I travelled back up the valley to Blaina a fairly hopeful young man.

After some days, which seemed to me like months, there was a knock at our door and that man Bob Evans loomed largely in the porch once more. Imagine my dazed delight when he informed me that I had been chosen for Newport's first XV in the opening game of the season against Penarth the following Saturday. At first I could not believe my ears, but then I realized that Bob was continuing with routine instructions and requesting me to arrive at Rodney Parade at 2.30 pm in time for a 3.15 kick-off. When he left I spent a few pent-up seconds treasuring private thoughts before rushing into the living room to tell my overjoyed parents and brothers. Great was the rejoicing in the Watkins household that night.

You will understand how keyed-up I was by the day of the match, though, when I tell you that I left Blaina at five minutes to twelve. The bus journey to Newport was a bare half hour or so, but I was beset by fears that there would be a break-down or traffic hold-up which would deprive me of my debut on Welsh rugby's big circuit. Of course the journey was totally uneventful, so that at the end of it I had oceans of time to kill. I sat in a café near the bus station kicking my heels and willing the minutes to pass.

Fearful in the end that I might be suspected of loitering with intent, I set off across the Usk bridge on what had blossomed into a balmy, warm September afternoon. Even when I arrived at the club-house, though, there was still an hour and a half before the match was due to start. Fortunately the late Bill Everson, a big-hearted and thoroughgoing secretary, was at hand and set out to calm the nerves of the new recruit by showing me around the Newport Athletic Club complex. It had grown to impressive proportions since its humble beginnings in 1875, and the aroma of tradition could almost be smelt. My eye fell upon a portrait of Roy Burnett, a stand-off half who had played 372 times for his club and once for Wales before retiring a year or so earlier — how could I presume to fill a berth that had been occupied for so long with such lustre and brilliance?

At length Bill, who had other things to do, deposited me in the home changing room, with its view over the tennis and bowls areas in the foreground to the rugby arena away in the distance. Once again my eyes widened, this time at the meticulous preparations made by the ground staff: smoothly laundered jerseys on hangers, with shorts, socks and freshly polished boots on a chair beneath. Spotting my own jersey — which bore a figure six, for numbering in those days began with the full back — I went to sit beside it, suddenly realizing that I was not alone. The room's other occupant I recognized as Des Greenslade, and I felt disconcerted at his failure to greet me. But I need not have worried: soon I was to discover that Des habitually shunned all human contact before matches, choosing solitude and seclusion as he prepared his mind for the fray.

Soon, however, some less highly-strung team-mates began to arrive, including the then Wales hooker and captain of Newport Bryn Meredith, who did the introductions. Again I experienced a feeling of great humility: here was I, shaking hands with men whom I had come to think of as giants in the past year or two. Many of them, indeed, were International Players. The back row forwards were Brian Cresswell, Geoff Whitson and big Glyn Davidge, a man who seemed not to have a care in the world yet invariably had to make himself physically sick before taking the field. There were Brian Jones, Peter Rees, towering locks Ian Ford and Brian Price, and the powerful centre Gordon Britton.

The respect and admiration must literally have radiated from my face, and yet I felt reassured by their presence too. These were men who would look after novices like myself and the other hopeful, Dick Uzzell, a boy the same age as I.

And the strange thing is that any tendency I might have had towards being overawed evaporated once we were out on the pitch and applying ourselves to the job of demolishing Penarth by 36 points to 3. Once a game gets under way, the other fourteen players lose their individuality and become simply team-mates. Such is the speed of the first-class game that usually you are aware of a black and amber jersey near you and precious little else.

I did myself a bit of good in front of the 7000 spectators that day, too. Early in the game a big Penarth lock, Elwyn Jones, came thundering in my direction, at first causing me to back-pedal rapidly. But then, summoning up my courage, I did the unexpected thing and snatched the ball from his grasp. Off I set on a counter-attack and just managed to reach the try-line after a 40-yard sprint. The crowd straightaway identified me as a cheeky chappie who had some potential as entertainment value, and I think that there and then the regulars took me to their hearts.

Having the crowd on your side is important and valuable, especially to a newcomer, and I tried to please people by correct behaviour off the field as well as by the tricks I could play on it. There is nothing I regret more than the constant barracking some players have had to contend with during their careers, even occasionally at Rodney Parade.

My family, who attended that first match, were given a warm welcome at the ground by Newport's officials and presented with season tickets. The process of making Watkins junior feel a part of the team continued with the issuing of a voucher enabling me to purchase a pair of boots worthy of a first-class player; moreover it was made clear that I should leave them at the ground after a match or training period to be cleaned by the ground staff. These were the first 'perks' I had known. On the other hand there was nothing to be made out of expenses in those days: half a crown was handed to me by the treasurer when I produced my 2s. 4d. return bus ticket from Blaina — but I was asked for the tuppence change.

The Press decided to be kind to Newport's new fly half. 'Is this the new Cliff Morgan?' demanded the headlines. Rodney Parade had to be patient about making up its mind, for our next two matches were played away from home, at Bristol and Leicester. On both occasions I was to salute the careful travel arrangements, master-minded as always by our genial match secretary of the day, Nick Carter. Packed lunches or snacks were always available to kill off the hunger pangs of youngsters with big appetites, while there was also the heady experience of first-class rail compartments (these were days before teams could motor into and out of England via the Severn Bridge) and taxi rides between stations and grounds.

In those days Newport always looked like a rugby team when they went away to play. Check shirts were enjoying a vogue at the time, and surreptitiously eying our senior players I decided that I must buy one just as soon as I could afford it. However, they were the sole idiosyncrasy permitted: everybody wore blazer and flannels, and we were never without ties. I know that times have changed, and when I look at the casual dress of today's generation of players I am the first to acknowledge that their gear is smart; but I do find myself wondering how intense is their team spirit and how strong their club loyalty.

Our Leicester excursion was memorable on two counts. Firstly, we went down to defeat by 8–6, my initial reverse in black and amber colours, so that our evening at the Bell Hotel was rather muted. Because I had scored a try, though, and put in two important cover tackles, my own inner self was not too unhappy. In the morning my spirits got a further boost from the Sunday newspaper reports, which declared that I had shone in a beaten side.

So when Bryn Meredith took me aside after breakfast before we left for home I expected the big complimentary treatment. Alas for my hopes.

'We were leading 6–5 until near the end, weren't we?' he said.

I nodded.

'I gave you a penalty kick to take, and asked you to find touch to relieve the pressure. I also suggested that you make absolutely sure of it, kicking the ball over the grandstand if necessary.'

My face fell, understanding beginning to dawn.

'You missed touch, David. Leicester set up a counter attack, and managed to get the winning score,' went on Bryn mercilessly.

I could find no words to reply, for I remembered the incident only too clearly.

'So,' continued the captain, 'you surrendered the tactical advantage to our opponents at a crucial moment in the game. That's no good to us at all. We need your individual brilliance, sure. But you must learn to do as you are told at times when it counts, and fit into the general plan. Rugby football is a team game.'

Close to tears I still could not reply. But Bryn had not finished with me yet. He pointed to the papers under my arm.

'You can forget about what the Press says,' he added. 'We will tell you whether you had a good game or not. That's all.'

My little world was shattered, and I felt that all the stuffing had been knocked out of me. But do not conclude that my medicine had been too strong. Not at all. That was the moment when I learned, once and for all, that the team counts for more than the individual. There can be no cause for rejoicing if you have played well but your team has gone down to defeat.

Before we broke up back at Newport Bryn had bought me a drink, as if to emphasize another aspect of team spirit: some sharp criticism had come my way, but I was still a valued part of the family. My morale climbed a little above zero-level, and I tucked the lesson securely away in my casebook of experience. Rockets have to be fired sometimes in rugby football, and Bryn's delivery had been a model.

Years later, when the Welsh selectors were searching for a full back to replace Terry Price who had turned professional, they asked Newport to play the rising star Keith Jarrett in the position for a match against neighbouring Newbridge. Reluctantly, for we considered that the future for this nineteen-year-old lay in the centre, we obliged and swapped him around with our regular full back John Anthony.

Keith will agree that, overcharged with confidence, he made a nonsense of things in the first half, especially with his missing of the high balls with which Newbridge tormented him. At the interval it fell to me as captain to take a difficult decision, restoring the two men to their normal positions. 'You will never, ever, make a full back,' I snapped at Keith. 'And, remember, you're no golden boy — you're just one of fifteen Black and Ambers.'

My decision was correct on the day, in the context of a tough local derby. But the Big Five chanced their arm and picked Keith at full back for the subsequent International against England, when he repaid them with a sensational performance that included a try and 16 points with the boot. However, I often think — and hope — that my hard words at him at Newbridge had gone home, with the same salutary impact as Bryn Meredith's lecture to me at Leicester. Brilliant youngsters, with all the arrogance and conceit of youth, need encouragement, but they must occasionally be brought down to earth. Good captains and coaches are those who can get the balance right.

My senior team-mates nursed their new recruit pretty well in that first season, and I also profited from some of the extra space a newcomer gets from the opposition before they have identified him as a danger man. In later seasons I was not to have things so easy. However, Newport went serenely along to win the unofficial clubs' championship, thereby being recognized as the uncrowned kings of Welsh rugby. All our games had been hard, particularly on the Welsh circuit where inter-club rivalries are so intense. But the most demanding had been our quartet of matches against Cardiff, our oldest and fiercest rivals. I must tell you about these fixtures, for in my experience they are unique.

For a start they date back to 1876, near the dawn of organized rugby in Wales. Since the first quarter of this century Cardiff have had the upper hand in the number of victories registered, though we have the best record of any club side in the world against them. They envy us the several invincible seasons we have enjoyed, never quite attained over at the Arms Park; we smart at the fact that more than once they have beaten us four times in the same season, a Grand Slam our club has never quite brought off.

Add to that the proximity of the two places, just ten miles apart, and you can grasp the reason for the hyper-tension that infects a clash between black and amber and blue and black. From Newport's point of view the atmosphere in our changing room before setting out to join battle with Cardiff is akin to an International occasion, and the stakes seem just as high. In the mid-seventies the two clubs reduced their annual encounters to two, but I cannot conceive of this diminishing the will to win of the modern generation.

A little extra piquancy accompanied my first appearance against Cardiff. My opposite number was Geoff Davies, who had been dislodged from Newport by my arrival and moved west along the coast. Since he had played the final dozen games of the previous season for Newport's first XV it was not surprising that he quickly became Cardiff's first choice fly half.

Geoff, playing outside the experienced Lloyd Williams, had the satisfaction of coming out on top that day. I was well served by the wily Bob Prosser, but had the disadvantage of being marked by that great flank forward Dai Hayward. In my view, Dai was the best of his era in his position, a man who used his grey matter during a game and was a bundle of restless energy. Some folk accused him of dirty play, but I would draw the line at that. When Dai saw a chance of hurting you, he took it — but in rugby football to hurt your opponent fairly is all part of the game, and you thereby go some way towards establishing superiority over him.

As a tactician, Dai was years ahead of his time, and I was not surprised that, when he took up coaching in later years, he trained the East Wales XV that robbed the 1967 All Blacks of a hundred per cent record. On the field, the pair of us developed a healthy mutual respect, which dated from our second encounter. I made a bit of a monkey out of him, leading him to promise as we left Rodney Parade, 'If you ever do that to me again I promise you I'll bury you several feet deep.' What is more, he meant it.

One of the great pleasures of Welsh club rugby is the comradeship and rivalry which develops over the years. One looked forward immensely to renewing combat with flankers like Dai, Omri Jones, Leighton Davies, and the great Haydn Morgan. However, I must repeat: nothing quite approaches the fervour with which Newport and Cardiff relish the prospect of locking horns. It surpasses even that generated when Wigan play St Helen's at Easter — and that is saying something!

CHAPTER 4

Stardom

To understand the problems I had to cope with as I entered my second season as a Black and Amber you have to understand that at this stage I was barely out of my teens. And although today's youngsters radiate more confidence and seem to be more blasé about life's challenges and opportunities, I don't believe that deep down they feel much different from the way David Watkins felt at the end of summer 1962: great expectations — yet tempered with apprehensions of all kinds, and the fear that my fortune was too good to last.

I had survived a year's molesting and buffeting at the hands of the great back row forwards of the day, perhaps because they had decided that they could allow this precocious newcomer a little latitude while they reserved their strong-arm stuff for our International players in the midfield. But now, coming out for season number two, I knew that I would be a prime target. The buzz had got around the wing forwards' union.

For 1961–2 had not been a bad beginning for me at all, prompting the veteran critic, Jack Davies to write in the *South Wales Argus*, 'He will be a great player when he has acquired the wisdom to ration his breaks. . . . Next season, given the chance, he could revolutionize Newport's back play.' I had made thirty-nine appearances, scoring four tries and three dropped goals, and had been shielded from much of the hurly-burly by back row team-mates like Glyn Davidge and Alan Thomas. But now progress towards maturity had to be made.

Davidge and John Anderson were great influences on me at this time. Occasionally I would be invited to join them for a post-match supper in one of Newport's hotels or restaurants, where perhaps we would play £1 each for a steak followed by cheese and biscuits. My eyes widened the first time such a bill was placed in front of us, but I tried to affect a nonchalant attitude as I put my quid on the table and mentally calculated the damage it would do to my weekly wage packet. A pound was a lot of cash in those days.

Other men to whom I listened attentively were Peter Rees, Brian Jones and 'Algy' Thomas. In their company, particularly at away games, I started to experience and savour the protracted, all-embracing conversations that can develop when a group of like-minded rugby men get together. Strategy, tactics, moves, techniques, defensive alignments — such subjects occupied us for hours and hours. Perhaps Brian owes a debt to such exchanges for the profound and keenly thought-out book which he published after his retirement in conjunction with another Newport great, Ian McJennett.

Long sessions of chat usually mean that a few jars of ale are sunk, and there are uninformed outsiders who imagine that rugby clubs are dens of drunkenness, peopled by near-alcoholics who play a match simply to work up a thirst for their intended evening consumption. Certainly beer is part of the rugby scene, wherever the game is played. It helps to lubricate the social side of Union and League, where post-match arguments and analysis are the delight of spectators and participants alike.

But I wince when I see new recruits trying to ape the ten-pint-a-night men, especially if they are backs whose careers are going to depend upon nimble, quick-silver movements and the retention of slim, trim physiques. Terry Price, the Llanelli-born full back who moved North after eight caps and half a Lions' tour, was a youngster of huge promise when he came onto the representative scene in the mid-sixties. But when I observed him matching his intake of beer with that of heavily-built locks and props I always feared that his game would lose its fine edge. And, it seems to me, that Terry, although he became a fine servant of the Bradford club, never quite fulfilled his great potential.

At Newport, no one was pressurized into drinking beer for social reasons and no unkind jibes came my way when clubmates found that I was a near teetotaller. Orange juice was my tipple, and for years I stuck to it as a drink that would not undermine my fitness or cut a foot or two off my pace.

Nor, to be honest, could I see the point of training hard for a couple of hours if one immediately retired to the bar and took in liquid which would swell the waist-line. I do not seem to have missed any valuable experiences through this discipline, and since those early days I too have come to relish a pint or two or a glass of wine as an aid to relaxing. But I am grateful to Newport for respecting my feelings as a young man, and I would like to think that most big clubs share that enlightened viewpoint.

In Blaina, let me admit, I could by this time have become an advanced free-loader, so anxious was the village to acclaim and rub shoulders with its favourite son. Businessmen, councillors, teachers, miners, shopkeepers, and all manner of folk whom I held in high respect now greeted me in the street, slapped my back, wished me well for my next fixture, or pressed me to join them for a drink. The local rugby club, which had advised me to spend a season or two with them before advancing to the first-class game (and are perhaps disappointed today at being unable to claim me as a former member) sank their pride and invited me to their annual dinner. I even recall a special sportsmen's service at our chapel, when the whole of the Watkins family occupied the pew of honour and an ornamental clock was presented to me. It ticks away on my mantelpiece to this day.

The upshot of all this was that I had to set about evolving an attitude to my new-found fame. The problem is one, I suppose, that is common to all who work in the public eye, be they rugby players, stage celebrities, TV personalities or men of affairs. The first manifestations of popularity can make a person feel overwhelmed and perplexed.

My initial response was to allow the humility that I felt take its course, and for long I behaved more like a mouse than a man. I spoke only when spoken to and passed an opinion only if it was asked for. At Rodney Parade I wrote a careful, earnest autograph for young fans at the final whistle, secretly envying my seniors who could dash off an indecipherable squiggle in the twinkling of an eye. I had a horror of being thought a big-head or immodest.

This policy on my part continued for some time, and perhaps I was rather dull company! Then, one spring day in 1965, I came to terms with it all. Having played a big part in the Welsh XV's success that season, I had been elected the South Wales Miners' sportsman of the year along with Lynn Davies from Nantymoel, winner of the long jump medal at the 1964 Olympics. As I accepted the gift of a collier's lamp and surveyed the huge gathering rising to applaud me, it suddenly dawned upon me that this was a two-way process: the mining community was taking huge pleasure at this opportunity to honour its champions. People evidently got a kick out of acknowledging their heroes in this and other ways. So — why did I not admit it to myself? Fame was an agreeable spur.

For their part, communities in South Wales take what almost amounts to pride of ownership in those who have made good. The Cliff Morgans of this world now earn their livings a long way from home, but back in the valleys they are forever 'sons of' the Rhondda. Phil Bennett 'belongs' to Felinfoel. And likewise with myself: although as a rugby player I am associated with Newport and latterly Salford it is Blaina which really claims me as its own. A claim that I do not dream of disputing.

There is an interesting contrast here between the village attitudes of Wales and those of the big suburban nexus to be found in northern England. There adoption — rather than ownership — is the in-thing, and warm, sincere towns like Wigan, Warrington and Wakefield like nothing better than boasting about how they have taken so-and-so to their heart. Footballers such as Georgie Best, Mike Summerbee and Colin Bell have experienced this vividly in the Manchester area. So have Commonwealth cricketers like Clive Lloyd and Farouk Engineer. And so have hosts of rugby immigrants from South Africa, New Zealand and Australia, not to mention England and Wales. It happened to me too

— indeed to Salford chairman Brian Snape, of whom I shall have much to say later, it sometimes seemed that I was almost a son.

I recall with mixed amusement and pleasure, too, the sentiment expressed by Lancashire cricket captain David Lloyd, speaking at a Merthyr Tydfil dinner given as part of Glamorgan fast bowler Tony Cordle's benefit year. Looking round the sea of expectant faces he cracked, 'Thank goodness there are a couple of Lancastrians here to keep up my morale!' He meant Jane and me!

So, in Blaina, I was happy to meet and greet anyone who wanted a chat, and was on Christian name terms with most of the village. Incidentally, I have always been 'David' (or, up North, 'Dave') to those who know me well. 'Dai' seems to have been an invention of the Press — perhaps of my old friend Tudor James of the *Sunday Mirror*. His newspaper has narrow columns! However, 'Dai' is not a nickname I have ever encouraged or particularly liked.

My parents, I feel sure, enjoyed their share of reflected glory. I suspect my mother was not too unhappy to be known as 'David Watkins's mam,' while my father would be bought an extra pint or two in exchange for the latest inside story on his son's progress. What pleased me most, though, was that my achievements and fame almost certainly contributed to his being picked out for less onerous work at the pit-head, which he badly needed in view of his poor health.

Men who have become famous, however, will recognize the slight feelings of guilt it is possible to experience about brothers on whom the limelight does not fall. In particular, Martin probably possessed the ability to have been my equal, but was discouraged by having to endure endless comparisons with his elder brother. 'David would have played it this way,' he would be told after a perfectly respectable performance. You can only take so much of that, and I conclude that it was a main reason for his failure to persevere at his game. He made an early mark at a Newport trial which was arranged for him, but after that life's social side seemed to attract him more.

Brian, in contrast, was never endowed with the talent to match his total enthusiasm for rugby. 'If only I had Martin's ability,' he would sometimes say wistfully. 'Or if only he had my drive.' Nevertheless, I always had whole-hearted support from the pair of them. And certainly they never turned down the occasional International match tickets which I could provide!

But, more and more, the focal point of my life was moving in the direction of Rodney Parade, and, if I was beginning to mature as a person, membership of that great club had much to do with it. Newport was an institution in the land, which inevitably boosted the pride and self-respect of its players. In return, enormous loyalty was generated and although I have sympathy for men whose ambition is to win a first XV place I cannot really approve of those who flit endlessly from club to club in their eagerness to fulfil it. I understand that you are entitled to wear the full blazer and badge paraphernalia of Pontypool after just six games for them, but I prefer the Newport system, where a great deal more effort has to be ploughed in before such rewards can be reaped. Thoroughly to be commended is the story of David Rogers, who played in the shadow of many a glamorous Black and Amber stand-off half before making the spot his own at the ripe old age of thirty-one — and going on to play in a Cup-winning XV.

You gained stature also because Newport thought big. Each year we played a special quartet of away games, at London Welsh, Blackheath, Harlequins and Oxford or Cambridge, for which the club treated us to a long weekend break that included accommodation at a first-class hotel. Once, tucking into Sunday lunch on a Paddington train home, members of the Aberavon side who had also been in London filed past us on their way for a beer and a sandwich in the snack bar. Our chests swelled a little at their open-eyed envy, and even more when they told us that after their fixture the previous afternoon each man had been given a couple of quid and told to find his own accommodation. That did not seem to me a good way of building team spirit. Newport's method was.

However, our pre-eminence cut both ways. In the Wales of the sixties, like Llanelli in the seventies and Salford in our great days, Newport was the club the rest loved to hate, which led to an intensity on and off the field of which one did not always approve. Once, after Abertillery had lowered our colours at Rodney Parade and I had cadged a lift on their coach back up the valley, I had to button my lip very tightly. All the drinks in the pub where we stopped en route were 'on' the club. It was like Christmas. Moreover a lot of vainglorious twaddle was being mouthed even by great players like Alun Pask and Haydn Morgan who should have known better. The reason? — simply that Newport had been beaten!

Fixtures against Bristol, Blackheath or Wasps, which we felt we could cope with straightforwardly, often came as light relief from the big Welsh circuit. I mean no disrespect, but the fact is that scores in the twenties were not uncommon on the other side of the Bristol Channel for our team, whereas from the Gnoll, Stradey, St Helen's or the Arms Park we counted ourselves lucky to return with a 3–0 or 8–6 victory. Crowds could be downright hostile, and I recall an afternoon at Newbridge, not far north of Newport, when the sheer venom coming off the terraces was almost tangible. A 5–3 win scraped by the visitors did nothing to improve the general mood.

The spleen of the crowd, however, soon found itself vented upon a very thick skin. I was deliberately cultivating detachment, the better to concentrate upon improving my game. Jack Davies's comment which I quoted from the *Argus* earlier was one of the first pieces of genuinely constructive criticism written about me in the Press, and I remember anxiously consulting team-mates to see if we could work out what exactly the journalist was driving at. My main mentor was Peter Rees, a wing who was studying for a degree and therefore considered by the rest of the boys to be a most erudite analyst. Don't forget that these were days before clubs had coaches to whom one could turn automatically for advice.

Peter gave it to me straight. 'Jack is right,' he said. 'You're a bit cocky, and the way you bait opposing wing forwards could get you into big trouble one of these days.

'Your fault is that having beaten them once you get so carried away that you try to beat them two more times in the same movement. That's like thumbing your nose at them, and it makes them all the more determined to nail you. Once is enough.

'I've noticed, too, that if an opponent tackles you really hard you start a kind of private vendetta, bent on getting your own back. That's pretty pointless, too.'

These were criticisms to which I gave increasing thought as my first-class career began to lengthen. It also started to dawn on me that, since the stand-off half is a major tactician in the Union game, much responsibility was mine for thinking out ways of plugging the opposition back, as well as enabling Newport's free-running rugby to flow.

This, of course, involved kicking, which was alien to my wish to run with the ball. But one day in my second season along came another of those small but vivid lessons. Newport went to St Helen's and lost to Swansea because of a careless display for which I was as guilty as anyone. On the coach going home I was told that Brian Jones would move up to fly half for the following Wednesday's match: David Watkins was to be left out.

I took it hard. The committee assured me that I was simply being rested, but it felt like being dropped. Looking back I see plainly that the decision was in my own interest, for I was having a surfeit of high-tension matches. At the time, however, I spent a few miserable hours contemplating leaving Rodney Parade and seeking my fortune elsewhere.

Swallowing my pride I took my seat in the stand to watch the boys play Bridgend. 'BJ' made few if any breaks, but gradually I found myself acknowledging how his astute tactical work with the boot was kicking Bridgend to their doom. His was a masterly display, enabling Newport to score a narrow victory.

That example rubbed off on me. Soon, back in the XV, I found myself in a pressure situation up at Ebbw Vale, a side with key men like Roy Evans, Carpenter at full back, and a gifted fly half in Wilf Hunt. I nursed my forwards, plying the touch-line in front of them, or causing the Vale to turn and chase back long, stamina-sapping distances in pursuit of precisely-placed diagonal kicks. The crowd totally lost patience with this dogged display of ten-man rugby and gave Newport the bird as we fought through to a first success up at the Heads of the Valleys for several seasons. But I felt a deep sense of satisfaction. I had proved to myself that I could assume a different role when the occasion demanded it — and another small milestone had been passed.

Having neglected kicking since my youth days, I now redoubled my efforts to perfect the craft, and soon began to take positive pleasure in doing it well. The new balls provided for our fixtures gave me a lot of pleasure by their appearance alone: there is something beautiful about a brand new, yellow leather ball, with its perfect proportions, smooth surface and agreeable smell. You can make it do whatever you like, and to achieve a screw-kick requires something amounting to a caress rather than the use of brute force. The situation is just as satisfactory in the League, where sponsors always fall over themselves to provide the match ball, which is therefore guaranteed to be factory fresh.

In my Union days, incidentally, I rarely took place kicks at goal. In my first three seasons I ran up 19 dropped goals (and 48 altogether by 1967) but the off-the-turf kicks were taken by expert colleagues like Norman Morgan, Ray Cheney and Keith Jarrett, while contemporaries such as Graham Hodgson, Keith Bradshaw and Terry Price did the job for Wales.

Subsequently, at Salford, Ron and Doug Hill were our principal performers, until the day when they could no longer command places in our XIII on playing ability. We experimented briefly with Maurice Richards, the signing from Cardiff, only to find that if he missed a shot or two at goal he worried about it, and the general rhythm of his game was disturbed. So chairman Brian Snape persuaded me to take on the responsibility. Instant success! — by the end of the 1972–3 season I had run up a club record of 493 points, which included 221 goals.

The aspect of training which never palled in my early twenties was the cultivation of speed. By that I mean the electric start and burst necessary to take a stand-off half on an outside break around opponents and across the advantage line. Let me tell you that among my mementoes is a Welsh International athletics vest acquired after running a 4 x 100 yards relay in the company of stars like Lynn Davies and the Joneses, Ron and Berwyn. But although I once did even time for the hundred, I wasn't too disappointed when that fine coach Ron Pickering, who worked in South Wales in the sixties, told me that I lacked the sheer strength of frame to become a top-class sprinter.

For it is speed over the first 30 yards that counts in rugby football, and as long as I could beat any rival over that distance I was happy. Years later, as a veteran League performer, it gave me great satisfaction to find that over a short distance I could more than hold my own with Keith Fielding, the crack England wing, when he came from the Union game to Salford.

Again, however, it is worth emphasizing that such searing pace can only be developed and sustained by constant, often cruel, practice. That fitness fanatic Peter Rees and I once spent every single morning of a week-long pre-season holiday at Bournemouth doing 30, 40 and 50 yard sprints on the sands between the north and south piers. Rodney Parade at lunch-time might find me engaged on a solo sprint-training period under the shadow of the grandstand, and after squad training the same evening I might stay on to punish my legs a little more. I wore spikes from an early age for this purpose, and I recommend their use. All Newport's players were issued with a pair, but it is the backs and back row forwards who reap the main benefit.

I needed speed to survive, you see, as a small man. Just occasionally an opposing flanker would manage to tackle me heavily (sometimes late as well, for the law affecting the tackle was not as stringently refereed then as it is today) but being on the move seemed to enable me to ride the impact. I also taught myself to fall properly, minimizing the possibility of breaking bones.

But pace was, and is, all-important to the launching of attacks. Flankers in the sixties lay right up on the halves, and to beat them on the outside (which is the best way to break) you had to move like greased lightning. Basic nimbleness allowed me to perfect the side-step which people described as devastating, thus wrong-footing many an opponent. And I always bore in mind that the ball-carrier calls the tune; the onus is on the tackler to guess what he is going to do.

For the benefit of flankers who have given thought to ways of stopping dodgy little opponents like me I will let out a trade secret here. In my Union days the man I found hardest to beat was my own club-mate Brian Cresswell, who would often be marking me in opposed training periods. His technique was simply to remain steady and properly balanced until the latest possible moment. Occasionally, with a grunt of 'Gotcha!' he might even envelop me without even having to move.

On reflection — and it is difficult for me to try and work this out, since I admit to having been an instinctive player — I deduce that in the tiny fraction of a second when one is deciding how to beat a tackler, one is on the look-out for the small, give-away clue that he has committed himself one way or the other and may be caught off balance if one makes one's thrust in the opposite direction. If that clue has not been telegraphed, the ball-carrier usually settles for drawing his man and passing the ball, or may even die with it still in his grasp. A fine defender, Brian had this all worked out, but not many flankers had thought out their approach as thoroughly.

Because I was quick and elusive the accusation was frequently levelled at me in these early days that I was difficult to play alongside and lost touch with my centre three-quarters too easily. There was some truth in it. I recall afternoons of arrogant immaturity, when I ran ball after ball, only throwing a pass when the way ahead was finally barred.

Thus I was fortunate to play inside clever men like Brian Jones, Gordon Britton and the under-rated Dick Uzzell, who made it their business to stay with me and often had the skill to turn a bad pass from their stand-off half into worthwhile possession. But sometimes my impetuosity strained even their tolerance, and the Newport midfield triangle echoed with sound and fury: 'You stupid little so-and-so,' the others would scream at me above the roar of the crowd.

'Let the bloody thing out!' It took two or three seasons to absorb the idea that one telling pass could often do the work of six flashy side-steps.

Having paid tribute to the men outside me I must now acknowledge the service I got from Bob Prosser, the scrum half who joined Newport just after myself and remained with us until 1965 when he signed professional forms for St Helens. The veteran Billy Watkins, who played half a dozen games inside me, went happily into retirement once Bob had arrived from University College Cardiff and begun showing his class.

At first he had to overcome the prejudice of senior committeemen. 'Two running half backs in partnership,' they warned. 'It'll never work. What we want with Watkins is a shoveller, not someone who wants to make breaks too.' Soon, however, they were eating their words, and I like to think that my three and a half seasons in harness with Bob were as successful as the period spent together by that brilliant pair Onllwyn Brace and Roy Burnett. Before long Bob and I were to play jointly in a Welsh trial—and I would not like to be dogmatic about which of us took the other in with him.

When he himself was not kicking or probing, Bob provided me with a service of above average length. It spun out perfectly, midriff-high and an arm's length in front of me, forcing me to hit top speed to take it. But its prime quality, at a time when flankers could hover so close to halves, was speed. I was constantly in his debt for the half-second's advantage that put me clear of the back row.

There was one occasion in 1962 when I had to do without the support of Bob and the other Black and Ambers. This was when the Barbarians FC chose me for the Mobbs Memorial match against East Midlands. Apparently the tireless running of the young fly half from Newport had led the Ba-Baas to conclude that I was tailor-made for their style of play.

My recollections of the game are few. In a high-scoring affair which we lost, a try came my way and I don't believe I played badly. My trip was memorable in two respects, however. I was overawed by everything, firstly by the journey alone to London and the need to negotiate the maze between Paddington and Euston, and also by the large, hugely self-confident Englishmen — doctors, lawyers, stockbrokers — with whom this coal miner's son from Blaina was rubbing shoulders for the first time.

I suspect that it is hard for the average southern Englishman, with his cool, calm detached air, to realize the tensions his presence can engender in the Welsh — and probably in the Irish and Scots too. We are volatile, noisy, and anxious for social recognition and interplay. If such instincts exist at all in the Englishman he plays them down mightily; and sometimes my countrymen find themselves behaving aggressively simply in order to force a reaction or a response in his company. But if at such times we can be described as larger than life, then I consider that the English are often smaller than life.

Secondly I recall falling for Barbarians-type sales talk, forking out pocket money for the club badge, tie and even blazer buttons. They hinted that it was infra dig not to have all these. This temporarily bankrupted me, but there was a chilly atmosphere when I claimed the taxi fare I would need to get from Newport station to Blaina that night. 'A taxi!' they said incredulously. 'Four pounds, Mr Watkins? Dear, dear.'

In the morning, however, a quick trip to the bank was followed by the purchase from the Co-op of a blazer onto which my badge was sewn by the local seamstress. That badge, with its gambolling lambs and insignia of the seven International Board countries, created a sensation in the valleys, and its short wearer felt six feet tall.

Not so agreeable, however, was my reaction recently when I looked up my name in a newly-published history of the Barbarians FC. I am not listed among the amateur 'W's, but in a separate category entitled 'Expelled having joined Rugby League clubs.' That struck me as apartheid gone mad. Amusingly, though, the apartheid did not extend to organizational details and for years after my departure for Salford I continued to receive annual reports from the Barbarians and circulars drawing my attention to forthcoming fixtures and events. The faces of their committeemen would surely have bloomed into a rare crimson hue had they thought that their notepaper with its attractive letter-head was actually being handled by a fellow from the paid ranks!

In one way and another rugby was making more and more demands upon me, something that is bound to happen to the amateur athlete who reaches the big-time. I had every sympathy with the three or four potential British Lions of 1977 — Gareth Edwards, J.P.R. Williams, Gerald Davies, Peter Dixon and one or two others — who found career commitments too heavy to permit their presence in New Zealand that summer. My own problem back in 1962 and '63 at RTBs was that the steel plant's shift system required me to work evenings, nights and weekends, something that became more and more incompatible with my rugby career. Usually a work-mate would change shifts so that I could train with Newport at Rodney Parade or make myself available for an important fixture. But it was complicated, and in the end embarrassing, to keep fiddling with a carefully prepared rota system.

And so, although I enjoyed my job, I was eventually relieved at the chance of a move. Newport put me in touch with Bill Joyce, boss of a Bicester-based tyre firm, who took me on as his Cardiff depot manager in charge of four fitters and a couple of secretaries. At £16 per week the pay held out no promise of my being able to afford a gleaming Mark 10 Jaguar like Mr Joyce, but I could augment it with commission payments of 2s 6d and 5s — about 12½p and 25p — depending on the size of the tyres I sold.

The joke was that at the time I could not even drive! But I worked hard to pass my test, knowing that it was the key to a £1700-a-year representative's job, with a company car thrown in. I was to remain with the firm until 1967, and was grateful for the five months' leave with pay that I received when I was invited to tour New Zealand with the 1966 British Isles side.

In February 1963, after a four-year courtship, I married a local girl, Jeannette Morven Jones, the only real girlfriend I had ever had. But apart from our upbringing in Blaina there was, in retrospect, little foundation for a lasting relationship between us. The Jones family was middle class, Jeanette's father being a secondary school master and youth leader, her mother Beryl M. Jones a woman with a literary bent whose book about the legendary Welsh outlaw Twm Shon Catti was well received by its youthful readership.

We set up home in a Cardiff flat, but all too soon there began to be arguments — small at first, then bigger and more acrimonious — about my wife's career aims, about where she thought we ought to live, and about the amount of time she spent with her parents. Came the day when she finally packed her bags, walked out of the house, and went off to London to live with her mother who had by then been widowed.

To say that the crisis left me unmoved would not be true. The marriage had clearly failed, which must be a traumatic event for anyone. However, I cannot deny that I felt as if a weight had been lifted from my shoulders. Soon my native resilience came to my aid, and I consoled myself with the thought that I could now devote all the time and energy at my command to my job and my rugby. This renewed bachelor status would have its consolations.

No attempt was made by either of us to effect a reconciliation, and I never saw my wife again. When Salford paid me their big signing-on fee to turn professional in 1967 a solicitor's letter came along suggesting that this was an opportune moment to negotiate a generous settlement with her, pending a divorce. Naturally I was not too interested in the idea, and replied in that vein. Our marriage was finally dissolved in 1969.

CHAPTER 5

The Lighter Side

So far the subject-matter of this book has been serious. We have been preoccupied with training and strategy and tactics and diagonal kicks and side-stepping opponents. It is time now for a brief change of tempo and mood — otherwise I shall fall into the trap of setting myself up as an Aunt Sally for those oddballs who accuse rugby men of treating their sport as a religion.

It is not like that at all. Like the weather, rugby may be a never-ending topic of conversation, in Wales as in Lancashire and Yorkshire, providing a welcome escape from the state of the economy or the latest national emergency. But in the end it is just a game.

Those who play it to a high standard, whether for money or not, are naturally out to win and at the same time, if possible, to enjoy themselves. But let no-one imagine that they are under any illusions about the ephemeral nature of rugby and the mortality of the stars who play it.

Moreover, once the 80 minutes' confrontation is over, there is nothing that boys enjoy more than a damn good laugh, a chance to bask in the company of some of the marvellously well-rounded characters of whom the rugby fraternity is full, or even a hilarious escapade of some kind. For the sake of appearances, ear-bashing by earnest fans is endured, but serious analysis is postponed until the next training session.

Looking back on what amuses me from the early days of my career I find that the fall-guy is often myself. My wide-eyed innocence and gullibility as a nineteen-year-old moving into senior rugby now astonishes the man-of-the-world that I suppose I have become. But of course as a teenager one does — or one used to — take every small bit of advice as gospel, being eager not to displease the giant figures beginning to swim into one's ken.

Ray Prosser was such a man, a larger-than-life tight forward who still today, as coach, rules Pontypool with a rod of cast-iron. During the build-up to a game for 'Pooler before I joined Newport I remember 'Pross' gripping me amiably by the collar and whisking me away to a quiet corner of the dressing room. 'Us forwards 'm elephants,' he told me. 'We'm not quick thinkers. Now you — you'm one of them fairies behind the scrum, and you'm got to look after us elephants. See?' I drew myself up to full height and nodded earnestly, not at all appreciative of the subtle mickey the eighteen-times-capped prop was extracting from me. But at the same time my morale and confidence had been bolstered no end.

It was at Ebbw Vale, as reserve in a Welsh trial match to Cliff Ashton and Bryan Richards, that I first learned how caustic fans can be behind your back. On arrival at the ground I went immediately to pay a call at the gents, there to hear the news that one or other of the International players had withdrawn through injury. An Ebbw Vale regular was broadcasting the information to all patrons of the rather cramped urinal. 'But have the selectors brought in our own Wilf Hunt?' he expostulated. 'Have they hell! It's to be this young twit from Newport, David Watkins. He's no bloody use to anyone. Is he?' he barked at me, digging my shoulder violently with an elbow. I kept my head lowered in dumb agreement with him.

Half an hour later, when I scampered from the tunnel clad in the white shirt of a Possible, I am sure to this day that I caught sight of his shell-shocked face, mouth gaping wide, close to the touch-line railings. But soon, no doubt, he had recovered his composure and could continue his acid comments on all stand-off halves who did not hail from Ebbw Vale.

Tours, however, are the settings in which a youngster's rough edges can really be rubbed off. In my Union days Cornwall was my favourite scene. The rugby was tough but oh-so-agreeable against hard opponents like Penzance,

Redruth, Falmouth and, a little further east, Plymouth Albion or Devonport Services. Cream teas were not a bad idea either, while after-match hospitality invariably included delicious Cornish pasties — the real thing — served piping hot from the oven.

Newport's west country trips included a ceremony in which first-time tourists had to stand up after dinner and answer grave, apparently serious questions from colleagues about why we cherished the rugby game, or why our club was really the finest in the land. Newcomers took all this as deadly serious stuff and dreamed up answers fit to grace the Pseuds' Corner of *Private Eye*. Older players went to great lengths to choke their guffaws.

But the best value in touring was that provided by the happy band who went — and still go — on tour early each autumn under the name and banner of the late Captain Crawshay, an austere military man who, while he was alive, cheered his men on from the touch-line garbed in a flowing cloak and protected from icy winds by a deerstalker hat. 'Crawshays' is the nearest thing we have in Wales to the Barbarians, a loose association of officials and players young and old who play a few show-piece matches each year and fulfil missionary fixtures with leading secondary school XVs.

Mind you, some of the kids can hand it out as well as take it. The story is told of that marvellous character Stanley Bowes, who propped with such distinction for many seasons at Cardiff, that he returned one evening with a large, purpling black eye after playing for Crawshays against Llandovery College. He had to endure merciless ribbing from his club-mates for letting a schoolboy leave such a trademark on that battle-scarred visage. 'And he got away with it?' they asked Stanley incredulously. 'No,' came the gritted reply. 'They're burying him on Tuesday.'

On the Cornish tour, convivial activities were a prime ingredient of the four days with Crawshays. And although I cannot claim to have been a great originator of rugby 'japes' it was in 1962 that I learned how to play a useful supporting role. After a defeat in Plymouth, a long coach journey to the venerable Victoria Hotel at Newquay and the consumption of much thirst-quenching liquid, I went out into the night for a breath of fresh air with David Hayward, Denzil Williams and Gary Protheroe of Bridgend. Here we conceived a desire to lasso a sheep and import it into the hotel kitchens, perhaps fancying roast mutton for lunch the following day.

The resourceful Hayward inveigled the seventy-year-old night porter into leaving his post by requesting an aspirin, whereupon the rest of us shepherded our woolly victim as far as the dining room. Here, however, bereft of further energy, imagination or — for all I remember — the use of our legs, we abandoned the terrified animal, which proceeded to wreak havoc during the night in its efforts to escape.

At the crack of dawn, so it seemed, the entire tour party was summoned before a panel of chill-faced elders chaired by Arthur Rees, a former Welsh International forward who was at this time Chief Constable of Denbighshire. 'All right,' he intoned, drumming the table-top fiercely with his finger-tips. 'Those who did it — own up. All of you.'

We culprits, heads bursting with hangovers, eyed each other anxiously. To do as the man said surely meant disgrace and an ignominious sending home. After a pause during which Arthur's eyes scanned the room like avenging laser beams four of us raised our hands. The Chief Constable's brows lowered, creased and — after an age — twitched and finally lifted.

'What are we to do with reprobates like you?' he thundered. 'We have to foot, gentlemen, a £60 bill for damage. The rustlers will find the bulk of it.' The tension in the room eased as small sniggers all round turned to ripples, then gusts, of laughter. Arthur stopped it with a gesture.

'They will,' he added, 'also return the sheep. . . . Well, at least they were original.'

Four young Welshmen felt that they had been left off the hook rather more lightly than they deserved, and sat bolt upright to absorb the rest of the scolding.

More serious was the fate of Dick Uzzell and Ray Gladwyn (who was in the Newport ranks for a time before going off to Abertillery for the bulk of his career). This pair 'borrowed' a motor bicycle for a jaunt around the clubhouse after a tour match we played against Birkenhead Park. As they set off, however, a siren mounted on the handlebars began to wail, and they realized to their horror that they were on a bike belonging to the Fuzz! Their inability to switch off the siren drew uniformed officers swarming to the scene from far and wide, and there was no hiding place for the luckless Black and Ambers. Ray, I recall, paid a fine, but Dick spun some clever tale that got him out of trouble.

Subsequently, though, Uzzell was not so lucky. In 1963 he played truant from St Luke's College, Exeter to accept the chance of a lifetime and play for Newport against the All Blacks. Not only did Newport score a famous victory by 3–0, but Dick was the hero of it with his never-to-be-forgotten dropped goal. His name (and picture) was thus plastered all over the front pages of the national Press, notoriety which got him into dreadfully hot water when he returned to his *alma mater*.

Sometimes, in my view, 'japes' were pushed by an overdose of strong beer far beyond the bounds of common sense. Often, had we not been 'rugger types' and therefore held to be basically law-abiding chaps, certain of my friends and acquaintances must surely have been locked away. A touring colleague once hurled several buckets of water over some innocent hotel guests in the belief that they were his mates. I have gone onto the field for a tour game with as many as twelve or thirteen team members still smashed out of their minds after being on the beer at lunch-time. There has been the spiriting away of souvenirs, often valuable hotel ornaments, for in their cups rugby men are not clever at distinguishing a priceless vase from a cheap-as-dirt lounge bar ash-tray.

This is known, I suppose, as sowing wild oats. All I can say in defence of rugby football's cowboys is that in my experience there were usually in attendance senior club officials who never hesitated to read the riot act. That way, although Rugby Union will always have its wild ones, high-spirited young men do come to discern the difference between harmless pranks and what amounts to senseless vandalism.

Tour experience, of course, further enlarged a circle of friends which was already spreading like a ripple as I came into contact with more and more clubs. Characters who still stand out a decade and a half later include that warm-hearted Aberavon prop Len Cunningham, who always wore a crew-cut hair-style on a skull as hard as the steel they turned out in the plant where he worked. In a drawn match against England Graham Hodgson, our full back, pleaded injury to decline a penalty shot which could have won the day for us. Keith Bradshaw took it and missed, but afterwards it was Graham's photograph that Len ripped out of the programme and multilated savagely in mock rage.

There was Neath's man-mountain Brian Thomas, who loved to play the part of a Roman emperor at pre-International match lunch-times, picking languidly at a bunch of grapes while reclining on the nearest available sofa. There was Cardiff's tough little hooker Billy Thomas, who ranted and raved at me for seasons alleging that I had deprived him of a 'grand slam' blazer: it stemmed from the year when Cardiff, having defeated Newport three times, were only robbed of a series whitewash by my winning dropped goal in the fourth fixture.

Outside Wales I came to know and enjoy the company of rugby stars from many other lands. England full back Don Rutherford — now the RFU's premier coaching officer — and stand-off Mike Weston became good friends. Ray ('lend us a quid') McLoughlin was my favourite Irishman, with Stewart Wilson a great Scot to have around. Keith Oxlee and John Gainsford were South Africans I liked, while the fine New Zealand full back Don Clark was a man with whom I kept in touch after our first meeting in 1963 and spent many happy hours on my visits to his country in 1966 and later in 1977.

CHAPTER 6

Big Dai

You may remember a pop song called 'Big John', intoned in a deep voice by some Transatlantic star, which did well in the charts of the mid-sixties. 'Big John' was, as I remember it, a gentle giant of a man respected for his sheer size and muscle power.

Inevitably, when I toured New Zealand in 1966 and had from time to time to stand in as captain, my fellow tourists adapted the ditty to suit their tiny, lightweight boss man:

> Each morning at the ground — see him arrive
> Only five foot six, weight one-forty-five;
> Not broad at the shoulders and narrow at the hip —
> Even so, the boys don't dare to give lip
> To Big Dai. . . .

There was no answer to this kind of banter, so I turned it into my personal party piece, with the addition of the following verse:

> On the day of the game he'd be at his best —
> That's when New Zealand would be put to the test.
> A crushing blow from his right hand
> Could send even Meads to the Promised Land —
> Big Dai. . . .

It is ironic but true that it was big Colin who nearly put Big Dai in the Promised Land with a knuckly swipe in the final Test. But more of that in a later chapter, when I shall also come back to playing against the All Blacks, touring overseas and playing for Wales. However, I quote the verse because it was that same 5′ 6″ Big Dai who, in 1964, was invited by the Newport committee to become club captain. After three seasons with the Black and Ambers I was being asked to take the reins — at the tender age, I might add, of twenty-two.

You may consider that I showed a fair degree of conceit in accepting the invitation without a moment's hesitation. No qualms? No youthful tremors? No second thoughts? Answer — negative. So distinguished was my club, and so great my respect for those who ran it, that I reached out and grasped the honour gratefully like someone plucking an apple from the bough. If Newport thought the time was ripe, then so be it.

I was taken aback at the time when I read the news in the local Press; those were not great days for communication between club committees and players. But on reflection it was always on the cards. During the 1963–4 season I had vice-captained the team under 'Ben' Price, generally organizing and calling the moves for the back division. Although Price had led us to our fine victory over Wilson Whineray's All Black tourists, I suspect that in that first term of captaincy he frequently rubbed the committee up the wrong way. Since they were looking for a successor, my name was the one that came logically to the fore. It is clear, incidentally, that by the late sixties the big lock had become a far more formidable leader, who took Newport to a championship title and Wales to a Triple Crown.

But I should like to set down here my view that a club captain — in League rugby as well as Union — should be allotted a minimum of two years in the job. He needs the best part of one season to get the players onto his side, to reach a sound, working relationship with the committee, and to adjust his own style of play to the extra demands being made upon him. Only after that is it fair to expect him to start achieving success consistently.

That was certainly true in the mid-sixties, and despite the coaching revolution — indeed, perhaps because of it — I have no doubt that it still holds good today. My view is borne out by the track record of men like Phil Bennett, Terry Cobner and Gerald Davies at Llanelli, Pontypool and Cardiff, each of whom retained the club captaincy over a substantial number of years. It is all very well to share the honours around, but undoubtedly some men make better leaders than others and deserve to remain at the helm.

To go a stage further I believe that the chosen skippers at International level, again in both codes, should be given one whole season in which to prove themselves, and that an announcement to that effect should be made before an International campaign begins. Captains have enough on their minds without the extra worry about whether they are playing for their places. The International Board countries do not seem to have got around to this yet, nor do Wales's rivals in the League game. But it made total sense to me, in autumn 1977, to be nominated as Welsh captain for the triangular tournament that we would play during the winter against England and France.

This whole question of continuity is so important. During 1977 I kept hearing of the management troubles experienced in New Zealand by the Lions, and could not help feeling sorry for 'Dod' Burrell and John Dawes, who had to feel their way along from scratch and learn from their own freshly made mistakes. And it seems clear that there were some things that they never put right between them.

Now although Union men are amateurs, for whom participation in an overseas visit means taking valuable time off from work, it would seem worthwhile exploring the possibility of including one management man from a previous tour. Would it not have been sensible, for example, to ask Syd Millar, who coached the Lions of 1974 in South Africa, to bring his experience to bear on the business of managing the tour of 1977? I was pleased that he got the post in 1980.

This is one reform that has got through in the other code. Reg Parker, our 'Welsh' selector on the Rugby League Council, managed the 1974 Great Britain tour of Australia, when record profits were returned. He was also given the job for the 1977 expedition 'Down Under'. As the coach on that trip I can report that the move paid off.

Anyway, let us come back to earth. Here was I, who might be expected to be a callow youth in 1964, entrusted with the leadership of one of the world's great clubs.

Now, maybe I had been trained in a hard school at Blaina, in those early days when I prevailed on boys with rugby balls to organize games the way I wanted them organized. Maybe in a sizeable family like ours you learn to look after yourself in an argument or a dispute. Whatever the reason, I seem to have possessed a streak of native cunning which I straightaway brought to bear on the battles I was going to be engaged in.

First of all I weighed up the personnel making up the selection committee on which I would sit. There were somewhat conservative members like R.T. Evans and Jim Hawkins, who would seldom permit themselves to show total enthusiasm about a new flank forward or scrum half, and who would need to be treated with great care and delicacy. Though I must confess that my respect for Jim's understanding of the rugby game took a dive when I heard him ask our scrum half Bob Prosser, 'Why do you always put the ball in on the same side of the scrum? — sometimes it wastes valuable time.' We had to give him a brief lecture, with the aid of fingers and thumbs, on the advantage of feeding a scrummage from your own loose head side!

Other men, however, like Bill Everson, Vince Griffiths and 'Nick' Carter, would be on my side. I believe they connected my presence with the unofficial title we had won in 1962; and their allegiance was cemented by the fine rugby, including a hard-fought win over the Barbarians, that the club produced in the second half of the 1963–4 season.

But however many friends I might have, argument and controversy were bound to lie in store. A definite policy would be required by the captain, who was the chief representative of the players in committee.

So I used to enter selectorial deliberations with the XV I wanted fixed firmly in my mind. In the back row, however, or the midfield, I would privately be happy with any permutation from several gifted players; so, although in these areas I might put up a show of resistance, I was always able to concede a point or two in the end and hence acquired a reputation for being a very reasonable fellow in debate. But when the crunch came, and positions were being discussed on which I held absolutely firm views (for instance, I generally preferred the direct methods of Peter Rees on the wing to the trickier approach of Dennis Perrott) I was able to assert myself and get my own way. It may have been a 'con' job, but to me it was an engrossing battle of wits.

I also set out to establish myself as a true friend of the players themselves, knowing that this would filter through from committee sessions and secure the loyalty of my men to their young skipper. Occasionally, for instance, one of the boys would take some stick in a committeeman's report for his performance in the previous fixture. Then I might step in and restore the balance by chiming in, 'Look, he was playing to orders. If anyone's head should be on the block, it ought to be mine.'

I was able to improve committee-player harmony, too, by assuming responsibility for relaying selection decisions to the men involved. If someone were promoted from the United XV he would be told and congratulated by the captain. If a player was to get the chop, he would hear personally from me before seeing the omission of his name on a noticeboard or in the Press.

This does not mean that my approach was soft. Once, near the end of a game which we eventually lost 5–3 to the Harlequins, I told the whole of the team that our only salvation lay in running every single ball. But in the very next phase of play a flanker kicked to touch with three or four colleagues unmarked outside him.

Afterwards we had a showdown. I said that my word was law on the pitch. He replied that he could not play under so autocratic a system. 'Very well,' was my response. 'Newport and you will have to part company for as long as I remain captain.' And indeed he left us for Abertillery (where, next time we played them, he managed to put me down very hard in a tackle and proceeded almost to bite my thumb off!).

I studied the character of all my men with the aim of bringing the best out of them. Gordon Britton, for example, was someone at whom you had to keep firing rockets to keep him on his toes. But Stuart Watkins required kid-glove treatment and had to be reassured every so often that he was really the best wing in the business.

In my time Newport enthusiastically embraced numerous new ideas and devices that were doing the rounds. We bought a number of Danish-made water-repellent balls which were fresh on the market. We acquired a scrummaging machine of the type pioneered, I believe, by Gerwyn Williams, a former Wales full back who was then teaching at Dulwich College. In the mid-sixties some alterations to the offside law prompted us to arrange some lectures from the late Vernon Parfitt, once a top-flight referee, to see how best we could take advantage of them.

It could be claimed, I consider, that we were moving steadily into an era when more thought was put into the game than ever before. As an example of the attention paid to detail let me cite the case of that outstanding young prop, Martin Webber, who met a tragic death in a road accident before ever fulfilling his great potential. The first time Martin played in a Newport-Cardiff game he was taken to the cleaners and back again by that stern scrummager, John O'Shea. Our poor recruit thought he was finished as a first-class forward.

But Newport threw everything into the re-building of Martin. On the scrummaging machine we got the positioning of his feet right and corrected the angle of shove. Our senior forwards spared no effort to restore his sagging morale. In his next clash with O'Shea he fought an honourable draw and was told later by the British Lion, 'You'll get a cap one of these days.' How sad that fate intervened to confound the prediction.

I believe that Martin was maturing into a prop who was years ahead of his time. The great props of the day — Cunningham, Waldron, McLeod, Jacobs and the rest — were essentially scrummagers, and I am cynical enough about the forwards then to add that all they did was scrummage. Locks treated the scrum as a place for a quick breather, while back row forwards leaned on and picked their prey from members of the opposing back division.

In Webber, though, Newport had a prop who not only learned to shove his weight but also moved very rapidly around the field. He could run, handle and think all at once, which ran counter to sacred and long-established traditions dear to props! He would have fitted supremely well into the Union game of the seventies.

One reform that had yet to arrive, however, was the introduction of coaching. A huge load had therefore to be borne by the club captain. I had to arrange training schedules and make sure every player knew about them. Once they began I was in sole charge and, besides driving myself hard, had to ensure that the players' work-rate was maintained. Since we trained as a fifteen-man unit I even had to oversee the efforts of the forwards.

On match days it fell to me, of course, to give the last-minute pep talk designed to lift and motivate the players. Borrowing a little from the styles of predecessors Bryn Meredith and Brian Price, a little from Clive Rowlands whom I was now partnering in the Wales XV, and drawing a little from deep within myself I learned to make my points crisply and bluntly, including a personal word to each man, and do not recall being lost for a sentence or suffering from shyness. Some people say pointedly that small men enjoy being bossy to compensate for their lack of inches — which may well be true! Having said as much, though, I must add that there was an inevitable expenditure of nervous energy, which took its toll of one's composure.

I must have brought team talks to an art over the years, however. Years later before the second Test against New Zealand's rugby league XIII in 1977 I so impressed Dennis Wright, our psyiotherapist, that he complimented me, 'I've never heard a better pep talk, David. I could go out there and play myself!'

During an actual game, of course, I had to ensure that my own form was at a peak and that fourteen other men were functioning to maximum effect too. Responsibility for tactical control throughout the 80 minutes lay with me, and solely with me. Lucky the team captain in a game like cricket, with the opportunity and the time to confer at the end of an over with a senior colleague if he is in doubt about his next move.

As if this were not enough, on away trips I had to decide the pattern of travel best suited to the fixture, and how long

Newport would spend fraternizing with the opposition before departing for home or retreating to our hotel. I was also the keeper of the beer kitty, which had to be deployed with immense care!

So all in all, despite certain reservations about their effect upon styles of play, I approve of the introduction of coaches to the Union scene. If he is conscientious and totally committed the coach can be a team manager off the field, relieving his skipper of many arduous chores.

The main fear I have is that bad coaches will produce a mechanical approach to the play in their protégés. If straightforward rugby works, all well and good. But what if the opposition is playing straightforward, effective rugby too? There will be an impasse, unless the coach has taught his men, through their captain, to search for alternative methods. This may be the time for an individual to forget all he has ever been taught and revert to instinct and native genius to crack the stalemate — and a good coach must make sure that he keeps this option open.

Although, too, I recognize that in rugby styles of play go in and out of fashion I consider that by the mid-seventies coaching in Wales had tipped the balance of priorities too far in favour of forwards at the expense of back play, at which the Welsh have traditionally excelled. Too often the backs were being used solely as crash-ball merchants, whose object was to set up ruck after ruck or maul after maul until a certain overlap of three-to-two or two-to-one could be achieved behind the scrum. Then a wing or full back would run in the try.

Thus much genius has evaporated from midfield play, and I find difficulty in naming a great, defence-splitting centre three-quarter since the time of D. Ken Jones who preferred to (and could) beat his opposite number than to sacrifice himself under a heap of forwards so that the second phase could begin. His play amounted to an art form; that of his successors rates as little more than a craft. (I would have exempted Gerald Davies from this criticism had he continued as a centre.)

I was in the crowd one evening in October 1977 when Pontypool, coached by Ray Prosser, relieved Newport of a long-standing ground record at Rodney Parade. The margin of victory would have been wider, it struck me, had not 'Pooler's inside backs persisted in running back to the pack without seriously extending the defensive capabilities of the Newport back division. During one movement I counted seven smoothly-rucked balls on the trot won by Terry Cobner and his men — yet I doubt if the total gain of ground amounted to 25 metres.

Prosser falls into the category of very great 'motivating' coaches, less concerned to tutor than to inspire their men.Turning to Rugby League Mal Reilly is a perceptive analyst of the game, while Derek 'Rocky' Turner and Roy Francis are other men for whom I have respect. At Salford the coach is less like his namesake in Rugby Union than the manager of a League soccer club. He advises the directors on the needs of the team, and whether they should dip into their pockets to enter the transfer market. He also represents the players' interests to the bosses.

I played under four club coaches with contrasting characters and methods. Griff Jenkins was there when I arrived, but I think that his bluntness made players wary and even fearful of him. On the other hand his successor Cliff Evans was probably over-influenced by his men. Yet he was a person who loved to take the game apart in conversation and put it together again, and out of consultation with him and the keen thought he put into his job arose my move from the stand-off position to that of a midfield back with the likelihood of more freedom and space to exploit. He was followed by Les Bettinson, who now oversees physical education in the schools of Cheshire, and finally by Colin Dixon, who practises on the field what he preaches in coaching sessions.

It would have been tremendous to have had any of the men I mention with me at Newport in 1964. However, what faced me was a one-man job.

CHAPTER 7

Team-building

19 September 1964 is the first meaningful date to me as I look back on my captaincy of the Newport club. After comfortable victories over Penarth, Bristol and Pontypool we were entertaining Neath at Rodney Parade. But the buzz was all through the changing rooms and along the terraces: representatives were at hand from the mighty Wigan Rugby League club. They had cash to put on the table — and their target was our number eight forward John Mantle, the holder of three Welsh caps.

That day Neath beat us, in my fourth outing as captain, by 21–5, a large margin in those low scoring days. The men from Wigan adjusted their sights and, instead of Mantle, signed a Neath lock called Peter Davies, dubbed at the time the 'iron man' of Welsh rugby. The iron turned out rather rusty, since Davies played a mere half dozen games up North before announcing his retirement from the game. For once Wigan had slipped up badly, failing to sign the best number eight forward, in my view, who ever played Rugby Union football.

Apart from height — at 6′ 1″ he could not dominate the tail end of a line out as completely as Pask or Mervyn Davies — John Mantle had everything: weight, to help project set scrummages forward at a rush; power, to rip the ball away from mauls as Geoff Wheel did in a later era; stamina assisting him to cover gaps and tackle when all seemed lost; and in addition, the ability to run with the ball and puncture defences close to the scrum or in open play. A versatile fellow, he appeared for Wales at number eight, blind side flanker, and as a lock in an under-twenty-three XV which played the Fijian tourists.

I dwell on John Mantle, who in the end left us for St Helens later that same season, because he was typical of the newcomers to Rodney Parade who were attracted by Newport's open style of play. And we needed fresh blood. In the decade before 1964 our team had been stability itself and if one recruit established himself during a season it was something to write home about. Now, abruptly, a whole clutch of clever and experienced men like Brian Jones, Glyn Davidge, Brian Cresswell and Bryn Meredith had hung up their boots or were unavailable for other reasons. So it was with relief, as well as gratification, that we greeted new arrivals like, first, Keith Poole, Vic Perrins and Alan Skirving, and subsequently Ron Bendall, John Anthony, Tony Hurford and Bob Phillips.

That is not to mention John Jeffrey, who joined us from Ebbw Vale. 'Poaching' players is not something I recommend, but in John's case I bent my principles and went after him. Having seen him in, of all places, South Africa, where he toured in 1964 with a Rhymney-Glynneath junior team, I decided that he was the number eight we needed to succeed John Mantle. And he responded, I like to think, because of what Newport stood for and the way we played the game. Ivor Taylor came to us for similar reasons, a man destined to become one of Wales's most respected midfield players.

On reflection, the collective exit of the senior players probably made it easier for me to impose upon my team the style I wanted, but it did not survive without some hard questions being asked in committee. For that home defeat by Neath was followed by a 17–3 drubbing in Swansea, which took club morale down several pegs.

But rugby form is as capricious as the ball itself. Five days later we relieved Cardiff of their ground record and set off on a run of eighteen victories. Our colours were finally lowered 6–3 at Coventry on the eve of a Wales-England match which deprived Newport of five players, 'Algy' Thomas, Price, Uzzell, Mantle and myself.

I must place on record, though, that the most satisfying result during my first season of captaincy was a game at Bristol that we won 25–3 in rather curious circumstances.

Taking place the same afternoon was a first Welsh Trial, at which I ought to have been. The selectors, however, had insisted on the previous Tuesday as the deadline for availability, and erring on the side of caution I had withdrawn because of an injury suffered some days earlier.

By the Thursday night my injury had eased no end, and in response to anxious pleas from the committee, who had released no fewer than nine other Newport men for the Trial, I decided to turn out for the club.

We were so pushed for personnel that, in addition to a clutch of young hopefuls, we had resurrected Ian McJennett to play at prop and coaxed veteran Haydn Mainwaring to turn out at full back. Yet, to my delight, we ran rings around opponents who included such performers as Rollitt, Pullin, Watt and Richard Sharp. The last-named, an outstanding fly half for Oxford University and England, told me later than Newport's team effort was the best encountered by Bristol that winter — and looking back on the result I am not surprised! It is a statistical reminder of the enormous club spirit that we were now nurturing and even strengthening.

So, for me and the club, 1964–5 was not a bad year at all. Besides learning to live with a new skipper Newport had got through a fair amount of rebuilding, ending up with 33 wins and only 11 reverses. Although we did not know it, we were laying the foundation of a side which would bring fresh glory to Rodney Parade by the end of the decade, with a championship title in 1968–9 followed by a victory over the 1970 Springboks.

When certain key players depart, however, even the best organized clubs can be thrown into confusion. Bob Prosser's move to the professional ranks left us without a dependable scrum half at the outset of the 1965–6 season — and me without my partner. After numerous experiments Cliff Williams came our way from Cross Keys to be a sturdy and resilient caretaker for a year before he too went North. However, he had helped us through a better-than-average season in which the quality of our play is again commemorated by the statistics: the leading try scorers were Stuart Watkins (19), Peter Rees (11), and

Dennis Perrott (10) — all wingmen. That proves that Newport were running the ball purposefully and stretching defences, and reflects well on our centres Uzzell and Britton. They, at least, were not crash ball kamikaze pilots.

The season's end was marred by the death of my mentor Bill Everson, a great club secretary. How he would have loved to know that three Black and Ambers — Price, Stuart Watkins and myself — were chosen to tour New Zealand and Australia with the 1966 Lions.

It was during that tour that I heard to my great satisfaction that I had been re-elected Newport's captain for a third term, but when I returned from the arduous six-month trip I should have liked a longer rest than proved possible. Defeats at Neath and Cardiff — a 27–0 beating, this — prompted the selectors to hurry me back into club colours against Blackheath in early October, when I dropped a winning goal. During another stylish year for Newport I was again somewhat discomfited by having to adjust to a series of hopeful partners at scrum half, which did not end this time until late in the season when little Gwilym Treharne joined us from London Welsh for what turned out to be a long stay at Rodney Parade.

My own was soon to be terminated, and after eight final appearances in black and amber colours at the beginning of 1967–8 I opted for the red jersey of Salford with its thick double vees sloping from the shoulders, a move we shall discuss in detail later on. Something special to remember was our 11–6 defeat of Cardiff in the last game I played against them.

By that time my International career was under something of a cloud, and I had been overlooked as a possible captain by the Welsh selectors as they prepared their side to meet the All Blacks. Barry John was the rising star, and I was not enjoying the experience of playing second fiddle after winning for myself twenty-one caps. But nothing of that nature can spoil my memories of days with Newport — golden days, perhaps with a rose-coloured tint as I look back.

Inevitably over the years I had to take some stick from fans, the Press and our committee. In particular there was a period during my second term as club captain when people said that I had lost all zest and inspiration, and that my play was pedestrian by my own high standards. There was, I admit, something in the criticism: this was a time when I was trying too hard and was obsessed with a desire to get everything right in the interests of my team. But dull care was ultimately thrown off, and in the long run I do not see that the demands of captaincy fundamentally affected my game. On the contrary it was a privilege that mostly brought the best out of me.

What the club gave me, in terms of responsibility, experience, satisfaction and sheer pleasure has by now, I hope, emerged. But I believe that the account is square: I turned out 202 times for Newport in just over six seasons, contributing 288 points — and I think my overall tally of 55 dropped goals will take some beating! A discernible lustre bathed the club as a result of my own efforts and those of my contemporaries. Tours overseas enabled us to uphold the name of Newport in the rugby fraternity the world over.

It was a good relationship. I am fond of saying that I was in the right place at the right time — and in the right company.

CHAPTER 8

Capped

If the club system provides people with a basic rugby education, then International, or Test, matches are the game's university. And as we begin reflecting on my Union career at representative level let it be said bluntly that David Watkins's arrival on the scene got the Welsh selectors out of a big hole. But before you accuse me of high conceit, consider the prevailing circumstances.

That key position, stand-off half, had belonged almost exclusively to the great Cliff Morgan in Welsh teams of the fifties. So good was he that even the brilliance of my distinguished predecessor at Newport, Roy Burnett, had been rewarded with only a single cap when Cliff was injured. For a variety of reasons that particular era was not one in which Wales were dominant — France and England were at least our equals — but there was no doubt about the Morgan genius, and his personal supremacy went unchallenged.

After he called it a day in 1958 with twenty-nine appearances to his credit, however, the Big Five lurched in all kinds of different directions as they sought to replace him, and the following four seasons saw no fewer than five men called on to occupy the stand-off berth. Twinkle-toed Cliff Ashton, of Aberavon and later Cardiff, played seven times. Ken Richards of the long legs and devastating side-step (sadly to become a car-crash victim in the prime of life) won five caps in 1960 and 1961. Alan Rees, the Maesteg man who went North like Ken, made three appearances and Bryan Richards of Swansea one.

The selectors were clearly at a loss, which in retrospect probably explains their decision to include me in the first Trial of autumn 1961 even though, at nineteen, I had barely established myself in the Newport XV. Extra piquancy was injected into the match by the selection of Geoff Davies (who you will recall had forsaken Rodney Parade for Cardiff Arms Park after being displaced by me) in the rival team.

Playing with the Whites, or Possibles, Geoff saw little of the ball and subsequently faded from the Trials scene. His fate, however, befell me in my next outing at Bridgend. With Alan Rees in the red jersey I picked up only crumbs of possession and was demoted to reserve for a final Trial which saw Rees and Ashton fighting it out between them. They shared the International matches of spring 1962, though it was significant that the final game against France found myself and a promising scrum half called Clive Rowlands seated on the reserves' bench. Of course in those days there was no replacement rule, and thus no possibility of either of us winning a cap as a substitute.

So it had been a season of Trials for me and I suppose that was the way the selectors wanted it, content for the up-and-coming boy from Blaina to sniff the heady air of Championship rugby from a short remove. Such was my youthful confidence, however, that far from feeling grateful at having progressed that distance I actually felt privately slighted that the Big Five had not cast the ultimate vote of confidence in me. J.B.G. Thomas wrote in Wales's morning daily, the *Western Mail*: 'The selectors are right to hold young Watkins back. As yet he lacks the experience necessary for International rugby.' I asked myself angrily how you were supposed to gain the experience without being picked to play!

Of course, one was careful not to reveal the least trace of pique, for the selectors held your fate and your future in their hands. Men like Ivor Jones of Llanelli and David Jones of Blaina were like demi-gods; and when the latter, acknowledging a youngster from his own village, asked 'How are you, David?' I felt as though I was riding on cloud nine. Equally, if one was ignored, then one's sense of deflation was enormous.

From my present-day vantage point I can recognize that rugby selectors are on a hiding to nothing, which explains how they can swing between extreme conservatism, retaining trusted players who may in truth be just over the top, and flights of fancy when they back the latest dark horses to be tipped by the Press.

In my time they could be swayed by a single brilliant display, and I am convinced that had I scored a try in one of those 1961–2 Trials then my first cap would have come along much sooner. Another of their foibles was patent horse-trading as between the different Districts of the Welsh Rugby Union which they represented — 'I'll vote for your star flanker if you'll back my nominee for the wing.'

Later, as my own International experience increased, I even developed doubts about their basic ability to sum up a man's quality, and was relieved by the entry into the selection committee of Harry Bowcott and Rees Stephens, men with whom you could hold a sensible conversation. The latter proved his class to me once and for all after an incident in which Wales conceded a blind-side try to England which was scored by their stand-off half: John Mantle, on the flank for our team, got it in the neck from fans and critics for missing the tackle. Rees Stephens was one of the few folk off the field who realized that Mantle had correctly taken the scrum half within our '25', and that if anyone had slipped up it was the Welsh number eight forward.

These days it is clear even to a comparative outsider like myself how much things have changed. Selectors are younger, and more in touch with the game. Contact between them and the players is easier and less formal. Squad selection means that candidates' form is scrutinized and assessed far more methodically. Such considerations make it all the more perplexing that the Big Five have stopped short at the final logical step and shrunk from ending the Trial system.

Before the seventies, which have seen important reforms, places in a Welsh XV were up for auction in a real sense far more than today. And crowds knew it. They believed that by turning up and opening their lungs to full capacity they could cheer their club hero to a cap. Thus at the Bridgend Trial to which I referred earlier some 8000 souls were present, many having come from Blaina to shout for myself and the other local boy, Alan Silk. For a Final Trial at Cardiff the stadium might be more than half full, as it was in 1966 when the young Barry John was challenging me at stand-off half. Every so often a roar of 'David Watkins' would erupt from the Newport supporters backing me, to be countered with a thunderous 'Barry John' retort by the faction from the west.

Nowadays even a Final Trial pulls a bare 3000 gate and the WRU no longer count it as a money-spinner. By the time they have printed programmes and paid the stewards they are running at a loss. The explanation is that supporters know that nothing they see in the Trial will affect the composition of the Welsh XV, which is now decided at squad training over a period of weeks — not in one happy-go-lucky 80-minute exercise. The participants know this too, so that the rugby on display is usually exhibition stuff consisting of two teams going through the motions.

Also, although personally I quite enjoyed Trials, I know that many players hated them, and still do. Some men were naturally afraid of injury, perhaps at the hands of a competitive rival. Others resented having to prove themselves in a one-off game, taking the view that their week in, week out club form was evidence enough. Occasionally a candidate would be less than fully fit, yet would hesitate to withdraw lest his replacement should play a blinder.

So I think the system should be scrapped. There are no Trials in Association Football and we do not have them in Rugby League, where the selectors base their judgment on observation of players over a long period.

The Welsh XV of 1961–2 had a moderate year, redeemed by a March defeat of France, who topped the Championship table, in which Kel Coslett got our three points with a penalty and Alun Pask's great last-ditch tackle of Henri Rancoule prevented a French reply. It may have clinched him a place with the Lions' party which went to South Africa in which the stand-off halves, I noted with interest, were Richard Sharp of England and Scotland's Gordon Waddell. That autumn, however, with Cliff Ashton at stand-off, Wales could only draw with Ireland, in a game postponed from the spring because of an outbreak of foot-and-mouth disease in the Republic.

As it turned out, the Final Trial of that winter was switched from Cardiff to Newport because of frost, and had we known it we were in for an arctic winter. But the temperature in our clubhouse was high and the mood expectant that Saturday evening, for the Big Five had been deliberating in an upstairs office and would shortly be naming their side to play England. I stood nervously sipping orange juice among a huge throng of enthusiasts, pretending to concentrate on the small talk but privately turning the prospects over and over in my mind: Ken Richards and Alan Rees had turned professional; I had had a good Trial game; surely a cap was now within arm's length.

The announcement that came over the inter-com system still plays occasionally in my ears as if taped on a cassette recorder — a voice interrupted half way through its message by an all-enveloping burst of cheering.

'Full back: Graham Hodgson, Neath,' it said. 'Three quarters: Robert Morgan, Llanelli, Ken Jones, Llanelli, Brian Davies, Neath, Dewi Bebb, Swansea. Stand-off half. . .'

This was it, I thought.

'. . . David Watkins, Newp. . .'

The rest of the announcement was drowned — and so, nearly, was I, by the sheer volume of sound. There were top-of-the-voice congratulations, the poppings of a champagne cork or two, slaps on the back and arms around the shoulders. My parents' faces stood out a little from the mass of folk, flushed, proud and happy. Journalist Tudor James beamed with delight, saying that the news would make a splendid story for the later editions of the *Sunday Mirror*, in which he was at pains to point out he had tipped me for honours a week or two earlier.

However, I must add that I was but one of six new caps, whose names now followed. My friend and rival David Hayward was one, as were Roger Michaelson, big Brian Thomas, and Denzil Williams, whom I had known since youth days in north Gwent. But the captaincy was also given to a first-timer in Clive Rowlands, a teacher from Upper Cwmtwrch who was then with Pontypool. He had revitalized the club after the departure of experienced men like Fenton Coles, Malcolm Price and Benny Jones.

People often ask me how Clive managed to achieve that distinction in his first game for his country. The answer is complicated by the fact that he was probably not the very best scrum half in Wales at that time.

What the selectors had realized, I believe, was that Clive was already a highly intelligent rugby thinker who could also lead and motivate supremely well. As a player he knew his limitations, compensating for them by exploiting the game and its laws to the utmost. Opponents would describe him as 'crafty', meaning not only his fine grasp of tactics but also the one-upmanship he practised unashamedly on referees and opposing players alike. Allied to these characteristics was enormous confidence: he never shrank from a good argument, even with a selector, and his reasoning was ever sound.

Clive is also one of the greatest patriots I know. Victory for Wales was his prime aim, and he brought it about ultimately, in an era of few truly great players, through a policy of sparse, utilitarian rugby without frills — which is another way of saying that many people found Welsh rugby at the highest level dull and uninspiring under his leadership. That, in my view, cost him his Welsh team place in 1966 and also a berth on the Lions' tour of that year.

My own summation of him, though, stems from something I have written earlier: rugby is all about winning, and Clive finally brought the Welsh a Triple Crown we had not worn for thirteen years. As for playing with him, I was quite happy about that. Since he had come to live at Cwmbran, we could always manage a joint training session when we needed one, and his service from the base of the scrum was perfectly adequate for my needs.

However, before we took the field under him against the English in January 1963 there were a few last-minute mini-dramas to be played out. The day after the team announcement the six new caps all reported to the BBC's freshly-opened television studios in Cardiff — very small and cramped compared with the gleaming white palace they occupy today — to be interviewed by Cliff Morgan who then presented a weekly sports programme. I remember angling my chest so that the Barbarians' badge adorning my blazer would feature on the screen! — but when my time came to speak and Cliff asked me how I felt about the prospect of a first cap I was barely able to blurt, 'It's a great honour — I feel . . . well . . . great . . .'

Cliff handled us very kindly, but I came away reflecting, as I often have since, how difficult it is for a casual guest to do himself justice on the 'box'. Even after much practice in later years, it is still hard to choose the right words and get the sentences flowing. After assisting Eddie Waring during televised match commentaries I have been horrified when it was pointed out to me how often I had used a word like 'tremendous'. For example: so and so's performance was 'tremendous', a try was 'tremendous', even the weather was 'tremendous'! Footballers interviewed on *Match of the Day* frequently seem to punctuate every other phrase with 'y'know'. It is a comfort, though, that even the pros slip up from time to time: Eddie Waring once commented, '. . . And the shadows cast by the floodlights grow longer as the evening wears on'! He meant, of course, to say 'sharper'.

As if anxiety about my International debut were not enough, the other fear that I experienced during the preceding week was about its possible cancellation because of the weather. Frost and snow interfered drastically with my training schedule, and I had to slog along treacherous road surfaces instead of turf. To put the lid on everything, having promised me a lift from Blaina on the Saturday morning Dai Hayward was delayed, persuading me in my panic to beg a ride to the Angel Hotel with a car-load of supporters. Dai made it in good time, though looking a bit white about the gills!

In the event the game ought never to have been played. Cardiff Arms Park was like Antarctica, with sharp frosty outcrops gleaming balefully between patches of snow that the tractors had failed to smooth away. When we took the field our studs literally clattered over the earth.

The conditions, however, could not spoil what was for me and five other Welshmen (not to mention England's seven new caps) the greatest day of our lives so far. I think its significance finally came home to me as I entered our hotel through ranks of well-wishers and reached the quiet seclusion of our team room. Here we could order whatever we felt like for lunch, but although others' choices varied from steak and chips to egg on toast I ate nothing. For most of my career I preferred to go into an important game with an empty stomach.

Then we tried to relax by watching the televised build-up to the match, until finally, an hour before the kick-off, it was time to cross Westgate Street and saunter along to the changing rooms at a Cardiff Arms Park which was already four-fifths full and a bubbling cauldron of sound and jollity. It was at the entrance that I was intercepted by a ferocious gate-man who knew little about rugby and utterly refused to accept that I was one of the players! There was nothing for it but to await the arrival of the better-known Alun Pask to bear out my story.

We had been given socks and shorts at the previous evening's team meeting but now, in the changing room, we received our Welsh jerseys. I donned mine and sat in a scarlet daze for fully five minutes, simply savouring its feel and the (upside down) look of the pert white feathers on its breast.

After a challenging and inspiring pep-talk from Clive we had to remain put to hear the crowd sing the anthems since the officials thought, rightly, that it was too cold for us to stand out on the field. Then followed the longest walk of my life: that day we trooped all the way from the North stand behind the West terrace to enter the arena from underneath the South stand. Most of the benefit gained by delaying our exit from cosy, warm changing rooms was cast away upon the bitter wind that sliced into us from over the River Taff.

In contrast, the next 80 minutes were the fastest of my life. England's 13–6 win was the last they were to register at Cardiff for a mightly long time, but I remember with clarity only two episodes in the play. First Robert Morgan dropped a scoring pass during our long opening offensive, causing his colleagues and the crowd to groan their disapproval.

But when I looked closely at him soon afterwards I could see the wide, raw frost-weal that began at his temple and disappeared under his jersey. 'It's down to my hip,' he confided, refraining from adding that his fingers were frost-bitten too.

Other players on both sides had ugly grazes on knees, elbows and faces, and after half an hour I reached the conclusion stated earlier: besides being a thoroughly painful experience the game was too great a risk to life and limb and should definitely have been postponed.

In the end, though, the English had cause to rejoice that it had been played. Just before half time they took advantage of a lapse in our concentration to score a breakaway try that came completely against the run of play. Malcolm Phillips broke the midfield defence, drew me into the tackle, and freed Peter Jackson to do the running-in. The score gave them an interval lead, to which they added in the second 40 minutes in spite of our non-stop defensive work.

Many of us, including me, were left wondering if our first entry onto the International stage was destined to be followed by a fast exit. My own low spirits, however, were boosted during the evening by the award of the coveted cap. Soft and sweet to the touch it was wrapped carefully in polythene and stowed away in my kit-bag for the return journey to Blaina, this time in a van driven by Denzil Williams. As I got out, I fell flat on my back in the drifting snow! — but the cap survived, to feature on its owner's head in innumerable photographs including that taken by Gameson's of Brynmawr which hung in their shop window for many months.

Roger Michaelson got the chop from our team for Murrayfield, but an otherwise unchanged formation of no-hopers proceeded to get a 6–0 victory. This was the first time that Clive Rowland's tenacious will to win revealed itself on the representative scene. Beforehand he had told us, 'One sure way to beat these Scots is to kick, kick, kick. That's what I'm going to do.' And he did, one of his kicks being a fine dropped goal.

For the record, the ball went out of play 121 times. I touched it on only five occasions: once to collect the Scottish kick-off, twice to pick up their grub-kicks ahead, and twice only to catch passes from my scrum half.

But we were richly content afterwards, glorying in the win that no-one could now take away from us. People tried to write it off, and the Scottish Press the following morning accused Clive of kicking the rugby game to death. As they retreated from Edinburgh, Welshmen voiced polite sentiments and told the Scots how embarrassed they were that their team had won with such tactics. But deep down few cared: it would be in the archives as a victory.

Reverting to the game itself, my final two milestones in that first International season were defeats by Ireland and France. Against the former I dropped a goal, but could otherwise make little headway in the face of close marking from stand-off Mick English, restored to the Irish XV to give it more defensive fibre. Mick tackled and covered like a fourth back row forward.

Once, in a match with England, he missed his opposite number. 'What happened, Mick?' he was asked.

'Simple', he replied. 'Horrocks went one way, Taylor the other, and I was left tackling the hyphen!'

Paris was the venue for our last game, where we went down 5–3 against a powerful French XV. 'Le Petit Watkins' got a few good mentions in the Press, but it was not really a satisfactory note on which to end our campaign.

However, I was now a 'four cap man'. That label is important to an International player, for as opposed to the 'one cap wonders' it means that he has retained the selectors' confidence over a complete season. It is a tribute to consistency. I relished my new status, and was flattered at being asked to open fêtes and crown beauty queens; but best of all was the tiny star that match programmes now printed next to one's name: 'International', it said. My father took advantage of the situation to broaden his horizons, and besides attending the two Cardiff games came also to Edinburgh and Paris, having previously not been far beyond the Welsh border!

His son, you might imagine, now felt himself to be a fixture in the Welsh team of the day. Nothing could be further from the truth. In my time no Welsh International player, however outstanding, ever left the arena believing he was a certain choice for the next game. Our selectors were too fickle for that. To guarantee any continuity three conditions had to be met: an individual had to do himself justice, the team had to play well, and we had to win. Otherwise you felt that your neck was on the block.

There was no planned approach, you see, and men could not always work out what was expected of them. Take, for instance, the composition of our back division in that first season of mine: I was chosen principally for my ability to make breaks leading to scores; behind me was one of the fastest three quarter lines ever to play for Wales — Robert Morgan, D. Ken Jones, Brian Davies and Dewi Bebb. Yet our captain, and the link between us and the forwards, was primarily a kicking scrum half! Privately I think each of us wondered whether it all made sense, but no authoritative guidance was given from above on how we were to combine and what style we were to aim at.

Selectors often contributed to the general unease by veiled threats. Once, near the end of a match in which Ireland were leading us narrowly, I tried to initiate a counter-attack from broken play near our try-line, considering it better to go down honourably than to throw in the towel before the final whistle. My sortie got Wales into more trouble, but at least we had had a go. Afterwards, however, the then selector Jack Young said loudly and bluntly, 'You had no business trying that on. Next time we'll pick a man who knows how to find touch.' Hardly a comment calculated to rebuild my confidence.

Dick Uzzell suffered a worse rebuff after an impromptu strip show he gave during the banquet following his last appearance for his country at Stade Colombes in 1965. 'You'll never play for Wales again, Uzzell,' shouted an angry member of the official WRU party. He never did.

All these things meant that, in an International as opposed to a club game, my generation took fewer of the risks encouraged by modern coaches like Carwyn James and John Dawes. If I found that a certain manoeuvre was countered easily by my markers I would shrink from trying it again, and play safe. I marvelled at the confidence shown under the circumstances by young Terry Price, which helped him to adjust with the minimum of delay to International football. Once, entrusting Terry with a penalty kick at goal in 1966, Alun Pask sought to impress on the full back how vital it was. 'Just shut your eyes and stand back, Alun,' was the retort. Ever the unruffled diplomat, Pask did as he was told.

Another factor at this level of the game was the unpredictability of the opposition. Over the seasons you develop a sound knowledge of how a rival club side will play, and can face Neath, Cardiff, Wasps, Harlequins and so on with a fairly precise idea of what you have to do to win. An International XV can make no such assumptions. You may have beaten Scotland, for example, convincingly during one year, and in the following campaign find yourself faced by thirteen of the same players. Yet the two newcomers may work the magic that turns the Scots into a world-beating combination which tramples all over you.

Also, as I have hinted, the 80 minutes of an International match pass all too quickly. In that time you are supposed to confront the opposition, test them out at all points and try to exploit the weaknesses you discover — all the while keeping your own guard high. That demands a lot of a team. With time running out there is a danger, too, that a highly-strung individual may decide that he has failed to contribute anything substantial and do something stupid or selfish in an eleventh-hour bid for glory.

Finally, I used to find that the pressure on the stand-off half in Rugby Union was — as it still is — greater than that on any other player. The opposing back row know that if they can neutralize him they have robbed his team of its pivot and fulcrum. Thus open side flankers made me their number one target. I could cope with the attentions of John Leleu, Leighton Davies and others in the domestic Welsh game, but I have to admit that such as Noel Murphy of Ireland, the Scot Ronnie Glasgow and France's Michel Crauste set problems of a higher order. Curiously, I never had much bother with the multi-capped Budge Rogers and rated another Englishman, Gloucester's Dick Smith, more highly, although he was never picked for his country.

International teams nowadays set out to minimize the strain and tension deliberately and methodically. But in the mid-sixties, Welsh team practice consisted of a quick Friday afternoon session, after which we went home for the night. Even on Saturday itself the team would disperse long before midnight after home games in order to travel back to Llanelli or Abertillery by a sensible hour.

So most of our high jinks took place on away trips, and occasionally went beyond bounds because such outings were rare. British Rail once caused a Paddington to Cardiff express to make an unscheduled Sunday stop at Bath while complaints by stewards about the behaviour of the returning Welsh XV were investigated. Our 'fire brigade' had made nuisances of themselves stampeding along corridors to extinguish blazes started by Brian Thomas (and cronies) who specialized in surreptitiously setting fire to newspapers being read by other people. I think that was the journey in which Ken Jones's case was sent flying out of a window. Presumably he had declined the join the 'closed shop', who took terrible revenge on blacklegs!

If Brian and Ken — respectively Cambridge and Oxford men — had too much to say, in their impeccable Oxbridge accents, there would be cries of, 'I say, knock it off, you Blues.' Alun Pask found a way of literally bringing the latter down to earth by removing the 'be-taller' padding from the short fellow's shoes. Ken was also ribbed unmercifully one day after he had been telling us about a recent match played on a very frosty pitch. 'They had to use brassières to thaw it out,' he told his astonished team-mates.

CHAPTER 9

Ups and Downs

In the sixties our Cardiff pitch for International rugby was a disgrace, partly because it was used incessantly as the home ground of the Cardiff Club and their several fifteens. The stadium itself also bore a seedy look. So in January 1964 a trip to Twickenham, which now looks rather dated compared with the majestic architecture of Wales's National Stadium and the Parc des Princes in Paris, was a heady prospect. The atmosphere and air of tradition about the ground was unique, and having played there against Harlequins I knew all about its excellent turf and the lordly changing accommodation, including sufficient bath-tubs for each man to enjoy an individual soak after a game.

These considerations, however, did not help me sleep any better on the night before my first game at 'HQ' for my country. During our Friday afternoon run-out at Old Deer Park the tension both among the players and the thousand-odd London Welshmen who had come along to watch was almost tangible. Bear in mind that Wales had lost four out of her five previous International outings, counting our autumn Test defeat at the hands of the New Zealanders, about which I shall write in a later chapter.

Thus the XV which returned to an early night at the Berners Hotel felt very much on trial, and that included its stand-off half. My play in the preceding year had been adequate for representative rugby without ever bursting into bloom. I had shown a few defenders a clean pair of heels, yet had not exerted control upon events as a man in my position ought. So, during those hours of darkness, I lay awake for what seemed hours, worrying about the opposition, worrying about playing before a crowd of 70,000, worrying about the so-called Twickenham swirl, which might play havoc with my line-kicking. And, most important, worrying about being dropped if I turned in a sub-standard performance.

People often asked me whether I had nerves before big matches. 'Nerves' is not quite the right word; it was more a case of anxiety that one should reproduce one's known form and prove that one's selection was justified. In later years I coped with this feeling without difficulty, but in 1964 I was still fearful of the selectors' fickleness.

After a sickening start in which England went six up in as many minutes we pulled ourselves together and fought steadily back to earn a draw, which could have been a win had we not missed a 'sitter' of a place-kick. I had a hand in both tries, which were touched down by wing Dewi Bebb. The first followed a satisfying outside break which left Budge Rogers floundering in my wake.

In the second instance, the Twickenham 'swirl' (to avoid which, the story goes, Cliff Morgan once used the boot to keep play within the shelter of the West Stand for the whole of a second half) intervened for the one and only time during the game. I dropped for goal; but as the England players stood momentarily turned to stone watching my shot gust past a post, Bebb sprinted through to pounce on the ball before it could bounce across the touch-in-goal line. He was a great wing, who could do the orthodox things correctly and always threatened to make something out of nothing too.

Having shared the honours we felt able to savour the post-match banquet to the full. England always do this function well. I approve of the invitations they extend to celebrities — that night Richard Harris was present, soon to make his name in the film about Rugby League football *This Sporting Life* — and in later years there were Dave Allen and Richard Burton.

Afterwards there was a dance at the plush May Fair Hotel, which the hangers-on had penetrated and where every other dancer seemed to be a lord or a sir or an admiral. Brian Thomas, John Mantle and myself found this a bit stuffy and took a cab to the Regents Palace where we knew that the Welsh supporters would have gathered. In the event many of them had drunk so much ale that they failed to recognize the dinner-jacketed newcomers. We three found ourselves treated as waiters, plying with trays between the Welsh fans and the bar, and even picked up a few tips!

Clive Rowlands, who had come out of his shell in the later stages of the Twickenham match, continued in a more relaxed mood against Scotland at Cardiff and allowed me to call more of the moves. Between us we worked a fine dummy scissors that allowed Keith Bradshaw to score without a Scots hand being laid upon him, contributing to an 11–3 win. It was round about this time that Clive acquired his 'Top Cat' nickname (after the American cartoon series on television) and no feline could have been more elated than he that night. It is a pity that he is remembered as a kicking scrum half, for he could and did play the running game when the circumstances warranted it.

In Dublin he said quietly to me before the start of our match against Ireland, 'If you feel good this afternoon, pull out all the tricks.' I obliged; so did our pack, spearheaded by David Hayward, and we finished victorious by 15–6. John Dawes, on his debut, got a try; so did Stuart Watkins, while my own came after a break in which I got around the Irish back row and Mike Gibson. This was a turning-point for me: I felt at last that I had established myself in the Wales XV. For that I hand some of the credit to Top Cat's understanding captaincy.

In March that year I played for the first time (counting Youth Internationals) in a Welsh side which escaped defeat at the hands of the French. But our 11–11 draw at Cardiff was only sufficient to give us a share of the Championship title, since Scotland also finished with six points. I was left reflecting how impossible it is to guarantee a good performance against France. Her players always look the part, bulging with well-oiled muscles and crisply kitted-out. Their upper lips often sprout fierce moustaches. They invariably seem to begin a game bursting with confidence, and when their handling is good it is very, very good.

Some nations have complexes in relation to other countries. New Zealand are always fallible against South Africa. The French, even when the calibre of their team is in no doubt, rarely do themselves justice at Twickenham. England now (though it was not always the case) view the Welsh as their hoodoo team. And Wales who commonly consider themselves in with a chance against England, Scotland and Ireland view the French with suspicion amounting almost to apprehension.

Just as French play on the field is unpredictable, so are their tactics off it. In my day their selectors frequently split the brilliant Boniface brothers, leaving opponents imagining that their replacements must be supermen. They played ducks and drakes with scrum halves, alternating Pierre Lacroix, whom Wales rated highly, with the pedestrian Lasserre. They allowed a feud to become so intense between Benoit Dauga and Walter Spanghero that those two outstanding forwards could scarcely bear to appear on the same pitch together.

British Rugby League XIIIs have never done well in France, either, though for a specific reason. I have no hesitation in branding French League referees as 'homers', ever anxious to please a partisan crowd. For the visitors to win, therefore, means that a French side has to be really sub-standard.

As an artful dodger of a back, however, in the style of little Gachassin, I have always seemed to please the French. Walter Spanghero, whom I considered the equal of Frik du Preez and Colin Meads, paid me the compliment of selection in his World XV. I have the book he wrote to prove it, presented personally by the author after an evening spent appreciating the bistros of Toulouse, where he runs a taxi business.

Wales got a mauling at the hands of South Africa that summer — again, I shall return to the subject later. But out of adversity came triumph — as in 1969 — and we returned to win a Triple Crown on British soil in 1965. It is significant that during the campaign we used a mere seventeen players, and the two new caps were both locks. In turn Bill Morris and Keith Rowlands replaced Brian Thomas who figured in our victory over England in January, the first time for my generation of Welshmen to beat the men in white.

Here I must pause to recall that Brian was the scapegoat for an alleged incident in that match when Geoff Frankcom, an England centre, claimed that he had been bitten. It is time to put the record straight: Frankcom was bitten — but not by Brian. The fangs belonged to another Welsh forward. It is a pity that the Big Five were persuaded by rumour and allegations to break up an eight which had overpowered the English and which was described as our best pack for over a decade.

Having had a satisfactory game against England I was somewhat mortified at Murrayfield to be caught behind my own posts by a Scottish second row forward, Mike Campbell-Lamerton, who made me look less than nippy. Games were now being televised, so that an audience of millions could chuckle at the discomfort of a star.

But Norman Gale's try near the end allowed us to return to Cardiff to play for a Triple Crown against Ireland. A crowd of 58,000 turned up to cheer us on our way against a powerful-looking visiting XV which included Ken Kennedy, Noel Murphy, Ray McLoughlin and the up-and-coming Willie John McBride in the pack with Tom Kiernan, David Hewitt, Jerry Walsh and Kevin Flynn behind the scrum. Dewi Bebb and I got tries, but the major contribution to our 14–8 win came from Terry Price. He kicked a penalty and a conversion besides dropping a monster goal from 45 yards out. Clive Rowlands had inspired us in the changing room and charged our batteries with exactly the right amount of confidence. We had taken the field convinced that there was no way the Irish could thwart us.

All forwards enjoy a chance to put backs in their place and although he later said he thought it something of a gamble, I believe Alun Pask revelled in the 20 minutes he spent as an emergency full back while John Dawes was off the field having stitches inserted. Alun showed his versatility with immaculate handling and kicking and, by going to full back, allowed Price to move up to centre and maintain Wales's positive approach to the play.

For me the Triple Crown meant another blazer, so to be

measured the team called at the Cardiff men's outfitters, Calders. My collection of blazers was mounting, and the new one hung in my wardrobe next to those from the Welsh Youth, the Barbarians and our South African tour. Newport, as befitted a great club, contented themselves with a mention of Newport's Triple Crown men in their yearbook, but in Blaina the celebrations were something special and I was presented with a wrist-watch inscribed: 'To David Watkins. Triple Crown. 1965.' From other well-wishers came a kit-bag and a suit-case.

If you think that I dwell over-much on such mementoes, remember that in 1965 Rugby Union football had not quite acquired the charisma it has today. Video-tape recordings had not become common, and great tries and victories could not be re-enacted endlessly on television as they are today. Thus an achievement like a Triple Crown melted speedily into history and players never basked in the afterglow of glory as they do today. Souvenirs were important.

In 1965 we would not have basked for long in any case, since the French unleashed a terrific first-half assault upon us at Colombes to run up 22 points. It was an absolute nightmare. After 40 minutes our proud hopes of a Grand Slam had evaporated, and as we sucked half-time oranges we looked wide-eyed at each other as if to say, 'How the hell is it going to end? How many points will they finish up with?' — a sinking feeling that rugby players at all levels will be familiar with.

Thankfully the Tricolours eased up in the second half. We ran in two goals and a try for a respectable 22–13 score-line at the final whistle. Although we were badly beaten, the scores by Stuart Watkins and Dewi Bebb meant that our wings had totalled six tries during the campaign, which says something about the aims and style of our play and the calibre of centres John Dawes and Dick Uzzell.

As it was to turn out, the years 1965 and 1966 were the high-water mark as far as my International career with Wales's Rugby Union side was concerned. In both seasons we topped the Championship table, though in each we went down to one copybook-blotting defeat. In 1966 it was Ireland's turn to humble (by 9–6) a team which had accounted for England and Scotland without too much difficulty and fancied itself as poised for another Triple Crown. Humble pie tastes no pleasanter to rugby men than to anyone else; but at least we had the satisfaction of defeating France at Cardiff by 9–8, thanks to a long try-scoring run out of defence by my Newport colleague, Stuart Watkins.

A prospective Lions tour, such as that which would take place in 1966, tends to dominate the previous home season and give players all sorts of complexes. In September 1965 many star performers were anxiously wondering whether they would receive cards from the Four Home Unions Tour Committee sounding out their availability for the trip. No-one need have worried, since it is standard practice for all men capped by their country in the previous year to be carded. But many of us, were edgy and irritable until the scrap of paste-board tumbled through our letter-box.

There was still the challenge of getting into the side, though, and the Welsh XV that met England in January was determined to make sure of excellent results that would sway the selectors in our direction. As far as I could see, the main competition for the stand-off berth would come from the Irishman Mike Gibson and England's Beatle-hair-cut star, Tom Brophy.

I must add, however, that senior players were always apprehensive lest a new comet should swim into our ken and upset everybody's calculations. Keith Rowlands had been taken to South Africa in 1962 as a lock to the disappointment of men with many more caps; years later in 1977 the sudden emergence of Clive Williams as a prop for the New Zealand tour probably cost the experienced Scot, Ian McLauchlan, a third British Isles trip.

And that, indeed, was the fate which now befell Clive Rowlands of all people, captain of Wales in fourteen successive International matches up until January 1966. After an indifferent Trial he was left out of the Wales side (never to be recalled) in favour of Allan Lewis. The Abertillery youngster, an old friend of mine, made the most of his chance, played through a Championship year with Wales, and duly packed his bags as a Lions scrum half along with ten other Welshmen, including myself.

I felt deeply sorry for Clive, who is one of rugby's honest men. 'If you don't win, you don't enjoy yourself,' was one of his sayings. I agree with that. The trouble is that you are not supposed to be quite so blunt in polite rugby circles. There were folk in, for example, the Barbarians' set-up who put the weird concept of 'playing the game' first; Clive never became a Barbarian — never moved into the sinister inner corridors of power frequented by men who have influence on the British rugby scene.

Sadly, 'sportsmanlike' thinking finally penetrated Wales's Big Five, and Clive had to go. Just think, now, what a difference his presence could have made to the tourists who went Down Under in 1966.

It was curious beyond belief gathering for matches with Top Cat as captain of the reserves. But further than that, one remained unaffected, relieved simply to be one of the survivors. Little did I dream that before long I would be going through a similar humiliation myself.

My final season for Wales was a shambles.

It was redeemed only by our high-scoring win over England in a do-or-die effort during April. This was the first season for the Five Nations' fixtures to be rotated, so that instead of a home match against the English we had to open our campaign with a journey to Murrayfield and an 11–6 beating at the hands of the Scots. Defeats by Ireland, 3–0, and France, 20–14, followed, so that our overwhelming of England at Cardiff by 34–21 was one of modern rugby's great upsets. It was Jarrett's game: the youngster ran up a record-equalling 19 points in his debut match, comprising 16 points with the boot and a try for which he sprinted 60 yards down the touchline.

That proved to be my last game for my country at 15-a-side rugby, and on reflection I am glad it turned out so well. For the buffeting suffered by the Welsh XV was nothing to the rough handling accorded to its dependable stand-off half of the previous four seasons.

Bear in mind that in summer 1966 I had played eighteen consecutive matches for Wales; that I had been the number one stand-off half for the British Lions in New Zealand and had assumed the captaincy several times; and that although I had returned to rugby earlier than the Big Five had wished, this had been in response to urgent calls upon me made by the Newport club, of which I was captain.

At a Cardiff hotel one night in early autumn I had taken some friendly banter from a group of Carmarthen students. They pointed to a fresh-faced member of their group and said, 'That's Barry John. He'll have your place in the Welsh team before long.'

Sure enough, the young hopeful from the west figured in the November Trial as stand-off half in a Possibles XV which nobbled the Probables side under my captaincy by 3–0. I thought him a good player, but did not feel my own form was below par and had no real fear that the upstart could unseat me.

The body-blow came a few days later.

Contrary to my usual habit I rang up a friendly journalist to learn what side the selectors had chosen to meet the touring Wallabies. When I put the question I was greeted by the sound of a throat being cleared. Then:

'You're not in,' he said. 'They've picked Barry John.'

My first reaction was disbelief. But gradually, as the voice on the line recited the other fourteen names it got through to me that I had indeed been ditched. I hung up, stunned and sick inside.

Mixed feelings of rage, indignation, embarrassment and despair churned away inside me, and were redoubled in the following days when I faced the world as a discard. I believed — and still believe — that Barry had been capped prematurely and that a big mistake had been made by the Big Five in dropping me. But of course you cannot go around telling people that sort of thing, so I just had to pocket my pride and try hard to appear appreciative of the sympathy which came from all sides.

One decision I reached was not to take it out on my successor. On the advice of Wally Talbot, destined soon to be my father-in-law, I sent off a good-luck telegram to Barry John before settling down to solve the private conundrum that confronted me under the circumstances: Did I want Wales and Barry to do well against Australia?

Did I want Wales to win, with Barry playing poorly? Did I want Wales to lose, with Barry carrying the can for defeat? I never quite worked out the answer to these questions, but I can assure you that they do loom large in the mind of anyone who has had a similar kick in the teeth from the selectors.

My mood was not improved when I joined the Welsh party as a reserve on the day of the Wallabies match. For a start I found my new status most embarrassing. In the days before replacements were allowed in Rugby Union a reserve felt himself to be a complete parasite.

Then, in succession, three of the five selectors approached me, slipped a sympathetic arm around my shoulders, and said quietly into my ear, 'I'm sorry, David. You had my vote.' Three out of the five! I ask you — how hypocritical can you get?

The records show that Barry played his first two matches for Wales in losing sides. Australia scored a surprise win by 14–11 and there followed defeat for Wales at Murrayfield. My rival took the field against the Scots with stitches still in a leg wound and was probably ill-advised to play. But he may have been afraid not to, such was the prevailing lack of confidence on the part of players in the consistency of selectors.

So this crazy year continued with my restoration to the Wales XV to play Ireland — and later France and England — as captain. Like Barry John, inside half Bill Hullin was left out and my old friend from Abertillery Allan Lewis took his place. For the last two games, defeat in Paris and the big victory over England, the selectors used their third scrum half of the season when they started Gareth Edwards off on his huge trail of caps.

The idea of turning professional had been preoccupying me for some time by now, and the events of the following autumn clinched my decision to join Salford. Yet again the Big Five revealed confusion and unsureness of touch when they picked a squad to prepare for the match against the 1967 All Blacks without naming a captain. I got the message: David Watkins had no certain place in their advance planning. The feeling I had was that they felt they could do without me.

With Wales I had known triumphs and tribulation. Besides plunging more than once to the depths, my country had also touched the heights; but when that happened I am bound to say, on reflection, that it owed more to luck than to sound mature judgment on the part of those who controlled events.

As I see the organized, methodical approach to modern-day team selection I admit to feelings of envy. The players of my era, I am sure, share those feelings.

CHAPTER 10

Foreigners

Throughout my career people have been kind enough to describe me as a gutsy player. And in truth, although big men have often used their size and weight to brush me off, I don't think I have been guilty of deliberately funking an important tackle. However, there have been times when my stomach has been so full of butterflies that it would have taken off had I been cut open. One of them was before the All Blacks tour of the United Kingdom in 1963.

From an early age likely lads in Welsh rugby have their fervour stoked up with tales of our country's rivalry with New Zealand. It stretches back to 1905, when a defeat by Wales at Cardiff put the only blemish on the tour record of the First All Blacks. Anyone reading Bleddyn Williams's autobiography, with its account of Cardiff's historic victory of 1953 is left in no doubt that New Zealand are Wales's arch-opponents.

If, at Newport, we were dissatisfied with the word of a mere Cardiffian, then we had Bryn Meredith to bear him out, a British Lion who had been Down Under in 1959. 'That's where the action is,' Bryn would say with conviction. 'That's where it all happens. We in Wales will have to pull out all the stops to match these boys.'

Our former hooker told us stories of the tall, raw-boned All Black forwards who would soon be stampeding around British pitches. They included established stars like Whineray, Nathan and Tremain, as well as a formidable new prospect called Colin Meads. The team's last line of defence would be a powerful full back who could float goal kicks through the posts from the half way line and beyond — one Don Clark.

Having myself seen the Springbok tourists of 1960–1 I knew that rugby visitors from the southern hemisphere were indeed cast in a giant mould. Hence the feeling I had in the late summer of 1963 – surely shared by other hopeful members of the Newport squad — was one of delicious apprehension.

Not that I feared getting hurt or sustaining physical injury, though it was clear that anyone taking on the 'Blacks' was in for a bumpy ride. What weighed more with me was the idea that we might somehow let down our followers by failing to acquit ourselves creditably. The reputation of Newport, victors over previous South African and Australian touring sides, was at stake. So was that of the county of Gwent. In a sense, too, we were carrying Wales's good name, since Newport would be the first side west of Offa's Dyke to meet Wilson Whineray's team.

With respect to Bleddyn Williams and his Cardiff XV of 1953 I must place on record that Newport's preparations for October 30 were probably the most methodical undertaken by any club side for any match up to that time. We began plotting our game at pre-season training periods in July. Two 'coaches', Bryn Meredith and Ian McJennett, were appointed to supervise our efforts in collaboration with skipper Brian Price. During September and October they had us out for extra practice on Sunday afternoons.

At length our team was chosen, and I reproduce it here for the record: Ray Cheney, Stuart Watkins, John Uzzell, Brian Jones, Dennis Perrott, David Watkins, Bob Prosser, Neville Johnson, Dai Jones, Graham Bevan, Ian Ford, Brian Price, Alan Thomas, Glyn Davidge and Brian Cresswell. For a number of our men, fine players but never destined to win caps, a chance to play against New Zealand was the highlight of their careers.

Our considered approach to the fixture continued when Ian McJennett and Brian Jones travelled to spy on the New Zealanders at Cambridge. They came back more than ever convinced that our basic plan was sound: we would be out to kill every loose ball, preventing the All Black pack from generating full momentum; and we had scrupulously to avoid errors within our own half which Don Clark might punish with penalties (in the event the big fellow got not a single shot at goal, so well did we adhere to our intention).

But before the match itself, to be played on a Wednesday, two severe blows befell us. First, we lost our Saturday game against the Wasps by 5–3. I gave an imprudent pass which allowed their wing, Hamish Keith to make a scoring interception.

Next our highly experienced flanker Brian Cresswell reluctantly declared himself unfit. Into the side, for only his second game at first-class level, came the twenty-year-old Keith Poole. Prompted by our Wasps defeat people drew the conclusion that we were now absolute no-hopers. In the event this may have stung us to greater endeavours. Certainly Keith was to play a blinder. As my friend Brian Wall of the *South Wales Echo* has written, 'He may have been a boy when the match started, but he was a man when it finished.'

The full story of our marvellous win by three points to nil has been properly and dramatically told elsewhere. That is just as well, since I retain only fleeting impressions of it. For instance, I cannot remember the morning before the match or the changing-room pep-talk at all. I do not recall the long gladiatorial walk along the old cycle track that has to be undertaken by teams at Rodney Parade to get from the pavilion to the pitch. I cannot remember so much as looking at a single All Black until they were dancing their 'haka' before the kick-off. This Maori tradition, incidentally, was great fun for the 24,000 crowd — the biggest I had seen at Newport — but it kept us Black and Ambers kicking our heels rather aimlessly in cold drizzle.

I do remember the immaculate figure of Gwynne Walters signalling the start of the match. A great referee, this, very precise and accurate. The advice we had been given about not conceding penalties was sound: infringements would not escape the eye of Mr Walters. But if you ask me who actually kicked off you will be disappointed — my mind is again a blank.

I can tell you that Newport's forwards, among whom Glyn Davidge played an outstanding game, more than contained the New Zealand pack, and it was from loose possession won by them that I was able to make the sole break of any consequence during the game. It created just enough room for Stuart Watkins to put in a cross-kick, and once more our eight secured the ball, for Bob Prosser to feed Dick Uzzell. Horror of horrors! — there was Uzzell dropping for goal, with two or three of us screaming at him to bring the ball to the left, where we seemed certain to have an overlap.

But his shot just squeezed its way over the cross-bar, for Dick to win instant and everlasting forgiveness. And, of course, it proved the decisive score. That was the historic moment of the game.

But perhaps the history was really made in the final 60 minutes when we had to hold onto that precious lead. That is when Newport demonstrated real heroism and nobility. Wave after wave of black-clad attackers rolled against us, only to be broken up by courageous defence that was inspired by the constant roar of our supporters, making us all feel ten feet tall.

I think I can claim to have played soundly enough, using our possession to the best of my ability. Chiefly I stuck to the orders I had been given — to probe and test the mobility of Don Clark with diagonal kicks, or to plug the touch-line. Just once, near the end, did I permit myself to think, 'These All Blacks are not so hot after all,' and to set off on a jinking run. Did I pay for it! Waka Nathan and Kel Tremain descended on me like two cartloads of New Zealand mutton, swiftly robbed the midget Welsh upstart, and pounded off upfield in a counter-attack which nearly brought an equalizing score.

Ages afterwards, or so it seemed, a magnificent tackle by Algie Thomas floored a New Zealander at our corner-flag, and just as we were asking ourselves 'How do we get away from here?' it was all over. Gwynne Walters blew up, the crowd invaded the pitch, and fifteen weary, battle-stained men of Gwent had earned the right to proclaim for evermore, 'We beat the All Blacks!'

It was pandemonium back at the club-house. Our changing room was so full of admirers and well-wishers that players could not find space in which to sit and unlace their boots. Outside the crowd refused to disperse, and kept calling for us to clamber onto the balcony and be serenaded by Welsh victory hymns. In Manchester in later years I have often watched with pleasure while City or United players paraded some trophy or other around town aboard an open-topped bus, but I have never envied them. They were not at Newport on October 30, 1963.

We got the usual accolades accorded to victors: messages of congratulation from fellow Welsh clubs and from Newport exiles everywhere, the inevitable blazer, and a celebration banquet or two. Our President, the late Lord Brecon, entertained the team privately at his pleasant country house near Abergavenny.

And perhaps you will understand and forgive when I admit that some Black and Ambers went to other grounds on the tour schedule simply to cheer for New Zealand, so jealous were we of Newport's achievement! At Bristol where the All Blacks were led at half time by Western Counties before recovering to win handsomely, Bob Prosser and I were for long the only Britons at the ground without a smile on our faces!

Mind you, Newport suffered during the succeeding months for our temerity in winning. For the rest of the season we had only to lose a game for the headlines to trumpet, 'Conquerors of All Blacks Plunge to Defeat' or 'Twelve of Side Who Beat NZ — But Newport Still Go Down' and so on. But we could afford to laugh it all off. We had known and savoured the most important single day in the history of our club. For me personally it remains an occasion that takes second place only to the day when I won my first cap.

Again you must bear with me when I describe the Wales–New Zealand Test that winter as something of an anticlimax. The Welsh side, like all British International teams of that time, were virtually a scratch outfit, not well organized and certainly not motivated as Newport had been. We lost a dull game 6–0, contriving only one threatening move during the whole eighty minutes — at the end of which Brian Price dropped a scoring pass.

This was the match in which our captain Clive Rowlands, having been put down ruthlessly by Colin Meads, had to leave the field, holding his back in apparent agony. My own view is that it was frustration at his side's inability to click, rather than pain, which caused Clive's withdrawal. Had he been playing for Pontypool in a Welsh club derby I suspect that Top Cat would have bounced back to his feet, had a rub-down, and continued.

That year was the first time New Zealand had managed to win at Cardiff, and once the disappointment of defeat had worn off we shared a little in their obvious delight. Another win in the Welsh capital was to come their way when the Barbarians were overwhelmed 31–3, Wilson Whineray scoring the final try of the match — and the tour — after a long run which included a dummy I would have been proud of. However, although I had expected to be picked to play at stand-off half, I was not at hand to clap the All Black skipper. My mini-feud with the Ba-Baas was by now under way, and Richard Sharp played instead.

The first major overseas trip of many was to come my way the following summer. Before Wales played France in 1964 the Welsh Rugby Union's secretary Bill Clement handed me a letter. 'Congratulations,' he said. 'Now read it.'

Excitedly I ripped open the envelope. Inside was an invitation from Dr Danie Craven and the South African Rugby Board to visit their country at the end of our home season and take part in the star-studded showpiece matches that were being staged to mark seventy-five years of organized rugby there. My face lit up — but that wasn't all. Added Mr Clement, 'If you are picked for the Wales tour as well you'll have a six-week holiday in South Africa, all expenses paid!' And as it turned out, my name was among the twenty-three listed by the WRU for our country's first-ever representative tour abroad.

I spent the month before departure in a fever of anticipation. Remember that by this time I had barely completed two years as an International player. The prospect of appearing with not only the great Springbok stars but also New Zealanders like Whineray and Clark, Wallabies such as John Thornett and Ken Catchpole and Europeans of Noel Murphy's and Ronnie Glasgow's calibre really set the blood coursing. Alun Pask, Wales's number eight forward, and wing Stuart Watkins were to be other guest stars from our part of the world.

Before the South African trip Wales had to cross the channel to Paris, a journey which obliged me to get a new passport. As I collected it I reflected that shortly its pages would be featuring an impressive montage of franking marks. So, ever the sentimentalist, I have held on to successive issues and treasure them as mementoes of my rugby travels.

After expecting to sit next to Alun Pask on our airliner, I found myself beside Mike Campbell-Lamerton as we took off from Heathrow. Two years later he was to be skipper on an ill-fated Lions tour and, since some critical things will have to be said about that in due course, this is a good point at which to state that I found the assured, jovial Scot very good company indeed. His world, as an Army officer, could scarcely have been more different from my small Welsh village, but he was the soul of charm throughout the long flight. Let it be remembered, too, that Mike was at that time a very fine lock forward. Colin Meads had already called him 'difficult' to play against, which is a whole eulogy in itself.

South Africa entertained her visitors royally. We stayed at luxurious hotels and ordered the food of our choice from big, mouth-watering menus. The white community all seemed to own detached villas where they held lavish barbecue parties in our honour and gave us the freedom of swish swimming pools. What with their generosity and the pocket money allowed by the South African Board I got through my stay for a personal outlay of just £25!

The only gift we were prevented from accepting was a blazer which the authorities wanted to give each of their guests. Scotland's rugby authorities back home got to hear of the proposal and, true to form, sent an acid cable saying that it would interfere with our amateur status. Did we stand for that? We did not! We got round it by suggesting to the South Africans that they paid us a little extra pocket money — out of which we then proceeded to buy our own blazers!

That stratagem shows that I was already familiar with some of the ways of the world. On the other hand, I was not politically aware, and although I had heard of apartheid, like most other twenty-two-year-olds I was not clued up about its finer points.

Occasionally things happened which made me furrow my brow. Once, travelling on a 'fifty-fifty' bus — that is, one carrying blacks and whites — I gave up my seat to an elderly coloured woman. For my pains I was told to get off the bus. Again, at the matches we played it soon dawned on me how the whites monopolized the grandstand seats while blacks were penned in the standing enclosure, often with the sun in their eyes. If a waiter spilt food or drink in a restaurant he was called all the names under the sun.

Today I understand the reasons for some of the things I observed in 1964, and deplore them. However, when so-called liberals demonstrate and shout the odds against South Africa it leaves me unmoved. I always argue that sportsmen want politics kept out of their games, and it is not for governments to decide who may associate, travel or play with whom.

The Rugby League, incidentally, has a clearer conscience than most. There is a long list of coloured men who have achieved distinction in our game, including Clive Sullivan MBE, Billy Boston and Colin Dixon to name but a prominent few. The latter is such a close friend that I do not think of him as coloured at all, and he too seems to be unselfconscious about it. Only once did I freeze with embarrassment, when we sat next to each other at a soccer match between Manchester United and West Ham at Old Trafford. 'Snigger, snigger, snigger,' bawled the crowd in a tasteless reference to the presence of Clyde Best, 'West Ham include a nigger.' Colin just laughed.

He has managed his career expertly since turning pro out of Cardiff's dockland at seventeen, prompted to do so by the struggle his parents were having to make ends meet. Now he is a successful publican in Halifax, who tells all and sundry, 'I'm not a Yorkshireman — I'm a bloody Welshman from Cardiff.'

Pause for a moment to see if you can think of parallels in

the Union game. How many non-whites have played for Wales, England, Scotland or Ireland?

Back to South Africa, however. The Jubilee games were tremendous fun, South African forwards being blended with overseas backs and vice versa. We played three spectacular 'Tests' in Johannesburg, Port Elizabeth and Cape Town, piling up points before big, enthusiastic crowds. The results did not matter, though for the record I played in two winning sides and was a loser once.

In June Alun Pask, now dubbed the world's top number eight forward, and I were joined by our compatriots for a short tour that was to include one Test. Alas, the old faults of poor preparation, organization and method told against us. We struggled to find form throughout, going down first to Northern Transvaal and later by 24–3 to the full South African XV. It did not help the Welsh cause that the Natal and Springbok back row expert Tommy Bedford had used the Jubilee matches to draw up a comprehensive dossier on my own attacking ploys, which helped to stifle Wales's midfield initiatives.

Thus the tour was a traumatic experience for Wales and her rugby pride. All I can say is that it clearly yielded dividends in the years to come. Our coaching revolution dates from 1964. And, in the short term, men like Clive Rowlands and Alun Thomas plugged the idea that a side which had hit the depths on tour could only improve if it was kept together for the Home Championship the following season. That was when Wales managed to gain the title and a Triple Crown to go with it.

A final word on South Africans as a people. In my experience you could get on well with folk from Durban and Cape Town, that is, the British stock. Men like Johnny Gainsford, Tommy Bedford and Keith Oxlee were good company. The Afrikaaners, however, were dour and withdrawn, given to gathering together in cliques to hold private conversations in their own language. So in general I never felt wholly at ease in their society, and rate them the least extrovert and welcoming of the many nations I played against.

*

New Zealanders, on their own soil, proved far different when I toured there in 1966. Although in play they are the hardest and most ruthless of opponents, the warmth with which Mike Campbell-Lamberton and his British Isles team were treated off the field was unsurpassed in my experience.

What a pity we turned out to be such an inept side on the field. Completely failing to give the All Blacks a run for their money, we went down to an ignominious whitewash, the first ever suffered by a British Lions touring party.

Although I am going to fire straight from the hip shortly, let me first say how thrilled I was to be invited to make the trip. Winning caps for one's country is fine, but it is selection for the British Isles that finally marks you out as the top player of your generation in your position. Fortunately I had played some of the best rugby of my career in early 1966, which drew generous and important backing from those two influential writer-critics, Clem Thomas and Wilfred Wooller. These factors helped me to beat off the challenge of highly-rated rivals like England's Tom Brophy.

The brilliant young Irishman Mike Gibson was to be the other stand-off half, probably clinching his place when the men in green beat a fancied Wales XV in Dublin by 9–6. Evidently I had done enough in our previous games for the defeat not to affect my chances; but in other respects this was a score-line that was to cost the Lions dear in later months.

For as a result Alun Pask, a leading candidate for the tour captaincy, was passed over as skipper in favour of Mike Campbell-Lamerton. Alun had led Wales well — but these were days before Carwyn James, John Dawes and Alun Thomas had proved that Welshmen could contribute successfully to the running of a Lions tour. Pask could have made a strong captain. He would have commanded a Test place, which Campbell-Lamerton could not. The only conclusion I can draw is that he was a victim of anti-Welsh prejudice.

Secondly the reverse in Dublin almost certainly led to the omission of hard, seasoned Welsh tight forwards like Brian

Thomas and Norman Gale, who would have enjoyed standing up to New Zealand packs and giving as good as they got. With hindsight, I now believe that the tour selectors were out to eliminate abrasive, rough-diamond characters such as these from the reckoning, in case they besmirched the image of the 'British sportsman' — and Dublin provided a marvellous pretext for doing so. For similar reasons I suspect that they overlooked the claims of Clive Rowlands, discarded by his country but another player ready-made for the harsh exchanges Down Under.

On the other hand some raw and inexperienced men such as David Powell, Frank Laidlaw and Ken Kennedy were picked. The selection, too, of Cardiffian Howard Norris, holder of just two Welsh caps, delighted folk in his home city but surprised them as well. And if you took an overall view of the forwards you could see that although they included some fine tight players they were distinctly lacking in fliers like Haydn Morgan and David Hayward.

Thirdly the management structure was absurd. The former Irish number eight forward Des O'Brien was put in charge, and given PE expert John Robins as his 'assistant'. John trained the team and got us fit, but had no brief to coach us or determine our tactical approach. Match preparation lay in the hands of O'Brien and Campbell-Lamerton who seemed unable to make up their own minds, let alone agree between them, what approach we should adopt. As a result of these things the Lions party on tour often resembled a ship with three rudders all steering in different directions.

We spent two weeks at Bournemouth before departure trying to develop team spirit. By today this anachronism has been dispensed with, and teams spend their pre-tour preparation period within the host country. These days, I also gather, the talk is all about winning; in 1966 we spent hours in negative, sterile discussion about how we could prevent the All Blacks from doing so.

In spite of all this maladroit ground-work, however, it is worth underlining that the party which left Britain in April was not short of talent. Besides some of the stalwarts mentioned earlier it contained backs such as D. Ken Jones,

'Sandy' Hinshelwood and Dewi Bebb; while, properly led and trained, Derek Grant, Gary Protheroe, Alun Pask, Jim Telfer, Ronnie Lamont and Denzil Williams would have been the nucleus of a formidable Test pack.

If you doubt my judgment, ask the Wallabies! We beat their national side comfortably in the two Tests played en route to New Zealand, by margins of 11–8 and then a sizzling 31–0. However, that second, giant victory was just about the worst thing that could have happened to us. It jetted us off to Auckland in a cocksure, as opposed to a confident, mood. It hid our deficiencies in team-work. And it left us all the more unprepared for the days of reckoning which lay ahead.

The first of these occurred at Southland, whose pack took the British Isles apart, pouring through the Lions' ranks like the tide through a broken sea wall. Our defeat there was one of three in the nine-match build-up to the first Test, a period in which we tottered from venue to venue, unable to make up our minds about what we were doing wrong or how to put it right.

In retrospect, of course, it is clear that the trouble was starting up front, in particular at the rucks, where New Zealand forwards reigned supreme during the sixties. Rucking was not coached in Britain at that time, and our forwards had no chance of achieving efficiency in the art, let alone matching All Black expertize. Little Ken Jones, a great theorist, did announce once that if you fell on the ball in a certain way you could not be rucked, and promised to demonstrate what he meant at the first opportunity in our next game, which was to be against Otago. I believe it was big Brian Price who watched Ken carry out his experiment before observing that he looked like something inside a tumbler-drier!

Mention of Ken reminds me how much he had enjoyed playing alongside the clever Irishman, Jerry Walsh. The pair of them were developing into a fine attacking combination when a bereavement cut short Jerry's tour. It also robbed the Lions of a partnership that could have been invaluable in the Tests.

Anyway, after some half-hearted tinkering with our tactical approach during June and early July we reverted for the first Test to the team and the style which had overwhelmed Australia. Predictably we were not good enough by a mile, going down to defeat by 20 points to 3, which was a huge margin in days before the sweeping changes in the laws and in scoring values.

That did it. Now we had a crisis on our hands. There was bitter and outspoken argument within our camp about who was to blame for our poor showing and why we had lost. Individuals took stick. There was a whispering campaign against the biggest national group: 'The Welsh are standoffish and arrogant.' This was rubbish! We mixed as thoroughly and conscientiously as we could. As for 'arrogance' — how is it possible to be arrogant when you are part of a losing side?

So it was in sad circumstances that I reached what many would deem the summit of achievement in the amateur game. The place was Wellington, the time was early August, and the second Test was a few days away. Mike Campbell-Lamerton took me quietly on one side after dinner.

'I've decided to drop myself, David,' he said. 'Will you captain the Lions against New Zealand on Saturday?'

For a tour captain not to lead his Test XV was tantamount to dropping a bombshell of unprecedented proportions. It had never happened before in the annals of British Isles rugby. I accepted the invitation, but my own delight was pretty well cancelled out by the wholehearted sympathy I felt for Mike. By this time he had been exposed as a lock who lacked the vigour and craft necessary to match All Black opponents. However, a captain can still be worth his place if he leads intelligently and inspiringly. In this, Mike's confidence had been undermined by constant sniping criticism from the New Zealand Press; and also by the huge social strain he was under as captain. He later calculated that all told he made 257 speeches on tour, gave eighty radio interviews and appeared on television thirty-six times.

So I agreed to take the helm, knowing instinctively that this was no time to rock the boat. Otherwise I might have said mischievously to Mike, 'Why don't you ask Alun Pask?'

Of course I knew that there was no way the management would turn to Alun in their hour of need. This would have been too close to admitting that he should have been given the captaincy in the first place.

The side which I led out for the second Test contained six changes from the XV that had played at Dunedin. There had been some re-grouping in the three quarter line, including the omission of Ken Jones, while my young compatriot, Delme Thomas, came in at lock, thereby joining the exclusive roll of men who have played British Isles Test rugby before winning an International cap.

Privately I considered that the team selection represented another lurch in policy by management, and could discern no constructive thinking at work. However, the boys and I talked long and earnestly beforehand about the need to restore our self-respect and they did not let me down.

True, we lost by 16 points to 12. But my team played some great rugby, leading at the interval by 9–6— and I will believe to my dying day that we owed our eventual defeat to some crass refereeing by an official called Pat Murphy. First Mike Gibson and later Colin McFadyean were brought back from absolutely clear-cut scoring positions for the Lions to be given the put-in at set scrums— meaning that we were not the infringing side! Murphy's rulings gave special meaning to the cry, 'We wuz robbed'. I was not at all surprised to read in 1969 that the same man was causing alarm and despondency in Welsh ranks during their tour of that year.

Murphy was undoubtedly influenced on the field by Colin Meads, by now a senior International player of five years' standing. A normal ingredient of his play was a running commentary complete with guidance and instructions to referees on every aspect of play from offside to forward passes. Of course, we have players in Wales who attempt the same ploy, but our referees seem to be made of sterner stuff.

Could the Lions, then, win the Third Test and gain a position from which to level the series? What did the manager think?

Manager? Mr O'Brien chose the week preceding this vital match to visit Fiji on a sight-seeing trip. He could have been busy rebuilding our shattered morale. He could have been cracking the whip, arguing team tactics, discussing team selection, relieving our skipper of some social chores. But no: Des was in Fiji, viewing the scenery. Since John Robins was now inactivated by an injured Achilles tendon and Mike Campbell-Lamerton was undecided about his own claim to a Test place, the British Isles were now totally without direction and purpose. Maybe that was why the selected XV for the Test included young Delme Thomas at prop (where he had never previously played), moved forward to accommodate the return of the captain to the second row.

Des O'Brien got back from Fiji in time to view our 19–6 beating, which meant that the series was lost to us for good. We were three quarters of the way towards whitewash.

Our hosts remained charming, indeed they seemed to redouble their efforts to show sympathy to the beaten tourists. If anything, that served to highlight our deficiencies — you can be smothered in sympathy! Often, too, in convivial gatherings the booze would set tongues wagging, and public concern would give way to the acid contempt in which New Zealanders really held this toothless group of so-called Lions.

Personally I rode the storm, knowing that my play had come up to scratch. The only barb which pierced my hide was fired by the Kiwi critic, Terry McLean. He had taken a fancy to the play of Mike Gibson, and saw fit to mount a campaign advising the Lions to play him instead of myself at stand-off half if they wished to avoid a 4–0 Test drubbing. In the years since then my countrymen and I have come to realize how difficult McLean finds it to praise anything Welsh, and his malign championing of this Irishman or that Englishman at the expense of a rival from Cardiff, Llanelli or Newport has become a predictable source of wry amusement. At that time, however, I was more vulnerable, and the thought that I might lose my Test place cost me some lost sleep.

But Mike Campbell-Lamerton, his confidence now completely broken, stood down again for the last Test, so that in the event I led the tourists once more and Gibson continued at centre, where he had already played three times against the All Blacks. Denzil Williams, back after injury, and Ronnie Lamont proved again that they could match anything New Zealand forwards could produce; 'Sandy' Hinshelwood and Colin McFadyean grabbed a try apiece; but in the end, after Alun Pask had snapped a collar bone early on, we fell to an inevitable 24–11 defeat.

We had been 'done' conclusively. We felt sick. We had touched rock-bottom, with no excuse for our whitewash, and no salve for our pride. That is how it feels in big rugby when you are really taken to the cleaners.

The fourth Test, of course, produced the great 'confrontation' between David (Watkins) and Goliath in the shape of Colin Meads, with Goliath reversing the Biblical result. Months later, at a school in New Zealand, Colin was asked why he had knocked me out that day at Eden Park.

'Self-defence,' replied the big fellow, with a poker face.

Actually, it happened like this. The Lions were awarded a penalty inside our 25-yard area, where Colin declined to retire the regulation ten yards. He even remonstrated when the referee attempted to push him back the full distance.

As I took the kick he charged me (which the laws forbid anyway) and put me down late. I jumped up indignantly, shouted at him and jabbed him in the chest, with a four-lettered suggestion that he should get back to his team-mates. That is when Colin knocked me cold. I never saw the punch, and it was two minutes before I saw anything at all except shooting stars!

However, most of the crowd of 52,000 did see the incident, and many of them howled for Colin to be given his marching orders. But the referee claimed that there was nothing he could do about it.

He was, he said, unsighted!

One of the great things about the rugby game, though, is that on-field rifts and feuds are swiftly healed after the final whistle. That night Colin and I sat at dinner together, chatting amicably and reliving the highlights of the series. Both of us, in fact, were guilty of giving vent to a short temper, and if our physiques had been reversed he would probably have been the one put on the deck. That, however, is not to condone the behaviour of either of us.

A couple of years later Meads was sent off the field after flailing wildly with the boot during a game at Murrayfield between Scotland and New Zealand. Appreciating how he must have felt I dashed off a short note of sympathy, to be rewarded with a genial reply wishing me well in my new Rugby League career. Our friendship endures.

There were one or two more dismal experiences in store for me before getting home to Wales. I suffered more than a touch of sunstroke during our Honolulu stopover, which confined me to hospital for a day or two. Then, as the Lions came through Canada bound for the UK, I volunteered to play in the fixture against British Columbia. Although I still felt sore, a number of our midfield men were out of the reckoning with more serious injuries. But I should have known better. The combination of effort and perspiration played havoc with my tender new skin growth, and when I stripped off my jersey before showering most of the skin peeled off with it!

By now we were a very homesick bunch of boys. We had left Britain on 20 April and it was 20 September before our jet touched down again at Heathrow. A tour of five months' duration was far too much for most of us; and even the 16-week visits undertaken by Lions sides in the seventies have been, in my opinion, too much for amateur players.

If I were a member of the Home Unions' tour committee I would be lobbying for eleven-and-a-half week tours. These allow time initially for a party to acclimatize itself and sort out its premier XV against provincial opposition — a very necessary exercise: some players react better to touring circumstances than others, and it is no good assuming that men with the highest reputations at home will be best suited to representative matches on foreign soil. Then, in the final five weeks, a series of, say, three Tests can be played, which is perfectly sufficient for a good, exciting rubber.

Although my stamina and zest for living remained at a low ebb for several weeks I found that I could look back on the tour with some pleasure. As a unit the whitewashed

Lions were in disgrace, but I felt that I had played to form and let no-one down. I was grateful to the rugby authorities for allowing me to broaden my horizons and see yet another part of the world.

Furthermore I had made a whole host of new friends. On a Lions tour the great camaraderie of Rugby Union football really waxes warm and strong. I welded lasting bonds with Englishmen such as Mike Weston, a great competitor and one of the coolest customers the game has known, with Irishmen like Roger Young ('Noddy' because of the way his head bobbed when he walked), and with honest-to-goodness Scots like Jim Telfer. He came close to causing an International incident when he announced after one game, 'I don't like playing against New Zealanders. They are thugs and cheats.'

I got to know some of my own countrymen better, too. Dewi Bebb, our choirmaster, was a quiet chap who often remained in the background puffing away at his pipe, but in his company you soon realized how dependable and reliable a tour companion he made. At the other extreme of liveliness was Terry Price, who came out as a replacement full back midway through the tour. We nicknamed him 'Sump' because of his large consumption of ale — but life was never dull when he was around. Technically I still rate him a better full back than J.P.R. Williams, though he lacked John's aggression and dedication.

A final note to put the whole thing in perspective. I believe that in the years between 1963 and 1970 New Zealand rugby went through one of its golden eras, and this is a view shared by many in that country. The results they obtained in the UK during 1967, and subsequently against a Welsh side which had captured a Triple Crown in 1969, convince me that the Lions of 1966 were not quite as feeble a combination as has been painted.

Back home I played my final two Union matches against overseas opposition for Newport and later the Barbarians versus the Wallaby tourists. Because of the popularity of the League game, which constantly denudes amateur rugby of its top performers, Australia has never touched the heights scaled by New Zealand and South Africa; but their 1966 party had its virtues and held Newport to a 3–3 draw. They then registered a shock win over Wales (from whose team, you will recall, I had been dropped) and ended their tour on a high note with a 17–11 victory over the Barbarians. Here and there I have hinted at my occasional exasperation with the Barbarians Club and their approach to rugby. But it is nice, finally, to record my gratitude to them for the 'consolation' invitation to a man who had just been dropped by his country.

CHAPTER 11

Crossing the Divide

Soon I will be telling you of the night when David Watkins felt like a walking Fort Knox — with a thousand pounds in tenners stuffed into an inside pocket. At least, it started as a thousand, but the number shrank somewhat as I pulled out enough to buy drinks for fans and well-wishers.

The date was October 1967 and I had just become a paid member of Salford Rugby League club. In addition to my signing-on fee the 'grand' had been tossed onto the table to cushion me against removal expenses between South Wales and Lancashire.

I had crossed the great divide, the rigid barrier which separates the amateurs of Rugby Union from the professionals of northern England. I was twenty-five; the price was right; and, looking back, it was probably the most positive and rewarding career step I have ever taken.

Even so it cost me enormous heart-searching at the time, and up until the moment my pen touched the contract I kept thinking of the wonderful Rugby Union fraternity on whom I was turning my back, and from whom I should henceforth have to keep a measured distance. This had been the major factor staying my hand on previous occasions when League representatives had contacted me.

There is a well-developed scout network which blankets South Wales and reports back regularly on potential League captures from the valleys. For me the approaches had begun in 1960 when I was still playing youth rugby, with a cap or two to my credit. I was outside our house in Club Row, Blaina, when a man came slinking up — that is the only way to describe his furtive manner. 'Psst,' he said. 'I know who you are. I'm a Rugby League scout. I represent Halifax.'

My recollection of our short conversation is dim, but it ended with my contact arranging to come and see me in action for my father's Rose Hayward Colliery VII in a tournament a day or two later. What I can remember is how my small chest swelled fit to burst. Me! — approached by a northern scout! I must be a player of some substance. This was certainly something to tell the boys about!

The euphoria lasted only until I checked the Welsh Rugby Union handbook to discover the full implication of the rules concerning amateurism. Their strictness is horrendous.

No-one may 'solicit, discuss or receive' any material reward for playing the game of rugby. Neither may he 'associate' in any way with a non-amateur club. Should he be caught doing so he forfeits all right, forever, to play, coach, referee or administrate Rugby Union football. My eyes popped out as I took in for the first time the absolute meaning of these words.

And I am afraid that my friend from Halifax got no joy when he came to watch my Sevens display. I avoided him like the plague, unwilling even to be seen talking to him. He had said that the possibility of a fee could be discussed — but I wouldn't have gone near him for a king's ransom. He evidently got the message, and troubled me no more.

You may imagine that by that time some kind of amateur idealism had taken root within me. It is true that many sportsmen in Britain, mainly among the middle class, have a horror of taking money for playing games. This attitude is common in Rugby Union circles, and is taken by numerous Welsh players.

However, it was to be some years before I thought such things out in any depth and reached my own, radically different conclusion. At nineteen my position was far simpler: I simply wished to continue my enjoyment of the 15-a-side game and make sure that I did not break any of its commandments. From an early age I felt instinctively that it had a lot to offer — and I was right.

Thus in 1962 I kept at bay the next expeditionary force from the north, this time from Leeds. By now I was a fully-fledged Newport player and had taken part in a couple of Welsh Trials. The Leeds delegation, headed by chairman Joe Wareham and coach Arthur Clues, pulled out all the stops. They dangled a £3000 bait before me, plus other incentives. They gave me a booklet published for the testimonial of Lewis Jones, one of their post-war Welsh signings, to demonstrate how bright my future could be at Leeds. But I turned them down flat in the end; this time my main reason was the full cap for Wales which I felt could not be far away.

A year later, when my tempters were St Helens, that target had been hit and I was recognized as Wales's leading stand-off half. This time club chairman Harry Cook and secretary Basil Lowe were accompanied by Kel Coslett, a former Wales full back who had become a big success in the League game. They did not mess around, and drove straight to Club Row in a splendid Mark 10 Jaguar which created a mild sensation locally. Blaina was not exactly flush with such vehicles.

And the pressure they put me under was greater than any I had known before. In our 'best' room, reserved for Sunday tea and VIPs, the three confronted my parents and me. Kel gave a reassuring little homily about how well I was bound to do with St Helens, at the end of which Harry suddenly plonked £5000 in crisp banknotes on the table between us.

I gaped. My mother's eyes widened. My father was speechless. We had never seen a tenth of that amount all at one time.

A long silence ensued — but if ever money talked it was in that little room in Club Row.

The Watkins trio retired to the living room, where my father came down in favour of my signing and said so. 'Where else could our boy get his hands on money like that?' he demanded. My mother demurred. 'Don't force him. David must make up his own mind,' she insisted.

In the end I played for time and told our guests that I would 'let them know' — a good Welsh habit which relieves one of the socially embarrassing necessity of turning a person down flat. In due course I informed them that I would not be signing for St Helens.

Why would a man turn down a tax-free offer of that magnitude, you may now be wondering? It took some doing, for the northerners had been persuasive, polite and plausible. They had pointed out that a job could readily be found for me; that large insurance premiums paid by the club meant that I need not worry about being injured while at play; that it would be a good feeling to provide some capital and security for my parents and dependants.

Stubbornly, however, I clung to my belief that the Union game as it was run in Wales could give me all I wanted from life. Moreover, like many South Welshmen, I was suspicious of strangers bearing gifts. The north of England was another world to me (remember that I had only recently discovered London, and places just across the Severn estuary like Bristol were still relatively new to me), and I had no desire to spend my early twenties being homesick. Wales is an affectionate, tight-knit community whose sons leave it only with reluctance.

Truly, I felt in need of advice. Normally when a young man launches out upon a new career wise words are available in abundance. But the potential convert from Union to paid ranks is almost totally isolated. On the one hand he hears the cloying words of men brandishing contracts and bundles of pound notes; but there is no balancing guidance he can seek, for to bring his dilemma out into the open may damage his amateur status. He is on his own.

With hindsight I probably put too much trust in the WRU powers-that-were. 'One-cap wonders' like Bobby Wanbon, Coslett himself and Colin Evans are witnesses to the absence of systematic selection in those days, and given the wrong sort of luck I could have finished in that category too. Also, from a strictly careerist point of view I think now that it is a good idea to learn the basics of a game like Rugby League at twenty-one, rather than at twenty-five when it is harder to discard Union habits and adapt to fresh circumstances.

To be blunt, even after the intensified TV coverage of League football in recent years, Wales has never been turned on by the game, and certainly showed no great interest in it in the sixties. I knew, for example, that the League game was played by teams of thirteen, not fifteen, and that it was reputedly harder than Union; but there my awareness of it stopped. As a matter of fact, until the time I joined Salford the sole 'live' League rugby I had seen was a quick view of the 1967 Wembley final as the guest of a commercial company.

Anyway, the word must have got around the North that David Watkins was no easy catch, and I was left alone for several years. During the British Lions' 1966 tour of Australia there was newpaper speculation that Ken Jones and I would be lured into League rugby with either Sydney or Brisbane. The alleged offer was for 20,000 Aussie dollars—about £10,000. But it was unfounded; no one even approached us. Commentator Eddie Waring, in that country at the same time to cover the Great Britain League tour, came to do one of our Tests against the Wallabies and sent home reports that several Lions would be prepared to sign for Northern clubs on their return hime. He too was a bit premature.

But the controversies that occasionally reared their head at this time left their mark on me and gradually crystallized my own attitude to professionalism. My contemporaries and I always undercut our expense claims, to the delight of club and WRU treasurers, for fear of the remotest possibility of our being accused of 'making money' out of playing. The modern players tell me that penny-pinching tactics are still employed today, even at International level. I once had to ensure that a lamp standard presented to me by an admirer cost no more than £5, which was then the limit imposed upon gifts to amateurs.

That rule was behind the row which blew up over a set of golf clubs, worth about £60, which some Cwmbran folk attempted to give Clive Rowlands after the Triple Crown success to which he led Wales in 1965. When the authorities got to hear about it 'Top Cat' was ordered to return the gift. I have noted earlier Clive's sudden departure from the Wales XV and his failure to gain selection as a British Lion; and I think that particular fuss knocked another nail in the coffin of his representative career.

My reaction was that people were simply being mean-minded. When one hears about the abundance of free kit and fringe benefits which accrue to the amateur players of the present it is not difficult to conclude that horses and carts have been driven straight through the old, strict definition of amateurism.

The other factor that finally prised open my mind to the real possibility of moving to a new rugby scene was my cavalier treatment by our selectors during late 1966 and spring 1967. You will recall that they first confined me to Wales's reserve bench, and after a defeat or two suddenly named me captain of my country. The last straw was their selection of a squad to prepare to meet New Zealand without the appointment of a captain. I decided that they must be a pretty mixed-up bunch.

My day of destiny, as it turned out, came in the Manchester area. Brian Price and I had flown there direct from a free-and-easy Wolfhounds tour in Ireland to link up with Newport clubmates and play as a 'David Watkins VII' in the Glengarth tournament staged to help local handicapped children. Since the competition was held on a Sunday, a day not recognized then by the WRU as proper for playing rugby, we could not play as 'Newport,' winners of the Welsh Sevens the previous spring — though our club did allow us to wear the famous black and amber stockings. However, our touch was as good as ever, and in the final we overwhelmed the Harlequins who were holders of the Middlesex Sevens title.

Glengarth has gone from strength to strength, with ever-increasing numbers of spectators attending each year. The area does not contain many glamorous Rugby Union clubs, so the tournament affords a tremendous opportunity to local fans of seeing a smattering of capped players and some quality rugby.

However, in the crowd of 6000 on this particular occasion the presence of one man in particular made all the difference to the life and times of David Watkins. It was our old Newport colleague John Mantle, who joined us afterwards for a few reunion pints.

After a while he took me a little way apart. 'A bloke from the Salford club has been watching you,' he said. 'Snape by name — he's their chairman. He's interested in you, and if he gets the chance he intends making you a cash offer.'

I inclined an ear.

'If he does, rush him for some more,' advised John.

I grinned and wrote down my number at the Newport office of Forward Trust, the finance company which had recently taken me on. 'There,' I said, 'tell Mr Snape to ring me if he feels like it.' Then I changed the subject. Nor did I give it a second thought as Newport's minibus zoomed south-westwards with its exultant but somewhat beery cargo of Sevens players.

I reached work promptly the following morning and was sleepily opening my mail at ten o'clock when the telephone rang.

'Good morning. My name is Brian Snape,' said a voice. 'I am chairman of Salford Rugby League club. I understand you would be prepared to consider a cash offer to play rugby for us.'

Instantly my head cleared and I pulled myself together.

'Just a minute,' I said. 'Firstly, I'm not at all sure that I want to get involved. Secondly, you must realize that I'm now twenty-five. My rugby career is half finished.'

'I know that,' was the reply. 'But I saw you play at the Sevens yesterday. I believe you could have a lot to offer us.'

They don't lose much time, I was thinking.

'Could we meet to discuss terms?' Mr Snape was continuing.

There was something in the voice. This man, I felt straightaway, was a different kettle of fish from the northern folk I had met years before. But— there was no need to sound too keen. I tried to stall by saying that I could not afford to get involved in a telephone call which might be overheard. Mr Snape replied that he had put through the call privately, and that none of his staff could possibly be listening to us.

'I need time to think,' I told him. 'Tell John Mantle to ring me.'

'All right,' said the man from Salford. 'He'll be in touch' — and he rang off.

John Mantle telephoned me in the afternoon.

'Did he mention money?' he wanted to know.

'No,' I said.

'OK. Leave it to me,' said John.

Mr Snape came through again the following day. The hunt was becoming remorseless. This time he said he was prepared to put £6000 on the table. Remembering what St Helens had offered me several years earlier, I told him boldly, 'You must be joking!' But next, in his own handwriting, he sent me a letter raising his offer to £10,000, which was negotiable. And he asked for an early meeting. This was it, I thought: now was the time for some really hard thinking.

In addition to this pressure, the newspapers had got hold of the story from northern sources and were trying to extract the truth from me. One evening after appearing for Newport at Cross Keys I was spotted at a telephone booth—making, as it happens, a perfectly innocent call to my brother. The following day's *South Wales Argus* carried a big 'exclusive' alleging that I had spent an hour on the 'phone completing final negotiations with a big northern club!

Remember the difficulty of my position at this time. There was no way in which I could make a clean breast, nor did I have the nerve to deny the rumours categorically. What I needed badly was some good advice. So in desperation I turned to the area manager of Forward Trust, Gwynne Walters, a distinguished International referee. In truth, he was a pillar of the Rugby Union establishment in Wales. However, to his everlasting credit, he leaned over backwards to be objective in my case.

'If you've really got an offer of £10,000-plus in writing, you have simply got to take it very seriously indeed,' he counselled. 'If you talk to Salford you can probably push the figure a lot higher. In that case, frankly, I don't think you can afford to turn it down.

'I think I can safely say that the directors of Forward Trust would be willing and able to grant you a transfer to our Manchester office.'

Those words helped immensely, and firmed my resolve. The time, at last, seemed to be ripe. I still had my parents to deal with, and curiously my father had by now become the one who sought to dissuade me. My mother was over the moon at the amount of money offered; while my father pouted and put up all the objections he could think of. Later I reached the conclusion that he had secretly savoured the 'perks' which, as an International player, I could provide for him and now foresaw a bleak future as one whose son had turned his back on rugby in his homeland.

However, it was a moment to stand on my own two feet and be decisive. I agreed to meet the Salford delegation on the 19 October 1967 at a hotel called the Royal Hop Pole in Tewkesbury. This venue seemed a satisfactory half-way house, besides being a safe distance from the Welsh rugby grapevine. On the eve of our rendezvous I played for Newport at Abertillery, experiencing acute pangs of disloyalty as I had two nights before when sitting with our committee to pick the team.

The tension I felt overflowed at one stage when an opposing back row forward tackled me late. Right in front of the referee I leaped to my feet and thumped the offender, an action which merited dismissal from the field. But, of all people, Gwynne Walters happened to be in charge that evening. He took my arm firmly and led me away from the other players. The crowd cheered loudly, believing that I was receiving a stern lecture.

But: 'Don't go out with a sending-off,' Gwynne was saying with a twinkle in his eye!

That night I spent at the house of my friends the Talbots, whose daughter, Jane, and I were keeping regular company by now, and she came to my room at 8.30 to wake me and say that she was off to work. She had a job getting through to me, for I had not slept a wink. Later, Jane admitted that she had not either.

My first stop after leaving Newport was Abergavenny, where I was to pick up Mr Morgan, my solicitor. In those days it was an hour's run, during which time I tried to collect my thoughts and work out an approach to these strangers who wanted to buy me, body and soul. As the Sugar Loaf mountain came into my sights, soon after passing Pontypool, I knew what the answer was. Disguising any eagerness or excitement I would push them as far as possible, preferably to £15,000. Then, if I liked the deal and the contract they offered, they could have my signature.

Mr Morgan and I drove into the Royal Hop Pole car-park at 12.25 and made our way to the lounge, where we swiftly identified the delegation we were to meet. The Snapes: Brian, and his equally suave brother, Keith, who was Salford's secretary; Griff Jenkins, the club's Rhondda-born coach; and the late John Berry, their solicitor. After greetings and some small talk it was he who presented me with the contract which would shape my future.

Tied up with green ribbon, it contained six pages of small print. As John Berry told me months later, 'Signing you was like buying a bloody house. And the money involved was the same — except that I kept trying to persuade Brian Snape that you weren't worth it!'

I held it; I felt it; I looked at it. And I decided that there was no way in which I would be able to get any food down me. Between my fingers I was clutching the key to a fortune.

'You go and eat, gentlemen,' I said with as much authority as I could muster. 'Mr Morgan and I will look through this document.'

Brian Snape and co. protested but eventually gave in. 'By the way,' I warned them quietly as they made their way to the dining room, 'this is going to cost you a few thousands more than you had bargained for.'

Mr Snape did not bat an eyelid. He nodded, and left the two of us to pore over the sheets of typescript which could turn me into a Rugby League slave. Full of suspicion, I insisted that we scrutinized every letter, every comma, for possible loop-holes — but can you blame me? After all, I didn't know Brian Snape and his companions from Adam. Truth to tell, I had only the haziest idea where Salford was, let alone what sort of club the place boasted. I still had that lonely, hunted feeling.

Three long hours passed while we went through the document minutely. Three times the head waiter appeared from the dining room to ask the reluctant guests if they required food, only to be greeted with shakes of the head. Not until long afterwards did it occur to me that my solicitor, for whom the occasion presented no particular hazards, was probably starving, while I was denying us a steak lunch with wine, brandy and cigars.

Occasionally he came up with an alteration, sometimes it was my turn. Never in my life, before or since, have I been so fussy. One sentence, for example, read, 'He will play for Salford whenever fit enough to do so.' I insisted that it be altered to '. . . whenever HE FEELS fit enough to do so.' If Salford thought they were taking white cargo on board, I for one did not.

The good people of Lancashire may find it strange that I was so mistrustful of four gentlemen of good repute from their county. I can only re-emphasize the solitary role that I was playing, and the fact that I was on the point of signing away many years of my youth. Nothing like this had happened to me before, nor did it subsequently. Nor does it fall to many ordinary mortals to sign a piece of paper that admits them to riches. That experience, and that whole day, retain an unreal quality in my memory.

At half past three by the hotel clock we were ready for the final confrontation. The Snapes and Mr Berry combed the contract which Mr Morgan and I had dotted with amendments. They endorsed them all, one by one, and I still smile to recall the laborious process whereby five sets of initials accompanied each tiny change of emphasis or meaning.

Four-thirty; we have pushed the signing-on fee to £10,000 plus £1000 at the start of the succeeding five seasons. Sheet six is pushed under my nose. It has spaces — for my signature, for that of Brian Snape, and for a witness from each side.

Welsh rugby is about to lose one of its star performers. Or will I pull back at the eleventh hour?

'All we need is your name,' says John Berry. 'Right?'

'Right,' I say.

I take the pen. My hand trembles a bit. I take a breath. Farewells flood into my mind — to Newport, to my career with Wales, to my homeland.

Then I write 'David Watkins' in a rather wobbly hand; and Brian Snape reclaims the vital document. 'Bloody marvellous,' he says with satisfaction.

I am a Rugby League player. I have taken the money. More money than has ever been paid before to a new signing.

But the Watkins cheek endures. Handshakes and congratulations all round follow, and Brian Snape queries a frown on my face.

'Well Mr Snape,' I say. 'You did promise that there would be some extra cash to cover my removal expenses up north and to buy furniture for a new home.'

'Ah, yes,' says the chairman, feeling inside his jacket. He fishes out a bundle of notes and tosses them onto the table. 'Don't bother to count them, David. That's a thousand pounds exactly.'

At last I knew that I could trust these people. I picked up the cash, feeling a warm glow of content. It, and the money, stayed close to my heart for the remainder of that amazing day.

That is how, after a thoughtful but happy journey back from Tewkesbury (via Abergavenny, where I slipped Mr Morgan a tenner to compensate for his lost lunch), I came to be carrying an inside pocket-full of loot at Tredegar and Rhymney Golf Club on 19 October 1967! On my way home I had carried out three obligations: as promised, I rang journalists J.B.G. Thomas and Brian Wall to give them the scoop they had been waiting for. And I phoned Jane.

'I've signed,' I said.

'My God,' she blurted. And rang off.

We had booked a table for that evening to celebrate her birthday. Inevitably it became the centre of attraction for every radio, television and newspaper reporter in South Wales. Poor Jane took a back seat, her coming-of-age presents shoved onto a side table to make room for tape recorders, cameras and note-books.

Everybody seemed to want to put the same question: 'How do you feel?' To each questioner I gave the same reply. I didn't feel any different at all. I was simply leaving to play a different kind of rugby, for which I would be paid. Nothing else had happened. I fenced off the hard questions: 'Will you regret being unable to play for Newport and Wales against the All Blacks?' 'What will you miss most about Welsh rugby?' and so on. Gradually the media men, still twittering with excitement, faded away into the night.

'I'm sorry about your party,' I said to Jane. Then I added: 'By the way, they've said I must make my debut for Salford tomorrow night against Oldham. I leave in the morning.'

She looked at me, wide-eyed. 'They don't waste much time, do they?' And then, firmly, 'I'll come with you.'

I knew that I had at least one close ally in my new career.

Forward Trust generously gave me a week off as breathing space in which to finalize removal arrangements. Much of the time I used replying to the myriad notes and cards from admirers and well-wishers. I understand how crestfallen Welsh fans become when one of their top players leaves the fold; but my mail-bag in that final week of October also showed me how quick they are to hide their disappointment and send a man on his way in good heart. Mr Clement's letter, on behalf of the WRU, sums it all up: 'I now express to you my appreciation and thanks for your tremendous contribution to Welsh rugby in recent years,' he wrote. 'You have been a credit to Wales both on and off the field, and our loss is the professional game's gain.'

Not one letter or telephone call hit a sour note, and I remain immensely moved by the respect and affection shown towards me. In those days, I suppose, we were judged entirely by our impact as players. Nowadays, following the intensification of rugby coverage on television and radio and in the Press, first-class players are far better known to their followers — with a correspondingly higher chance that some folk will take against them for personality traits revealed on the screen or in statements to the Press.

Young men, unused to the artifices of reporters out for a story, can often place themselves in a bad light with an immature or ill-chosen comment. As a player of the sixties I escaped such pressures, and my standing with the bob-bankers remained agreeably high.

So only my father said grumpily, 'You are on your own now. I shan't bother to come and see you play.' Later though he became a convert, and latterly looked forward to week-ends at Salford.

However, one sentence written by Bill Clement preserved a sense of perspective. 'I am sure,' wrote he, 'that in due time we will again be able to fill the serious gap in our playing ranks as a result of your departure.' He was right, of course. Soon Barry John came good, and Wales were once more well served at stand-off half.

In this life, no-one is indispensable.

CHAPTER 12

The North

To this day the number plate of the vehicle which I drove up the M6 in October 1967 to my new life is imprinted on my memory: MAX 133E. It was a Ford Anglia — but I might as well have been piloting a spaceship for all I cared about the little car's performance.

Even Jane, in the passenger's seat, found me uncommunicative. She knew that my brain was whirling with a myriad questions which clamoured for an answer. How would I fare in the evening fixture against Oldham which awaited me? What sort of welcome could I expect from the Salford players? Most pressingly, would I recognize the club chairman Brian Snape, whom I had arranged to join at the Knutsford service station? Yes, I had met him the previous day, when he had written me a five-figure cheque — but my mind had been in a daze and at its least retentive.

For fear of missing him in the hurly-burly of the cafeteria Jane and I sat in our parked car to wait. I need not have worried, for top people have ways of signalling their arrival. Soon a low, sleek Aston Martin DB5 purred its way into the car-park, and I knew that this was it. 'Mr Salford' was here.

A broad grin creased his face as he spotted us, and leaning out of the window he gave instructions to follow him to the hotel where we would be lunching. That was when I cursed my little Anglia, racing up and down the gears as I tried to keep in touch with the sports saloon sprinting through Cheshire's leafy lanes. It was a relief when the old mansion house that had been converted into Stanneylands Hotel hove in sight.

Here we sat at table with Brian, his brother Keith, Griff Jenkins and — when he could escape constant interruptions

— Vernon Darby who managed the hotel and was a director of Salford. He was to be my landlord until I could find a property of my own.

The ice was swiftly broken, and the atmosphere became totally different from the cat-and-mouse manoeuvrings of the previous day at Tewkesbury. But soon Jane was whisked off on a shopping expedition by Mrs Peggy Snape and the time had come for this new catch from Wales to be paraded in front of the northern Press.

And, to the astonishment of the old dears and retired colonels who habitually passed pleasant afternoons sipping tea and relaxing at Stanneylands, the media now mounted a full-scale invasion. Television cameras whirred, floodlights flared into the autumn afternoon, reporters rapped out brisk, no-nonsense questions. Don Mosey was there, along with Keith Macklin. Jack Bentley from the *Express* introduced himself, as did Jack MacNamara of the *Manchester Evening News* — the last-named a close friend of Salford who became a firm friend of mine too.

I recognized the same eagerness to probe and disclose with which I had been familiar in South Wales where J.B.G. Thomas, Malcolm Lewis, Brian Wall and the like ruled the roost. These were men who could help to make or break me. So I dealt scrupulously with them, giving them the quotable lines I knew they wanted and parrying questions which it did not suit me to answer too bluntly.

Sessions with the Press and TV can be exceedingly exhausting — especially when they ask you to pose for a coaching lesson from the club coach on how to play the ball after a tackle. I felt a bit of a fool grubbing around on an expensive hotel carpet in a 'piggy scrum', heeling a gleaming white rugby ball for the benefit of the cameramen.

Brian Snape, thank goodness, recognized it. 'Right, gentlemen,' he said kindly but firmly, 'that's enough for now. You've got your quotes and pictures. David has a job to do tonight.'

And to me, as the reporters went on their way: 'Off to bed now. Get an hour's kip. I'll call you in good time.'

I was escorted to, would you believe, the bridal suite! Now I was really married to Rugby League. But I could not sleep.

I lay back and fondled the soft leather of my boots, the sole item of kit that I had brought from South Wales: would they serve me as well on this new alien turf as they had in my homeland?

Mr Snape and I left for Salford after tea — and if I had been worrying about my debut it was clearly nothing to the torment the chairman was feeling. He chain-smoked furiously, at one point tossing a butt-end through what he thought was an open window. It struck glass and bounced into the back seat. We stopped the car and lost five minutes retrieving it.

His ability to judge a player, you see, was about to be put to the test by the wider world. Our negotiations had been secret until the end, and Salford's top man had plotted a lone course as he went after a player who he hoped would bring success and big gates to his club. It had cost money. Was the investment to pay off? Would this miniature Welshman from an obscure mining valley repay his faith? Or was Brian Snape about to be crucified by the watching world of Rugby League?

Meanwhile I was experiencing my own private agony. Wilmslow and the Cheshire plain had seemed lush, fertile pastures, agreeable to the immigrant. But suddenly we were quitting the new motorway ring-road and approaching Salford via Eccles along the road parallel to the canal. I was thinking, 'My God. Is this what I have let myself in for?'

Demolition and slum clearances have changed the face of this part of the world in the past decade. But in 1967 all you could see from the road were row upon row of tiny, terraced houses garlanded by lines of washing, hanging not in the back gardens, for there were none, but across what appeared to be main streets. 'This is hell,' I was saying frankly to myself. 'It makes the South Wales valleys seem like Utopia.' Such bleak thoughts occupied my mind until we swung into the Salford car-park at 6.45, three quarters of an hour before the kick-off of our match against Oldham.

There were more photographers' flash-bulbs to blind the pair of us as we disembarked, and a microphone or two thrust beneath our noses. But a couple of steps took us through the crowds into the changing-room area and, as far as I was concerned, out of the frying-pan into the fire. Salford's £15,000 capture confronted his new team-mates.

My eyes widened as Brian Snape went through the introductions. Joe Southwood, a wing, stood there on crutches. Terry Ogden, a forward, had a cracked knee-bone swathed in plaster. As David Evans (now a painter and decorator back in Penclawdd) bent forward to tie a boot-lace he revealed a scalp so criss-crossed with red weals that it resembled a road-map. I might have imagined that I was in a casualty clearing station, except that the room itself put me in mind of a prison cell.

However, to my relief, the greetings of my fit colleagues were friendly enough. That first evening I recall shaking hands with Peter Smethurst, Charlie Bott (a Bachelor of Arts and Salford's 'intellectual'), Paul Jackson, a wing, and Aidan Breen and Stuart Whitehead who were to become firm friends. In response to my apprehensive questions they replied, 'Yes, this game is tough all right. It's for men. But it's not too tough.'

Most of the boys, though, were donning shoulder-pads, which seemed another ominous sign to the Welsh novice. I tried on a set for laughs, but found them lumpy and top-heavy. My biggest thrill came from tugging on a crisp red Salford jersey with its smart white vees.

Before the match I noted with interest that our captain, scrum half Jackie Brennan, had little to say, leaving the final pep-talk to our coach. Nor were Griff Jenkins's words anything special compared with the spirited mini-orations I had been used to delivering in the Newport changing-room. He seemed to concentrate on warning us of the threat posed by individual opponents in the Oldham side such as Tug Wilson, a prop of Gloucestershire extraction, and Michael Elliott, a man from, of all places, my own Youth stamping ground at Cwmcelyn. In Rugby Union the object was to motivate your own men. Never mind about the opposition, let them worry about you. Griff's method struck me as rather negative.

His one valuable word of advice to me was to guard against being late-tackled after passing or kicking the ball.

'Opponents will come through onto you willy-nilly,' he said, 'so keep on your toes and don't present them with a sitting target.'

As with my first International match for Wales, so that first outing with Salford passed like lightning and it is difficult to recall many of the details. One impression, though, is of the big crowd; instead of the gate of some 7000 that was the norm there were about 15000 spectators packed into the ground. Then it occurred to me uneasily that 8000 of them had simply turned up to see the new man from Wales put through the mangle.

Still, it wasn't a bad debut, although I say so myself. The result was an 11–6 win for Salford, to which I contributed two dropped goals and a try which crowned a long solo run from our own 25. That seemed to get the crowd on my side straightaway, and they cheered lustily afterwards when they heard that I had been named 'man of the match'. I echoed their cheers silently, since this meant a John Player award of £6 and put me on course immediately for their big 'man of the season' prize of £200 to be handed out at the end of the winter.

Technically I had done moderately well. Union players, of course, release the ball on being tackled, whereas in League you must usually hang onto it so that possession can be retained. I slipped up in this respect just twice. Critics also commented that I ran across-field too much in the search for openings, whereas a golden rule of the new code was to go forward at all times.

I got one bump after dropping my second goal which hurt a bit, and ticked myself off for standing still to admire my kick instead of heeding Griff Jenkins' advice to step smartly out of the way. Apart from that Jackie Brennan kept me well protected from trouble.

Two other differences were brought home to me. First, linesmen have a duty to assist referees. I approve both of the custom and of the professional expertise of the linesmen, who are expected to pass an examination before taking up a flag. In Rugby Union touch judges are frequently no more than helpful committeemen without special qualifications, so a similar system might be impracticable to

Watkins country: but my mother was unwilling for me to become a miner.

Skipper of Cwmcelyn Youth in 1960. After Under-18 caps for Wales, the big-time was now beckoning.

The break that helped Newport beat the 1963 All Blacks. With the New Zealand defence disorganized, the cross-kick that followed allowed Dick Uzzell time to drop his historic goal.

After scorching wins in Australia, plus the acquisition of a ten-gallon hat, I arrive in New Zealand for the 1966 Lions–New Zealand Test series. But the hat had to be doffed to the vastly superior All Blacks.

Right-hand man of the five seated Barbarians. A club with which I had a turbulent relationship, but their invitation to play against Australia was agreeable compensation for being dropped by Wales!

Followed by the young Gerald Davies and Gareth Edwards I lead out Wales for my last International match as an amateur *v.* England in 1967. Our 34–21 victory redeemed a season which, for me, was a shambles.

On the way to a shower after my dream debut for Salford on 20 October, 1967. The law protects me from autograph hunters.

Salford triumphant in the Cossack Sevens of 1968. My skill at the mini-game brought me the club captaincy.

Players standing, left to right: Ken Halliwell, Doug Hill, Les Bettinson, Stuart Whitehead.

Front: Bob Prosser, Jackie Brennan, Chris Hesketh, DW.

A Blackpool bubble-bath for DW, Trevor Rabbit and Jackie Brennan as we prepared for Wembley. Alas the 1969 Cup Final was a cold-water occasion for Salford.

Spot on target.
But unerring aim
comes only after
endless solitary
hours of practice.

A try against Wigan: in the end their fans stopped shouting 'fairy' at me!

A Wales–England League duel featuring four great contemporaries: (*left to right*) Roger Millward, Bill Francis, Jimmy Thompson and Mal Reilly.

Mel James and Parry Gordon loom over George Nicholls, but cannot prevent the 1978 'Man of Steel' from delivering his pass. George was a player I greatly respected.

Australia's defence relaxes for a second, and Roger Millward is through the gap. 'The Dodger' was idolized Down Under.

Ball-carrier Robin Whitfield's progress is abruptly halted. Once we tangled angrily on the pitch but now Robin is one of the League's top referees.

The evening of my career, but still the kids want autographs! My 1979 debut for Swinton and only the third club jersey to be worn by me.

introduce. But it may turn out to be invaluable at International or Cup games, where a qualified ref on the touchline can now advise the official in charge about off-the-ball incidents.

For the first time that evening I also experienced the half-time retreat to the changing-room. Some readers may wonder whether there is a danger of a player going 'off the boil' or getting cold and stiff during a ten-minute break. But I decided straightaway that there was much to be said for this chance to sit and think hard about the game, talk tactics quietly with team-mates, or simply replace a wet, muddy jersey with a warm, dry one.

On the whole the Salford camp seemed genuinely pleased with my display, and there were slaps on the back from directors and season-ticket holders when we gathered afterwards in the VIP lounge bar. It was hereabouts that a Pressman put to my team-mates the question I had been dreading: what sort of feelings did they have about this new arrival who was starting his career at Salford with a silver spoon in his mouth?

I don't suppose that at that stage the fee I had been paid was common knowledge. However, as it had been hailed as a record, the boys knew that I must have banked a five-figure cheque. Other men who cost a lot have since confided to me their awareness of feelings of jealousy harboured by local players. And when men who have turned pro for a couple of hundred quid or less rub shoulders with one who got many times as much for his signature, you cannot blame them for feeling that life hands out some raw deals.

So I was hugely relieved when I heard Peter Smethurst's answer. 'We don't care what he's been paid,' he said flatly. 'It looks as though he'll help me and the boys to make money. We're happy.'

A further indication of acceptance came when Terry Ogden, Aidan Breen and Stuart Whitehead invited Jane and me to visit a night-spot with them and their wives. We dined, drank and danced well into the early hours.

Brian Snape had quietly thanked me, saying that he was a happy man. Then he had left, discreetly allowing the process of integrating David Watkins into the Salford team to continue. But before I slept that night I gave much thought to this man who had introduced me so smoothly to the northern scene.

Over the years he has impressed me as something of a model chairman. All I knew of him in 1967 was that he was forty-five years of age, and that two years previously he had succeeded his father whose term as Salford's chairman stretched back to 1935. Mr Snape senior had owned cinemas as far apart as Manchester, Blackpool and Bournemouth, and when cinema-going began to decline in the sixties had responded robustly. He and his sons had adapted some of their premises to take advantage of the eating-out habit which was fast catching on, and converted others to bingo halls. Also, recognizing the need for service industries close to the booming Manchester airport, they had branched out into hotels. Stanneylands was acquired in 1964 and before long the 150-acre Mottram Hall, a stately home, became the pride of their chain.

The Snapes made big profits, but large helpings of the cash went into improving our club and the lot of its players. Nowadays, compared with the somewhat austerely furnished club-houses of big Union teams, Salford's is a palace. The décor in its main bars and reception areas would grace a five-star hotel. It boasts sauna facilities, squash courts, and a magnificent hall where 1500 can sit in comfort to enjoy performances by top entertainers like Lulu, Bob Monkhouse and the Three Degrees.

Brian is a man who has always set out to make his staff feel special. In 1967 he was paying £25 for a win — and that was £5 more than the then average wage in the UK. He introduced overnight stays before big away fixtures, to relieve players of a long, tedious bus journey on the morning of a match. He insisted that we all ate an evening meal on the way home together, so fostering team spirit.

He was perceptive enough to win players' wives over to his way of thinking, establishing a crêche where toddlers could be looked after while mum sat in the grandstand to watch dad playing. In Rugby League, as I quickly understood, his methods were revolutionary, and it has taken many other clubs a whole decade to catch up with Salford. Some of them still haven't.

For these reasons Brian Snape has made enemies in the rugby world at large, and has been misunderstood. Not that I am claiming that he is without his faults. Wealthy men such as he are often accused of playing puppets with a club and its players, enjoying the sense of power derived from manipulating them. To me it has sometimes seemed that he wanted a finger in too many pies.

He demanded to know every last detail about players' wages, and the size of our gates. He frequently interfered in team selection. He could be generous to a fault: there was one occasion when, instead of a £15 payment for a defeat, we all found £50 in our wage packets. 'I felt sorry for you,' explained Brian. 'You all did your best.' Fine — but how, then, can men be motivated to win?

Some individuals exploited this trait of his. Bill Kirkbridge signed for us, soon to find that he could make plenty of cash simply claiming travelling expenses from Halifax. So he confined his appearances for Salford to a mere one in every three fixtures. Johnny Ward was a great forward who, in my opinion, never pulled out all the stops for Salford and would have responded better to some cracking of the whip.

Curiously too, for a man up to his neck in so physical a game, Brian has a horror of violence for its own sake which has led him to take some controversial decisions. One year we signed Derek Clark from Swinton for £9000 because the coach decided that we needed some steel in the pack. Soon Derek was quoted in a newspaper article describing his methods of clobbering opponents — but when chairman Snape read it, he had to go. Derek was sold off to Leigh for a bargain-basement price of £3000.

My own relationship with Brian, however, has always been warm and friendly. He has two delightful daughters, Julie and Jill, and it has sometimes occurred to me that I stand in the place of the son he would have liked as well. Other Salford players have noted our friendship in the last decade — and sometimes used it to their advantage, exploiting my persuasive powers with the chairman to push through some reform. At other times they have contented themselves with a sly gibe in my direction such as, 'What does Snapey's boy think, then?'

I owe Brian Snape a big debt. But looking back I can say with confidence that I began repaying him the moment I first trotted out at Willows Road. Crowds of 10,000-plus started to be the norm, and even at places like Whitehaven and Workington a visit by our XIII doubled gates to around 6000. Salford, with their new Welsh signing, were set to become the Manchester United of the Rugby League.

CHAPTER 13

The Glittering Prizes

Have you ever come into money? Had a big pools win? Cleaned up on Ernie? No? So you don't know how it feels. Well, sit back and find out from one who does.

Now, I must first of all be honest and admit that I had not really been on the breadline during my days as an amateur player. But my bank balance had never overflowed with riches either. Like most people, I invariably had to think carefully and exercise caution before buying an expensive item. And some desirable luxuries remained beyond my reach.

As late as summer 1967, holidaying with Jane and her parents in Bournemouth, I can recall peering wistfully into a car showroom which featured a trim Sunbeam Alpine sports model. The price tag said £700. Jane and I looked at one another, agreed what fun it would be to zip around the byways of Gwent in such a vehicle — and sadly ruled its purchase out of the question. I had some £500 put away as a nest egg, but there were other priorities that stopped us from doing more than dream.

And yet before that year was out, my fiancée and I were able to pay £1095, in cash, for a nearly-new MGB GT. By 1970 we could afford to lay out twice that much on a low, rakish E-type Jaguar. Days of worrying about money were in the past.

Now, having signed professional for Salford, I could suddenly indulge whims and fancies and buy exactly what I — or we — needed. It helped a lot that we spent our first six months in northern England living virtually rent-free at Stanneylands Hotel, where my standard of living zoomed skywards immediately. Instead of coming home to bacon, egg and chips I chose steaks or poultry and wine most evenings from an ample, gourmet-style menu. Laundry cost me nothing. If Jane and I felt like a Saturday night 'hop' we mingled on the hotel dance floor with the nobs of rural Cheshire.

This meant that our savings for buying and equipping a home grew even faster. So, when the time came to purchase a property in early 1968, I was happy to pay nearly £5000 for a flat in the expensive Wilmslow suburb, just about the most fashionable area of the whole north-west of England. We spent more cash in a large city store, taking just three hours to choose a dining room suite, furniture for the lounge and curtain fitments down to the last rod. Our Stanneylands connection came in useful when buying carpets, for we paid only cost-price to the firm which supplied the hotel.

This dramatically heightened mode of living — and spending — was the biggest difference turning professional made to me and, I should think, the greatest change in my circumstances there could ever be. At times I compared my new lot with that of my parents, who had always had to wait for something to wear out before replacing it. But then, such are the values of our society that I had probably banked more money simply by signing a piece of paper than my father had made in thirty years of toil as a miner. I should add that I did my best to assist mam and dad to acquire new material possessions, but I think that should remain a matter between them and me. At Christmas time I have usually tried to be as generous as possible to my family and old friends.

Jane and I bought well. Some of the furniture and fittings we chose still do good service in Newport over a decade later. But at the same time we gloried in the sheer sensation of dashing off cheques. In the past, for instance, I had contented myself with chain-store suits at £15 a throw; now, I was visiting boutiques and paying the earth for them. I bought shirts, about which I am a fanatic, half a dozen at a time as if they were going out of fashion.

Mind you, my feet remained fairly firmly on the ground. Jane has always been a steadying influence who would put a brake on my wilder impulses. For down-to-earth financial advice I depended heavily upon her uncle Philip Owen, an accountant who had once been a bank manager. He initiated me into the mysteries of the stock market — and only one share he ever tipped has failed to make the grade!

Let me now explain where all the money was coming from, bearing in mind that the figures I quote should all be roughly trebled to take account of the inflation Britain has experienced between 1967 and the end of the seventies.

Its foundation was, of course, the £11,000 in all which I had been paid to sign, with the prospect of an additional £1000 payable at the beginning of the next four seasons. My employers, Forward Trust, were paying me £80 a month, money for which I was really working hard. In South Wales I had been able to trade on my reputation as a rugby player to make an impact on clients; in Manchester, deals had to be done with hard-headed businessmen who had never heard of David Watkins.

However, I could afford to let my salary flow untouched into the bank, so lavish were the money-making opportunities now opening up to me. Salford paid its players £20 and £25 for home and away wins respectively (just to update those figures their 1977–8 equivalents were £50 and £55). For losing we got £8 — but we weren't losing often. In addition, when I became club captain, I reached a private financial agreement with Brian Snape for accepting the responsibility of leadership.

Later, after my initial contract ran out, I renegotiated my pre-season retainer payment to £1500, and you can perhaps appreciate the value placed on me at Salford by comparing the £800 paid to Keith Fielding, £700 to Maurice Richards and £600 to Mike Coulman.

All four of us are, of course, ex-Union men, and this retainer scheme is not commonly enjoyed by northern-bred players. Their best chance of making a quick killing is their ten per cent share of a transfer fee, on which the club normally pays the tax.

Salford's players, I found, could also earn half a crown — twelve and a half pence — for every point scored over and above the opposition's total. That is, if we defeated Wigan

16–8 we would find an extra pound in our pay-packets. Sometimes, on the spur of the moment, the management used to strike a half-time bargain with us, offering a £3 bonus if we prevented our opponents from scoring again. Besides hard cash the club also clothed us, supplying well-tailored suits and blazers which we were expected to wear to away matches.

Numerous outside firms wanted to be in on the action, and operated juicy incentive schemes of which the Mackeson Golden Egg appealed most to the players. It worked like this: at the outset of every season the names of every club went into a hat, from which one was drawn out. That club, Salford for example, became the guardian of the Golden Egg, initially valued at £50. If we could defeat our first opponents, Widnes say, the value of the Egg doubled to £100. Another victory would make it worth £200, and so on. As you will realize, if you were lucky enough to possess the Egg and could then turn in an unbeaten run of five games, there was £800 to be collected. When your colours were finally lowered the losers shared out the bonanza, and the winners started the whole process again with an Egg now devalued to its original £50.

Other gimmicks which can boost the earnings of League players include promotion and publicity jobs. The Milk Marketing Board would pay £100 or so to photograph a big, husky forward clutching a Pinta. A Wolverhampton firm which manufactured rugby boots paid me £150 for a signature to adorn their product, with the guarantee of a 12½ pence royalty on each pair they sold. I must admit that this scheme did not live up to my expectations, for a mere trickle of cash came my way as a result. In my early, innocent days of professionalism I often undervalued myself or omitted to read the small print on deals that were offered to me.

Another source of cash is the media, such as the Canadian film company which rewarded me generously for appearing in a film called *The Gladiators*. Players did not charge journalists for quick post-match 'quotes', but northern newspapers were ever ready to fork out £25 for so-called 'in-depth' interviews. The *Manchester Evening News* once suggested that I write a weekly column for them at £20 a crack. It would not have been hard work, for my thoughts would have been shaped by a member of their sports staff, but at the time the idea did not appeal to me and I let it drop. Today I enjoy stringing words together and am not averse to picking up the £50 various rugby magazines are prepared to pay for a 500-word contribution.

In 1968 I got my first experience of serious broadcasting, joining Bernard Ganley and Keith Macklin to share the BBC's sound coverage of the Wembley Final between Leeds and Wakefield Trinity — and a pretty unnerving afternoon it turned out to be. At half time the two 'pros' handed back immaculately to the studio and then told me that they were off to the Press bar for a quick snort to slake their parched throats. Since I had done far less talking than they, I was left to hold the fort, with head-phones clamped to my ears.

Suddenly, to my dismay, a voice penetrated the ether.

'Hello, Wembley,' it said brightly. 'This is the World Service. We want a quick minute's contribution, please, summarizing the first half. Stand by — we'll come to you in thirty seconds from now.'

'Hell,' I thought. 'The World Service! How many millions does that mean are listening in? And what on earth am I going to say?'

I glanced desperately in the direction of the Press bar. No help from that quarter — just the sound of the scribes and commentators jugging up happily. I was on my own.

How, I will never know, but I managed to get through that 'quick minute' without drying up. I remember exhausting my recall of the first half of the Final in fifteen seconds dead by the stop-watch my colleagues had thoughtfully left nearby.

Next I babbled about spectators wearing macintoshes and holding umbrellas to ward off the rain. Then I turned my attentions to the Guardsmen who formed the band. 'Very nice they look,' I commented lamely. 'They're playing a popular song called . . . called . . .' — and there was no way I could bring its title to mind. Of course, it didn't really matter, since the music could be clearly heard by the audience!

Somehow I 'stretched', as the professionals say, and the World Service announcer thanked me politely via the head-phones. But it had been a terrifying baptism, and I unloaded a piece of my mind on the unfortunate Keith and Bernard when they returned. They laughingly apologized — but I don't think to this day they realize the nature of the ordeal they left the novice to endure!

Since that time I have broadcast often enough, and visited Wembley every year (except 1969, when I was a participant) at the BBC's expense. A free grandstand ticket, plus a couple of London hotel bills settled by the Corporation, in exchange for a word now and then on the progress of the big match? Nice work if you can get it.

Recalling the incident recounted earlier concerning Clive Rowlands and the bag of golf clubs the reader will not be surprised when I write of my great, unalloyed relief at being able to accept money for commissions like these with a clear conscience. This came home to me after an appearance I made on BBC2's *Late Night Line Up*, compèred by the delightful Joan Bakewell. The late J.L. Manning of the *Daily Mail*, former Welsh International centre Wilfred Wooller, Lord 'Wakers' Wakefield, once captain of England's Rugby Union XV, and I had been arguing the toss as to whether professional rugby players should be allowed re-instatement, if they wished it, in the Union game.

Although Lord Wakefield, a north countryman, appeared to accept my case that they should be, Wilf opposed me determinedly and vehemently, saying in effect that Union players who turned League placed themselves beyond the pale and were traitors to the amateur tradition. In no way should they qualify for a return to the ranks of the unpaid. I finally floored him by asking what difference there was between my playing a game for money and his writing or broadcasting on it, also for fees. 'Moreover, Wilf,' I added, 'You should know how it feels to be a part-time pro, for your main job is as Glamorgan cricket club secretary, not in journalism.' I must have struck a raw nerve or two, because Wilf declined to stay on for the usual post-programme nightcap.

That last point is a very important one. Agreed, some

Union refugees prove unable to adapt to the League game. But neither does it follow, as Wilf was trying to argue that evening, that they are wash-outs or failures in life. A Rugby League man always has his main-line career to fall back on — Keith Fielding his teaching, for instance, and Glyn Shaw, the 1978 signing, his job in mining. It is my view that many more Union stars might have come North had they appreciated this fully.

But I have been digressing. By now you will be aware of the glittering new life-style to which I was becoming accustomed. You will imagine that I must have been asking myself 'Why on earth didn't I do this before? Why waste all those years turning on superstar performances with nothing to show for them but a few caps? Whatever did I hesitate for?'

Not true. The seven years spent in the amateur ranks at Newport and the wonderful afternoons when I wore a Welsh jersey will never be regretted by me. I must admit that within a season I seemed to have Rugby League in the blood, and was relishing my prosperity — but I could still feel wistful when viewing a Grandstand TV production showing Wales at play on Cardiff Arms Park. I was actually in the crowd when Maurice Richards scored four tries against England in 1969, and it was a thrilling experience.

There was one, and only one, day when I actually wished I were still eligible for the Wales XV. That was when Gareth Edwards ran out to collect his fiftieth cap at Twickenham in 1978. And here I am going to make two bold assertions.

Firstly I have no doubt that, had I remained a Union player, I and not he would have been first to the half century milestone. Despite all my griping about selectors and their inconsistencies I feel sure looking back that I could have regained their complete confidence and consolidated my number one position on the ladder of stand-off halves. And wouldn't the archives of Welsh International rugby football have looked odd without the prominence now enjoyed by the names of Barry John and Phil Bennett!

Secondly, I doubt whether I would have retired as early as did Barry. I see no reason why I could not have played

Union football into the late seventies, exactly as I have continued at Salford. What a partnership Gareth and I would have made once we got to know each other's play! And what a delight to have welcomed him into the exclusive ranks of fifty-cappers, just as I nursed him through his International debut in 1967.

However, enough of such speculation. Seriously, within six months my move from unpaid to paid status seemed as natural as the one I had made years earlier from Cwmcelyn to Newport. I felt a huge contentedness at having done the right thing at the right time. I enjoyed being generously paid. I liked the company of my clubmates. I relished the admiration of the crowds. Life seemed perfect.

Of course, I was a top performer, enjoying star status, and my income was way above that earned by workaday players with lesser clubs. This differential prompts some people to wonder whether Rugby League needs a players' union to get a better deal for the weaker brethren. Indeed some years ago Ray French of Widnes and Great Britain, now head sports master at Cowley Grammar School, tried to start one. The issue at the time centred around payments received from the BBC from their televised floodlit matches. Players in the half dozen or so wealthy clubs thought the fees, and consequently the share-out, should be a lot bigger since the televising of matches kept paying customers at home and off the terraces. Representatives of smaller clubs were satisfied with the pickings, however, since appearing on TV was one of the few ways open to them of boosting their income and basking in extra limelight.

So the impetus petered out, and I doubt whether League men generally will ever seriously consider the idea of a union. Our game is too small, its resources are finite, and the cake cannot be made larger simply by shouting the odds and waving banners. Again, the payment of a weekly 'sub' would bite deep into the wages of men with less fashionable clubs. Though Salford's staff are paid handsomely, their opposite numbers at Doncaster, for example, collect only one-third as much.

The other factor which helped me to settle down was the

appeal of Manchester as a city. It boasts excellent musical and dramatic entertainment, and also good places at which to eat out, which was rapidly becoming a favourite way for Jane and I to spend an evening. Also, when you were on the town, there was no telling who might be at the next table. Once we were dining at The Mandarin, a Chinese restaurant which was at the top of our list, with relations of Jane's called Sue and John Thomas. As we began our meal the wine-waiter arrived with an ice-bucket containing an expensive bottle of white burgundy. He stilled my query by explaining, 'Compliments of Alan Ball, Mr Watkins'. And sure enough, grinning broadly at us from an alcove, was the then glamour boy of Everton and England himself. John could hardly wait to get back to Govilon and tell the locals of his evening with a man who had recently helped England to win the World Cup.

Some of my earliest memories, you will recall, were of watching league soccer in South Wales with Bampa. Here again, in Manchester, I could indulge a taste which had been latent for years. Since Salford usually played on Friday evenings I could watch United or City in action the following afternoon.

Soon there followed invitations to train with the soccer fraternity and meetings at Maine Road with the likes of Colin Bell, Francis Lee and manager Tony Book. This contact had its practical advantages, for if our part-time masseur Bob Sladdon was tied up at the Walkden Centre for Industrial Injuries one could count instead on a rub-down at the hands of City physio Freddie Griffiths, once a member of Sale RUFC. At other times it would be a trip to Old Trafford for a gossip with fellow Welshman Jimmy Murphy and half an hour's attention from Laurie Brown.

It was a pleasant surprise to discover that the respect between the two codes was mutual. Manchester soccer stars such as Alex Stepney, Pat Crerand, Denis Law and Bobby Charlton enjoyed watching Salford in action, and frequently visited our VIP lounge afterwards for a chat. Denis, a much smaller man than I had realized, told me: 'You rugby men are heroes. I wouldn't let anyone knock my nose about the way you lot belt each other.' Since his nose was long and thin, that was just as well.

Bobby Charlton, too, was most agreeable the first time we were introduced. I cannot claim to be an intimate friend of his, for he is a taciturn fellow. But he has done me good turns such as inviting me onto a brains trust at Manchester Town Hall and ensuring that some rugby questions were put which I could answer. Years later, too, I met his brother Jack for the first time at a BBC *Sportsman of the Year* show in London. 'Oh yes,' said the tall fellow, 'I've heard all about you. "Our kid" often mentions your name.'

But I suppose the brightest star of the lot was George Best. Strolling through Manchester one morning a friend and I spotted the Irishman enjoying the sunshine in the doorway of his boutique, The Edwardian, which he ran in partnership with Mike Summerbee. My companion knew George well enough to perform the introductions, and so I made the acquaintance of a man who from the first struck me as basically quiet and even shy. I certainly warmed to him, though, when he invited me to choose a suit off the peg! — and subsequently when he came to watch Salford. 'Watkins,' he told me afterwards. 'You're the greatest thing since sliced bread.'

Handsome, eligible and a jet-set mixer, George was always an easy target for journalists out to sensationalize. When I met him his current girl friend was Eva Halsted, a Scandinavian beauty, but the Press never shrank from pairing him off with any girl seen sharing his company. His alleged sexual antics made cheap copy by the mile, and although George tried to laugh it all off I believe the continual glare shining on his private life disturbed as well as damaged him.

He played remorselessly into the hands of the gossip columnists simply by being himself. At one of Manchester's exclusive night-spots, the Blinkers Disco, mere mortal males had to wear a suit and tie and be accompanied by a lady. George would turn up on his own, dressed in jeans and a tee-shirt — and they let him in, for they knew that his presence guaranteed publicity and magnetized the young bloods with money to spend. The place was poorer by thousands of pounds when he stopped going there.

I liked George on his own but, once the entourage of hangers-on and parasites closed in, any normal relationship became impossible. This helps to explain why he eventually turned into a lone wolf, shedding one genuine friend after another. People like Mike Summerbee gradually drifted out of his orbit and went their own way. How George's life will turn out in the future is anyone's guess, and he still seems to slide from crisis to crisis. I shall remember him as a simple man, who like myself came from nowhere to stardom. Whereas, however, I bless my ration of Welsh common sense, George could not cope with the three-ring circus in which he performed.

So much, then, for a thumb-nail sketch of the new world I had entered. A world where money was no object, overhung with stars. And David Watkins was up there, twinkling with them.

CHAPTER 14

Settling Down

In Blaina up until 1967 the sight of a track-suited David Watkins jogging along the main street or sprinting in the park was commonplace. I would wave to fans whom I passed, pausing for a chat if I felt puffed. As a Welsh International player, and a senior one at that, I held court on my home patch as and when I chose.

As a public figure in Manchester, and especially out in my Wilmslow suburb, I was a far more reluctant hero. For a start I abandoned lone, pavement-bashing training sessions. It did not seem quite right for a perspiring professional rugby player to disfigure the smooth avenues of my posh new surroundings.

Although I took great delight in driving it, I even had a hang-up about being seen at the wheel of my MGB. It sometimes struck me as flashy and over-flamboyant compared with the workaday saloons owned by my team-mates at that time. So I would park it some distance from our ground on training nights lest it remind them too forcefully of my bank balance.

In short, I experienced a kind of personality change. Whereas at Newport I had become a confident, authoritative member of the rugby 'establishment', in the early days at Salford I spent much time inside a metaphorical shell. For here is the point: although, as we have seen, I now enjoyed wealth, status and stardom, at the same time I was indubitably a complete novice in my profession. This contrast between my material well-being and my limited usefulness on the field was for long hard to come to terms with.

I have acknowledged that my welcome was warm. True — but on the other hand the northerners lost few chances of scoring a point off the newcomer from Rugby Union. Second row forward Peter Smethurst went into print in the Football Pink to the effect that I lacked the physical attributes to survive even a single season in the League game. Came a day when he also wrote, 'David, you've kicked all your critics into touch, including me' — but that was several years later.

Some seasons after my Salford debut Griff Jenkins, my first club coach, sent me a telegram congratulating me on breaking the League goal-kicking record. 'Well done, David. There's no way they can take that away from you,' it said. But initially he too, although a fellow Welshman, made it clear that in his opinion Rugby Union imports were not equipped for the rigours of the 13-man game. He, too, criticized me to the Press behind my back. During training he would match me with young sprinters, with the aim of demonstrating to the world at large that Watkins was not as fast as he had been cracked up to be. The word 'softies' was freely bandied about to describe myself and other ex-Union stalwarts like Doug Hill and Alan McInnes.

There was — and is — you see, this myth that Rugby League players are harder, stronger and better-trained than their amateur opposite numbers. It is high time that it was undermined, if not totally demolished. For a start, let us put training methods under the microscope.

Now, admittedly, attendance at Monday and Wednesday practice periods with Salford is compulsory. This is a general rule with northern clubs. After all the players are being paid, and training is part of the working week. At Newport, inability to get a baby-sitter or sickness in the home were usually accepted as legitimate excuses for absence. Not so at Salford. If you didn't train, you didn't play — and didn't earn.

Having said that, I can truthfully report that training at the Willows in 1967 did not compare with an average session at Newport as far as commitment and method were concerned. On Mondays we did so-called stamina building exercises: lapping the pitch, a few sprints and some rather aimless physical jerks. Only at the end did we indulge in a few minutes' 'tick and pass', or touch rugby. On Wednesdays we shortened the preliminaries in order to make time for a game against our 'A' squad. Then we briefly ran the rule over our scheduled opponents for the following Friday evening.

I am certain that most Rugby Union players, especially those nurtured under the regime of WRU coaching organizer Ray Williams, would find such methods both boring and frustrating.

Let me list the missing elements. There was little or no emphasis on perfecting ball skills such as passing, catching and kicking. Hardly any scrummaging took place, even though good packing and shoving can both ensure regular possession and reduce opposing forwards' capacity for running and covering. Also, since the rules oblige a scrum half occasionally to put the ball into a scrummage on his opponents' 'head', you can see the enhanced value of good techniques. Yet Rugby League's general apathy about this set-piece means that scrummaging is about as unsatisfactory as the Union line out.

Another oversight concerned the working out and practice of 'moves' and tactics. Put very simply, the art of attack in Rugby League is systematically to commit or exhaust the opposition until an overlap can be engineered, giving a back enough space to reach the line. Ball-playing forwards —your Clawsons and Battens—take out as many opponents as possible, after which it is a half back's job to shout the 'move' and feed the backs. There are umpteen ploys which can result from such a situation, but at Salford when I arrived they were neither exploited nor even discussed in training. They were simply left to senior players to initiate when they judged the time to be ripe. The club was fortunate indeed to possess a captain like Jackie Brennan who was more original than most.

Again, although I am not sold on blackboards with diagrams dictating where players should be at certain moments in a game, there are certainly 'routes' which can be taken on the field which will help men to be correctly positioned at critical times. Often in my early seasons up North a ball-carrier who had wanted to find me with a pass would bawl as he was tackled in possession, 'Where the hell were you?!'

Inexperience had prevented my being well placed to support him. Yet in training such finer points were not covered for my benefit or that of other new recruits.

Take the rules of the game. Since 13-a-side is fairly complex, and as different from Union as baseball is from cricket, you would expect clubs to provide a book of laws for its players to consult. I for one would have found it invaluable — but if Salford did own one, I was certainly never shown it. There is no equivalent up North of simple Union manuals like 'Know the Laws' or 'Why the Whistle Went'. It is as if players are expected to know by instinct what they may and may not do, augmenting their understanding by trial and error — frequently error! Incidentally, I did buy books on Rugby League, such as Keith Macklin's essays and Vince Karelius's memoirs, but found them lacking in real insight into the game as far as a beginner was concerned.

Finally, no attempt was made at Salford to boost team spirit with a few post-training pints in the company of fellow players. This custom is taken for granted in the Union game, but at Willows Road we usually had a shower, got dressed and left for home without really getting to know each other any better.

You may wonder why we did not drink together in the club-house. The answer is that if one of us had a bad game the following Friday, members would be tempted to say, 'No wonder bloody so-and-so is off form. He was smashed out of his mind after training on Wednesday.' So, except after matches, we tended to shun the club lounge, but I still think that an hour's descreet companionship in a nearby tavern would have been a good thing.

For most of these shortcomings, which are commonplace in the North, coaches must shoulder the blame. They are the reason why I add that I do not consider Griff Jenkins to have been a good coach. Sure, he took me under his wing when I arrived at Salford, showing me around and performing the introductions; but all the while I felt like a new toy which was being shown off. The subtleties of the new code were not illuminated for me by him.

All this is not to say that Salford players did not, and do not, train hard and conscientiously as individuals. Jackie

Brennan adored his pints of Guinness but was never less than one hundred per cent fit. Peter Smethurst could not wait to close that butcher's shop of his and get to the Willows for an evening of perpetual motion. Another fanatic was Charlie Bott, now emigrated to Melbourne but at that time employed in the research department of Hawker Siddeley's. 'We just aren't training hard enough,' Charlie would groan if we lost a match.

Several of the boys had great senses of humour, and mickey-taking was the rule rather than the exception. Often Griff Jenkins was the butt, for he used to come out with some extraordinary phrases. We once heard him telling a player that there were more ways than one of beating a man. 'Work on them,' he advised. 'Then you'll have more irons to your bow.' On another evening he called out to a bunch of us in training, 'I want you to jog towards me in single file, two abreast.'

On the eve of one important away game we were dining at a hotel in Blackpool. Before the meal Jackie Brennan, as captain, rose to say he had an important announcement to make. 'It's from Griff,' he told us. 'He says that bread and potatoes must not be eaten tonight because of tomorrow's big game. However, I asked him on your behalf whether we could have toast and chips. He says yes.'

One man who had a unique sense of humour was Frank Collier, who won the Lance Todd Trophy at Wembley with Widnes before joining Salford near the end of his career. At one hotel his gaze was caught by a large stag's head mounted on the wall. 'I thought the coach's orders were that no women came on this trip,' he said to one of the players. 'What's your mother-in-law doing here?'

Our clubmate looked mystified. 'Well, let's put it this way,' explained Frank. 'If your mother-in-law lived in India she'd be sacred.'

Getting to know these guys was great, and their womenfolk were equally lively and entertaining. It pleased me that Jane could prove now and again that she was cast in the same mould. Once, however, her outspokenness caused me some discomfort.

On a night when I was having an indifferent game, a

group of season ticket holders decided to give me a verbal roasting from the grandstand. Jane, a newcomer and not known to these men, had to sit gritting her teeth as they shouted 'Go back to Wales, Watkins! What did Snape think he was doing when he bought you!'

When I joined the supporters in the VIP lounge afterwards though, everything was sweetness and light. The critics tried to put an arm around my shoulders. 'Great game, David,' they told me. 'Have a drink on us.'

It was all too much for Jane, who leaped to the attack. 'How two-faced can you get?' she demanded of them. 'You've just spent an hour and a half pulling David to bits behind his back. Now you're all over him with smarm. You're a disgrace to the club!'

Her victims retreated in disarray, shamed and embarrassed by her outburst. Not, however, as embarrassed as I. Unbeknown to Jane, the three men were all clients of my other employers, Forward Trust. There were some delicate diplomatic manoeuvrings to be undertaken next day!

But in general the northern crowds were tolerant towards me in that first season. The club itself also found ways of guarding its small crock of Welsh gold. The management were keen to shield me from fixtures that promised to be torrid; for instance in December 1967 they left me out of the XIII to play a hard away game at Workington. Their decision meant that I turned out for our 'A' team at home, in a match that I remember for another of life's amusing moments.

Because I was included, the fixture drew a host of spectators, who cheered the two dropped goals which I kicked early on. Then, handing me the ball to take a penalty, our player-coach Ernie Critchley demanded quietly, 'Give us an up-and-under, David. Drop it near the posts.'

In my anxiety to oblige I punted the ball too hard, so that it passed over the cross-bar. To the astonishment of all twenty-six players the referee whistled for another dropped goal, ordering Workington despite their protests to kick off at the centre spot. Having glanced away momentarily as I struck the ball he had looked back in time to see it pass between the posts, and assumed that the lethal Watkins' boot had put in a drop kick! Nobody on my side made a move to own up, so I too kept my trap shut deciding that when in Rome you did as the Romans did! Privately I decided that the 'score' compensated for an occasion at Swansea when a dropped goal by me which could have won the match for Newport was disallowed by Gwynne Walters, who claimed to have been unsighted by the setting sun.

Like the management, the Salford players helped me immensely in my transitional season, particularly in the man-to-man marking discipline which is automatic for an experienced player but which a beginner finds hard to get right. It is not always clear where precisely one should stand. Time after time men like loose forward Aidan Breen would appear out of the blue to plug a gap I had left. At other times, covering acrossfields like a fiend, he would literally push me away from my man with a shout of, 'Leave him to me,' rather than let his midget team-mate take the full force of some Goliath on the rampage for our opponents.

The boys would also warn me about other teams' hard men — not that the warnings always worked. 'Watch out for Frank Foster,' they said one day before a match against Oldham. 'When the ref isn't looking he'll land one on you just for fun.' So whenever he came close I watched Mr Foster's fist like a hawk. Alas. Soon, while I was eyeing his knuckles warily after a tackle, he managed to plant his weighty boot on my hand, breaking two fingers. Their joints are swollen and thickened to this day!

But I took the knocks, and as far as I can remember did not shirk tackles which I had to make. If anything, I was more vulnerable when I myself was tackled, for a reason I have mentioned before: at such times it is second nature for the Union player to release the ball, and my hold on it was seldom tight enough for the League game, in which you must retain your grip in order to put in a heel and re-provide possession. Knowing this, opponents frequently tried to knock the ball from my grasp, often with success.

I could have cleared up many of these points and improved my technique by asking a lot more questions. Because of the diffidence of which I wrote earlier I was not as inquiring as I ought to have been. My advice to anyone starting out in Rugby League, and other games too, is to make a perfect nuisance of yourself to get things straight. Your coach may become impatient, but you will progress faster. Likewise players with experience should put themselves out to assist novices. You do not have to be an International player to know something valuable which you can pass on to learners.

Mind you, there were some great players in the land at that time. One by one I came across them during that first season on the big circuit. Billy Boston, a fellow Welshman and a marvellous wing, was having a final year at Wigan — but I was too shy to make conversation with him when first we met. How could I expect one of the kings of the League game to exchange small talk with its rawest recruit?

Eric Ashton was at Wigan with Billy; Hepworth and Hardisty were at Castleford; Murphy at Leigh, and Cliff Watson at St Helens. At Bradford Terry Price was consolidating his reputation as one of the best full backs that club had ever had, while Neil Fox, Harold Poynton, Bev Risman and Charlie Renilson were other names to conjure with.

Just as it was marvellous meeting such men for the first time, so visiting the great clubs in succession was enthralling. I quickly recognized Wakefield Trinity, for instance, as the ground used in the film version of David Storey's novel *This Sporting Life*, with Richard Harris in a convincing lead role. In 1967 a trip to Wakefield was worth making not only for the game but because visiting teams automatically qualified as guests at the local variety club, which shared premises with the rugby folk. Most of us were bitterly disappointed when the rugby side of the partnership fell upon hard times, causing it to be dissolved. It is good to see Wakefield making a come-back to the big time — but I can assure them that their visitors still miss the post-match cabarets!

Leeds I shall always remember for its fine changing rooms. It was one of the few places where the standard of comfort provided for the visiting team matched that of the home side. I could not even exempt Salford from this criticism, and it was not until 1975 that we could persuade Brian Snape to spend some money on improving our facilities. Nowadays, I am happy to claim, they compare favourably with those at any of our away venues.

Just as Salford now have pictures of great moments in the club's history, so the Leeds club-house is distinguished by fine murals on a similar theme. But my readers outside the north of England will be surprised to learn that the rolls of honour, captains' boards and team photographs which hold pride of place in Union club headquarters are conspicuous by their absence. The secret is to call at a nearby pub like the Irwell at Salford: that is where you will find walls and panels hung with time-honoured archive material — pictures of former stars, yellow and fading hoardings advertising special fixtures, and match programmes from bygone years. Never forget that Rugby League has always been a working man's game, in which cash for club-house decorations and other luxuries has not always been readily available. In fact, just as The Rolling Mill did duty at Blaina for many a long year, so friendly public houses are the traditional gathering places for northern fans.

I shall now take a poke at Batley — which I trust the good people there will accept with a good grace since the scene at Mount Pleasant is now so much more agreeable! The first time I went there it seemed like the absolute back of beyond. The date was Boxing Day 1967 — and I was already in a bad temper. After spending a day or two with our families in Wales Jane and I made a special effort to travel north on Christmas Day itself in order to get a decent night's rest before the following afternoon's match, only to find Stanneylands Hotel locked for the night. Presumably the night porter had nodded off after the festivities, so the pair of us had to spend an uncomfortable night in the car.

So when I reached Batley to discover that on a freezing afternoon we had to change in what amounted to a pigeon loft, you can imagine my discontent. This was a changing room which made even Salford's old premises seem like the Hilton! My morale was at rock bottom before we ever stepped out onto the pitch.

A couple of seasons later we met Batley on an afternoon

that ranks among the very coldest on which I have ever played. It was so Arctic-like that, with one or two backs practically suffering from exposure, we begged the referee to shorten the game. He refused, and the only thing that kept us going was the thought of hot tea, warm changing rooms and a hot bath after the ordeal was over. Would you believe it — on that day the Batley club had a burst pipe, and none of these simple comforts was available. We spent some three hours just thawing out, never mind getting warm again. However, they are a friendly lot — and I forgive them!

My live-wire geography lessons continued with trips to Barrow, Workington and Whitehaven. Travelling through the southern fringes of the Lake District gave one a tremendous uplift, but to reach these Cumbrian townships represented a let-down. All around was heavy industry, the evidence of coal mining, and some scruffy dockland areas. However, I had to admit to myself that this was no different really from arriving at Llanelli or Newport following a breathtaking journey through the Breconshire National Park.

One had, of course, to learn to live with the caustic northern supporters, who seemed to be breathing down one's neck at places like Workington and Featherstone. The latter's pitch is surrounded by iron palings which seemed perilously close to the touch-line; I always used to imagine that a hard tackle would send me flying right through it to end up on the other side like a plateful of chips.

At grounds like theirs the crowd is very close indeed to the action. If someone decides to give you the bird, you can identify him with ease. In my early days, lacking the confidence to give a Harvey Smith type of gesture back, I just gritted my teeth at some of the more pointed remarks ('Hit him with your wallet,' someone once advised me after I had missed a tackle) and tried to retort with a demonstration of genuine skill, preferably resulting in a try.

Later on I used to wave cheerily at my critic or give him a grin, for I made a most important discovery: when a man is booed or jeered at by the other team's fans he should feel highly honoured: that is a crowd's way of betraying fear that a visiting star will run rings round the local heroes.

This is true of the supporters of the club which made the biggest initial impact on me and has retained my respect throughout my years in the north. The Central Park fans have cherry and white eyes, which cannot see any merit at all in the opposition. Even Cardiff supporters normally greet some Newport skill with polite applause, but would a Wigan man clap a try by Salford? — not likely! It is even said that before allocating an International match to Central Park the authorities wait until the English team has been picked. Should the Wigan representation be non-existent or small, they know that the match might as well be played elsewhere. Wigan supporters will not turn up.

I must now be quick to add that at Wigan, whose club was formed back in 1872, I always felt as if I was in Rugby League's spiritual home. There is no local soccer club of note to divide people's loyalties, and even the exploits of suburban Orrell RFC excite only passing interest in the town. It is not the most beautiful of places, nor does its legendary pier, a grubby edifice, do anything to enhance it. But, as usual in the north, fine rolling countryside is not far away.

Because of the Wigan club's greatness the highlight of my first season in the paid ranks was a 37–0 victory over them at The Willows on Good Friday 1968. For years our opponents had used Salford as a chopping block, and it was a great feeling to be one of a team which had taken them apart.

Perhaps that last recollection will prove that after a short while I felt involved in the wider world of the Rugby League and was committed to it. I was soaking up the folk lore of my new environment. Lying in bed on Sunday mornings I still flipped through *The Sunday Times* and the *Express* to find Newport's result; but a close second in the order of priorities came the match reports from Leeds, Wigan, St Helens and Salford's other rivals. It was easy to be carried away by a competitive atmosphere that could almost be touched. Never at any time did I experience homesickness or tell myself, 'Time to jack this in.' Within a year I had come to terms with the pressures of a new career.

I was certainly sustained by the great traditions of my own club, the 'Reds'. Eavesdropping on the conversation of the old hands I constantly experienced that feeling of buoyancy which I had known at Newport and which derives from membership of an exclusive band of men. Consider the names that cropped up — Risman, Lance Todd, Emlyn Jenkins, Barney Hudson, to mention but a few. Soon, with luck, my own might be mentioned along with this illustrious company.

So, to return to the theme with which I began this chapter, the only thing that troubled me was whether I was developing fast enough for Salford's liking. Now and then I would manage to run in a try from 60 or 70 yards; and privately I would pray that this would keep the fans happy for the next two or three matches, when my performance might be no more than adequate. I suppose this is a feeling which bugs all sportsmen who have large money tags dangling around their necks.

In view of that I think I may justifiably quote a single statistic here, which is not a bad comment on my first season at Salford: starting with my debut match against Oldham we embarked upon a sequence of sixteen victories on the trot, which took us well into the New Year. Looking back, I like to think that this run of success was not unconnected with Salford's injection of Welsh blood.

CHAPTER 15

Carrots and Sticks

If you pressed me hard for an opinion I would probably admit that Rugby League football, even at the highest representative level, has nothing that quite compares with Rugby Union's International matches. England versus New Zealand at Twickenham, Wales against Scotland at Cardiff or Murrayfield — these are unique competitive occasions.

Outside the International scene, however, the League game wins hands down. The amateur code in England and Wales has discovered during the seventies that knock-out cup tournaments can be fun, while in Scotland they run a league which I am told is fairly successful. But in general the true meaning of competition and the extra spice it injects into a sport is scarcely dreamed of, let alone exploited.

The 'tables' featured by various newspapers are legion, wholly confusing, and, in my view, quite unfair. Pontypridd — good luck to them — have won the 'unofficial championship' title a couple of times in recent years. Yet as far as I can see their fixtures are less demanding than those of Cardiff, Newport, Swansea or Llanelli; nor are their ranks regularly decimated for International matches. Yet their team is the one kitted out in presentation blazers at the end of the season, theirs are the men fêted, wined and dined by sponsors who have jumped onto the bandwagon. Cardiff and Newport players, who may have met a major touring side and a Barbarians XV during the winter, not to mention playing each other a couple of times, can only look on enviously and wistfully from the sidelines.

Other so-called tables would cause the average League fan to fall around with laughter. They are complete lash-ups: for instance, some of the participating clubs do not actually play each other during the season. It is possible for a club to finish top of one table and sixth or seventh in another.

I suspect that Union folk mistrust the word 'league' itself, since it reminds them too forcefully of the existence of the dreaded 13-a-side rival game. There must be prejudice of some kind at work, for a few years ago the Welsh Rugby Union's committee designed for its clubs a league system that would have dove-tailed neatly into existing fixture lists. Smaller clubs like Blaina and Whitland were enthusiastic, seeing the scheme as offering a chance of forcing their way into regular contention with the giants. But the glamorous élite, numbering a dozen or so teams which regularly draw big gates, gave it a contemptuous thumbs-down — drawing strength from the knowledge that without their participation no league in Wales could work.

I mention these points to illustrate how the amateurs sense that League men are onto a good thing, yet cannot bring themselves to take yet another leaf out of our book. They have adapted our touch-kicking rule to advantage; they now permit replacements for injured players (though they do not yet allow coaches to substitute men for tactical reasons); they have introduced our 're-adjustment' compromise to replace their rigid knock-on law. Yet they will not contemplate the establishing of a proper competitive framework.

In the North competition is everything, the Vitamin A of Rugby League. After more than a decade with Salford it flowed in my veins — and I assure you that its thrill meant at least as much to me as the cash rewards. If our team left the field victorious my first reaction was always, 'Good, we'll move up the table a couple of places tonight.' Only later do professional players think contentedly, '. . . and we've won ourselves sixty quid into the bargain.'

The year starts with the Lancashire and Yorkshire Cups at stake, with the two sides of the Pennines duelling separately. These competitions are over by October, but a good run can be very important to a club since it fuels spectators' enthusiasm and boosts gate receipts for the whole of the new season. It also guarantees lowlier clubs like Blackpool and Doncaster a crack at Salford, Warrington or Wigan every so often.

The Captain Morgan Cup was, you might say, rather a rum affair as well as being somewhat short-lived. It is now defunct, nor do I suppose that people miss it very much. Like the present John Player Number Six competition it never caught my imagination, failing to carve a real niche for itself during the winter.

I have already noted, however, that BBC2's Floodlit Trophy is quite popular with players. We enjoy showing off our skills to a wider, United Kingdom audience, and it helps to compensate for the pathetic Press coverage of Rugby League football outside the North Country. I know that in Wales they are grateful for the chance to keep tabs on a local hero who has gone off to seek his fortune in the paid ranks.

That is not say, however, that I am altogether happy with the way television treats our game. For a start, the coverage on BBC2 is run from London where media people generally insist that anything transmitted from the Provinces must conform to a naive metropolitan stereotype. Just as London decrees that screen Scotsmen must wear kilts and eat haggis, with Welshmen shouting 'look you' every few moments, so it sees Rugby League as a game for ape-like creatures watched by gloomy men in cloth caps. To London 'the North' is one long Coronation Street where everyone devours daily helpings of Yorkshire pudding and Lancashire hot-pot. The League grounds are rather seedy arenas where twenty-six gladiators knock each other around in order to earn enough for a bag of chips and a pint of dark ale after the match.

This homespun image, ludicrously out-dated, is perpetuated in the folksy approach and broad vowels of the League's top commentator, Eddie Waring. Now Eddie has a heart of gold and will do anything for the game. He works for charities connected with it, and drives hundreds of miles to show a film and make a personal appearance in aid of a player's benefit fund. On the screen he is conceded by most people to be a strong character, able to dominate events with his voice. He has ridden the Rugby League bandwagon to fame — and has helped to guide its destinies too.

It suits Eddie, however, that coverage of the game remains static and unimaginative. Players and spectators alike look enviously at the thoughtful, arresting analysis projected by Jimmy Hill and his soccer colleagues on *Match of the Day*. Viewers in Lancashire and Cheshire who can pick up BBC Wales TV know the merits of in-depth interviews and discussions that are mounted by this Channel in its coverage of Rugby Union in the Principality. Often the contributions are set in the cheery *bonhomie* of a club-house — whereas for all the TV authorities seem to care, Rugby League might not have a social life at all. And certainly the desire of viewers to be stimulated to think more deeply about the game in general and a televised match in particular is not catered for.

I have to choose my words carefully here, since I have broadcast from time to time and hope that I can contribute more to the media in retirement. Nor do I wish to underestimate the value of the Waring effort down the years — anyone who is paid the compliment of being imitated by Mike Yarwood is clearly a character to be reckoned with. But I must state my belief that to complement the projection by cameras and commentators — and the excitement generated by the Floodlit Trophy — television presentation of our game must now advance to embrace its tactics, strategy, structure and leading performers. There is plenty of expertize which the broadcasting authorities could readily tap.

The Blue Riband of the Rugby League game, in my view, is the Championship. Many may wish to question that, citing the Challenge Cup as the top trophy. But the League is the ultimate test, favouring the team with endurance, resilience, all-weather skills and strength in depth. You also need a slice of two of luck during the long trek from August to April; not to mention the stamina to cope with a flurry of vital late-season games postponed because of mid-winter snow.

If you doubt me, take the example of Widnes, who were inclined to pooh-pooh Salford's championship title of 1974, claiming that their Challenge Cup victory of 1975 was the greater feat. When they themselves subsequently won the League they could not change their tune too quickly: 'This is the big one,' they proclaimed. 'This is really the one that everybody wants to win!'

For once I agree with Widnes! Notice too that in Association football the club which wins the FA Cup attracts the glamour and the ballyhoo, whereas the genuine respect of the soccer world is reserved for the team which comes out on top after the exhausting forty-two match league campaign. This is reflected in Europe where the prestige of the Cup competition for League winners is greater than that of the Cup Winners' Cup.

Teams I particularly salute for consistency in League competition are Leeds and St Helens, often title-winners in my time and never far from the top of the pile. Equally regular occupiers of bottom positions are clubs like Huyton and Doncaster, and they, I believe, should move over to make room for up-and-coming non-League sides such as Thames Board Mills, Ace Caravans or Pilkington Recs who have shown promise when imported into the first round proper of the Challenge Cup. We need new blood. The trouble is that a two-thirds majority of votes is required at Rugby League Council meetings before the club structure can be altered in any way. The system is a conservative one, tending to favour the status quo.

However, I was delighted at the reform of 1973 which split the League into two. It introduced the excitement of promotion and relegation battles into the newly-created borderland between the Divisions. In the old days a middle-of-the-table side which had been dismissed from the Challenge Cup competition simply coasted its way through the remaining League programme. Supporters drifted off in other directions knowing that there was little at stake. Nowadays that has changed in two ways. Firstly, loyal fans will still turn up to shout for a team which is struggling to avoid relegation. Secondly the prospect of promotion to Division One can generate as much enthusiasm on the terraces as the run-in to the Championship title itself.

I come to the Challenge Cup competition last of all, perhaps because I have been putting off the evil moment of describing what was just about my biggest disappointment in two decades of top rugby: Salford's failure to win at Wembley in 1969. To have reached the Final, to have held such high hopes, and then to lose to Castleford: this was a shattering experience. And our downfall was all the more painful because of the colossal build-up that always precedes a Cup Final.

Wembley in May is often sunny and summery. But, I found in 1968, the trail starts in mid-winter when the nearby hills may be capped with snow or low clouds ooze a thin, cold drizzle, as they did when Wakefield came across to Salford for what was to be my first appearance in a cup-tie. We knew what we were up against, for Trinity had reached Wembley the previous year, losing by a single point to Leeds. Our coach Griff Jenkins put in a reconnaissance to watch our opponents play Featherstone, and for all I know the men who wear a 'W' on their jersey had sent spies to see us in action.

We lost — but I had certainly been blooded and knew what Cup fever was all about. Salford had prepared exceptionally thoroughly, with extra training periods. Punctuating them were searching TV and Press interviews, followed by hysterical previews on the morning of the match. 'Will Newcomer Watkins be Salford's Weak Link?' Yorkshire newspapers demanded provocatively. 'Watkins Could Be Salford's Ace' trumpeted the Lancashire Press in reply.

The Willows was packed with 15,000 spectators that day. Milling with white and red favours they seemed to throb with something approaching frenzy. We knew that many folk had crossed the Pennines by coach and car to root for the visitors, and it all intensified the spine-tingling sensations our XIII experienced in the changing room.

Came the 1968–9 season at Salford, and with it a splendid Cup run. Again one could not help feeling extra-special 'vibes' as the competition gathered momentum. It became our custom to head off for Blackpool and special training on the sands before each tie. The club compensated those players like Bob Burdell, a Post Office worker, whose employers declined to pay their wages. For the professional men in our ranks such as myself there was a simple deduction from our annual leave. It was worth it at the time.

Our home victory over Workington in round two was important to our morale, for the 18,000 fans who packed the ground made it clear that they thought this could be Salford's year. They were the biggest, noisiest crowd in front of which I had played to date in the North, and certainly inspired their favourites to great heights.

But even that occasion paled by comparison with the semi-final played before 25,000 people at Wigan in which our opponents were Warrington. This time their brilliant yellow favours provided the contrast to the red splashes of Salford colour around the ground. We were too good for Warrington, thanks to a great display by Stuart Whitehead who got a try himself and laid on others for Paul Jackson and Billy Burgess. Brave Jackie Brennan played through much of the match with a broken nose.

And there in the tunnel as we wearily left the pitch was a delighted Brian Snape, happily waving a magnum of champagne and blinking tears back from his eyes. 'We're off to Wembley, we're off to Wembley,' was all he could burble happily. 'Well done! Well done!' His excitement reminded me of my first outing for Salford eighteen months earlier when his faith in me was vindicated.

That night's celebration party back at our club-house lasted well into the early hours. The players were paraded as heroes, their wives sharing the glory and the acclaim of supporters. It was all very reminiscent of the aftermath of a Wales-England clash at Cardiff. Someone remarked to me, 'Many players never sniff Wembley during a lifetime of service to the game, David. You've made it after less than two seasons here.'

We were on the crest of a wave. Because of the four-week gap between semi-Finals and Final, however, a reaction inevitably set in. Afraid of suffering injury, players tended to hold themselves back, and some odd results occurred such as our defeat in early May at the hands of lowly Huyton.

There was also the strain of super-star treatment to bear.

At every ground where they play, the Finalists are welcomed officially by loudspeaker and must acknowledge the ovation of the crowd, not to mention suffering the jeers if they fail to come up to scratch. There are endless media interviews to cope with, as well as photo-calls when men who are highly strung and perhaps irritable must produce toothy grins at the click of a shutter. Commercial promotions have to be undertaken; receptions must be attended at which the whole world, it seems, wants to slap you on the back and wish you luck.

Players are also pestered for tickets, a demand which became particularly acute when 1968 emerged as the first Wembley sell-out for ten years. Salford were generous with their allocation to us, but there was still pressure to endure — especially for the miner's son from Gwent. Many of my friends and admirers back home decided that they would like to watch the local boy play at Wembley. Suddenly my father became important again as a kind of Blaina Cup Final agent, forwarding orders for hundreds of tickets to my Manchester address (whether Blaina folk ultimately lost a packet to the bookies after our defeat I do not know, but the fact is that the ticket operation left me with bad debts of some £80 which are unpaid to this day!). As a collier, Watkins senior also figured prominently in a *Coal News* article about mining town Castleford, giving plausible and authoritative comments on my form as an opponent.

After more hard work at Blackpool the Salford Cup Final party travelled south on the Thursday. It seemed a good omen when the bus driver at Euston turned out to be the same agreeable employee of Evans Coaches who used to ferry Newport around on their trips to the Metropolis. On this day he took us to a quiet, rather sedate hotel south of the Thames which had been patronized by FA Cup Finalists Manchester City the previous week-end.

On Friday, crisply turned out in specially tailored Cup Final blazers, we rode as far as Wembley to familiarize ourselves with the Stadium and its playing surface. The soaring stands there make a single human being feel like a dwarf; but at least the turf felt reassuringly normal to our feet. Horse trials had been held there not long before for the first time, generating controversy about the damage suffered by the pitch, but to the starry-eyed Salford players it looked as smooth as a bowling rink.

So back to dinner and an early bed. But sleep did not come easily. There were too many thoughts whirling around my head now that the moment of truth was almost upon us. The biggest anxiety centred on the display that I myself would give. Not only was I a key player; I was also by now Salford's captain. Could I crown my first season at the helm by leading my men to a Cup triumph?

This, I thought, would silence those hard-bitten supporters who had found difficulty in accepting me as skipper from the very day eight months earlier when Brian Snape had appointed me. 'OK, so he captained Newport, Wales and the British Lions,' they had objected. 'So what? That was in the other code. He cannot even put his own game together consistently up here. What hope has he of bringing the best out of twelve team-mates?' Such criticisms found their way to my ears frequently; my sole defence was to tell myself that the club chairman usually knew what he was doing.

Brian Snape's decision was based on my leadership of the Salford VII which had won three big tournaments in seven days at the fag-end of the 1968 season — we romped home at Leeds, Halifax and in the Don Close Memorial Sevens. I imported some of the expertise which had made Newport formidable Sevens practitioners in the sixties, and Salford's team responded nobly to my guidance and generalship (so nobly that the authorities actually saw fit to change the rules: a team which has scored a try must now also kick-off to re-start the game, in order that its opponents may have a sniff of the ball!).

Besides leadership on the field, I sensed that the chairman believed my personality to be in keeping with the new image he desired for Salford. He valued my ability to converse easily and on equal terms with councillors, businessmen and sports administrators who visited the Willows. He was aware that I could make a passable speech in public. He knew that I could hold my place in the team, and that there was no question of my transferring to another club. And he shared with his players the belief that I would make a reliable go-between.

So, feeling flattered and somewhat overawed I trusted Brian's judgment and accepted the post. To my surprise it carried a 'perk': before each match a white envelope containing ten pounds was slipped into my grasp by the chairman when he thought no-one was looking. 'For the extra responsibility,' he would whisper tersely.

I worried for a while about the attitude of my predecessor Jackie Brennan. Would he sulk over his relegation to the ranks? Was he now ten pounds a week out of pocket?

As it turned out there was no problem. Jackie gave me one hundred per cent loyalty, and I suspect that Brian Snape made sure that his weekly pay remained the same. For long I continued to accept his tactical decision-making at scrum half. The only time he protested was when I first delivered a pep-talk on the lines of those I used to give at Newport. 'Blimey,' he exploded. 'Not only have the Welsh provided us with a stand-off half — they've sent us one of their poets as well!'

I would not go as far as to say that Jackie enjoyed being relieved of the captaincy. But I think there were certain off-the-field duties he was happy to shed. Also, words for motivating his men did not spring easily to his lips. He preferred to lead in a simple, uncomplicated manner, by playing as well as he possibly could and trusting that the rest would follow his example.

Almost always, of course, Rugby League professionals do. In the amateur game, where nothing but fun and the club reputation are at stake, you sometimes have to tear a strip off players who are not pulling their weight. Northern pros know that if they give less than their best they may deprive team-mates of a winning bonus, so the only time a skipper may have to read the riot act is if his team, finding themselves well beaten fifteen minutes before full time, seem likely to sit back and let the points pile up against them.

This makes leading a League XIII easier than captaining an amateur XV — provided you know the game inside out. That was the one thought which caused me to toss and turn on the eve of our Cup Final. 'Please,' I thought to myself, 'let me not make some dreadful tactical boob in front of 100,000 people.'

The other concern I had was about marking Alan Hardisty, a great League stand-off half. Summoning up all my reserves of Welsh self-assurance I told myself firmly, 'You can tackle as well as Hardisty. You are a better kicker than he is. And a better runner with the ball. You're going to come out on top.'

Then the counter-argument would spin dizzily around my brain: 'Yes, but think of all that experience. And remember — Alan Hardisty is a bloke who can idle his way through seventy-nine minutes of a game, and sink an opposing team without trace if they let him loose for the remaining sixty seconds.' Alan always was a great opportunist, and was to prove it the following day.

Our opponents also had loose forward Mal Reilly, who went on to reach world-class before becoming Castleford's coach. They had Keith Hepworth, one of the two or three best scrum halves with or against whom I played, a man who never stopped working and goading team-mates to greater efforts. There were Johnny Ward and Brian Lockwood, who toured with Great Britain in 1971.

The team at large boasted a terrific spirit, drawing strength from the compact and vigorous character of the town itself. Several members were products of the famous Normanton Grammar School, a crack rugby nursery which has supplied many Internationals to the England Schools Rugby Union.

I finally dozed off counting Salford's plus points. Chris Hesketh and Billy Burgess were backs who could swing a game, while I felt sure that Colin Dixon would give his all — rightly as it turned out, since although on the losing side he came close to winning the coveted Lance Todd individual award. Our loose forward Ron Hill would be out to prove a thing or two against the club which had discarded him a year or so previously. And I hoped fervently that our latest Rugby Union capture, Moseley's British Lion Mike Coulman, would reward our faith in him at lock, where he had won preference over Peter Smethurst.

We awoke to find that the morning papers had made Cas' favourites, basing their prediction on a recent league victory over us. In no way did this dim our hopes as we set off for the Stadium, linking up on the North Circular road with a second coach bringing wives and girl-friends from their central London hotel. We vied like schoolboys to be the first to spot the twin towers ahead of us, regaining our dignity in time to acknowledge the cheers and boos of the rival supporters trooping in a phalanx along Wembley Way. Everywhere you looked was a painter's palette of red and white or orange and black and white. It was dazzling and tremendously uplifting.

I suppose that everyone imagines Wembley's changing rooms to be the height of luxury. Well, I am sorry to disillusion you, but the accommodation is no more than spartan compared with the space and comfort of Twickenham. No individual tub, for instance, in which to soak tired muscles after a game; at Wembley there is just the one large bath for the whole team.

But I had little time to worry about the décor. Press and television reporters buzzed around the room until 45 minutes before kick-off; there was sparkling new kit to be admired and tried for size; old Salford players were at hand to wish us well; while it fell to me as captain to open a massive pile of greetings telegrams. Many of them were from friends and admirers in the north, not just Rugby League buffs but also people like Bobby Charlton, George Best and the Manchester United football team. Most touching, though, were those addressed to me personally from old Rugby Union pals such as Stewart Wilson, Ray McLoughlin, Rees Stephens, Des O'Brien and Cliff Morgan.

So the time fled away, and soon we were following Brian Snape and his brand new trilby hat down the tunnel and out into the sunshine. Even I, twenty-one times a Welsh International, was unprepared for the noise that now assaulted our ear-drums.

At Cardiff, Twickenham and other Rugby Union strongholds the huge crowds who attend roar their heads off as the teams take the field. But the home crowd is always in the ascendant, so the sound they make has an even, steady quality. At Wembley that day Salford supporters were at one end of the ground, Castleford's at the other; and the volume generated by each group as they glimpsed their heroes came rolling across the turf to meet like a gigantic thunderclap somewhere above the half way line. Then the sound waves beat their way around the stadium, trapped beneath the big stands. It was a deafening and quite unique experience.

Soon, however, we had shaken hands with guest of honour Harold Wilson (much to the delight of Charlie Bott, a fervent Labour party man) and with a final wave to families seated above us we bent our attention to the Cup Final. I agonized over the reasons for our defeat in the months that followed, and of one thing I am certain: Salford lost the game at the kick-off when the burly Dennis Hartley ruthlessly clobbered our star wing, Billy Burgess. Had the referee seen this appalling act, a sending-off must have resulted. As it was, for the next quarter of an hour Billy dropped passes or failed to exploit the spaces we created for him, until it dawned on us that he was now suffering from concussion. Even then we were unable to substitute him, since our replacement back was a scrum half, Bob Prosser; and in any case, Billy kept insisting that he was fit to continue. But his brilliance when fit was one of our main attacking weapons, and we had to play the full eighty minutes bereft of it.

Ron Hill kicked a penalty for us, Howe replied with a try for Cas', then Ron restored the lead to us with a second penalty which sent us to the changing room with a 4–3 interval lead. But soon after the re-start the referee disallowed a try by Chris Hesketh, ruling that the ball had been grounded on the wrong side of the goal line. This was a second important factor in our defeat. Points at that stage would have ruffled Cas', and I believe that we would have won. As it was however, Alan Hardisty snatched one try, Hepworth got another at the end, and our opponents claimed the victory by 11–6, Ron Hill's third penalty providing our only score of the second half.

If only because they scored two tries to our none, Castleford deserved the Cup. But that was a conclusion I reached much later. You don't have the stomach for that kind of reflection when you can scarcely see your runners-up medal for the tears in your eyes.

The calibre of Brian Snape could again be appreciated in the wake of our defeat. Once the media had claimed their pound of flesh and the changing-room commiserations were over he whisked his despondent players away to the Royal Garden hotel, where almost all Salford's Wembley profit had been spent accommodating every last wife, girlfriend and close relative. Here, successfully, we drowned our sorrows. Sympathetic Pressmen who called on us after visiting Castleford's celebrations even said that we had the better party!

The chairman's remarks at our banquet were also a model of graciousness and magnanimity in defeat. 'Before the game,' he told the gathering, 'I said to the boys that, win or lose, they were to enjoy their afternoon. Sadly, we lost — but I know that they did enjoy playing at Wembley. They made me a proud man simply because they reached here.

'Their reward was to be £150 a man if they won, £25 for losing. Because I know they did their best, the club will pay them the full £150.'

Any Castleford players listening would have been green with envy. Their winning fee was all of £125.

When our train was pulling into Manchester the following day the Salford squad fell silent. Each of us feared that, like Scotland's disgraced world cup soccer team of 1978, we would be disowned by our fans, none of whom would turn up to welcome us home. How wrong can you be? Some 20,000 folk came to greet us at the civic centre, with banners which proclaimed 'Dixon for King' or 'Watkins for PM.' The Mayor gave us tea, and then we had to tour the area twice — by public demand — in an open-topped double-decker bus. We were forgiven; but the display of affection made every player realize even more fully what high hopes of us the supporters had held.

Was there any other reason for our defeat? In later years, when I knew the League game better, I formed the view that the Salford side of 1969, though able, was not a great one.

On the day a hard core of fine players had been unable to carry the rest, who fell into two categories. There were inexperienced men such as I truly was then, and certainly Mike Coulman, a disappointment in the pack. Others were definitely over the top, like Martin Dickens, at hooker, and our prop Terry Ogden. Paul Jackson was sold before long to Swinton, while the club soon decided that Stuart Whitehead was not really up to the job of playing centre.

All these men gave their utmost, but to win at Wembley you need players who are in their prime. Next time Salford play in a Cup Final I feel certain they will have them.

More than once during the seventies I have thought we were Wembley-bound, only to be foiled by an unlucky bounce or a lapse of concentration. Against Wigan in the 1971 tie we led at half time, only to relax fatally later. In 1974 we fell for the notorious dummy scissors which Sid Hynes and Alan Smith loved to pull off for Leeds. Somehow Maurice Richards failed to keep Sid in his sights and we conceded points that swung the game against us.

Then there was the second round tie of 1975 when, after my 75-yard run through the St Helens defence, the full back got a fingertip in the way of the scoring pass I tried to supply to Chris Hesketh; moments later, with a blind side move called, Kenny Gill inexplicably hurled the ball away to the open side. There it was intercepted, and the Saints went on to get a decisive score at the posts. Salford's cup rugby in the last decade has been glorious but, alas, unfulfilled.

Still, it is great to have participated at Wembley and also to have witnessed other classic occasions on this greatest single day in the Rugby League calendar. Leeds versus St Helens in 1978; Leigh, the no-hopers, inspired by Alex Murphy to that incredible victory over Leeds in 1971; Featherstone's rout of Bradford Northern in 1973 with a display of power play that yielded a near-record 33 points. These I pick out as the great Finals of my time.

But how poignant also to have seen Don Fox's horrendous mis-kick in front of the posts at the close of the 1968 Final, thus handing Leeds a one-point victory over Wakefield Trinity on a plate.

Don and I have at least one thing in common.

We know how awful it feels to lose at Wembley after having come so far. And we can only guess how it feels to win.

CHAPTER 16

Acceptance

As a person the new arrival in northern England is assured of a warm welcome. As a rugby player, I have hinted before, it takes longer to win acceptance.

Soon I will explain how Lancashire and Yorkshire finally took me to their hearts. But first it is worth considering some expensive signings which went sour on the clubs and individuals concerned. The League game has had its share of costly failures.

Sometimes the clubs have been at fault, writing large cheques to buy stars from another sport simply to draw the crowds and bask in reflected glory. Remember sprinter MacDonald Bailey's short-lived career? And that of the ambitious shot-putter Arthur Rowe, who wanted to become a great wing? Oldham begged to differ and asked him to try the second row. The grafting and the bumps did not appeal at all to Arthur, who decided that he would rather go off to Scotland and toss cabers.

But often the fault has lain with players themselves, declining to re-sit their 11-plus at Rugby League and learn the new game thoroughly. Resting on laurels never works.

Take the case of Raymond 'Chico' Hopkins, a very sound scrum half in Wales and a British Lion whom Swinton were delighted to capture in 1972. Up north Chico was too heavily marked for his liking, nor could he put his main skill to use in League — tactical kicking in support of his pack. He soon got fed up and went back to Maesteg. I thought it a pity that after returning he chose to knock the northern game and claim that it was dying.

Sometimes medical factors which ought to have come to light beforehand have cut short a star's career and prevented clubs recouping the money they spent on him. Ireland's Ken Goodall arrived at Workington in 1970 and quickly won praise for some hard play. But an arthritic knee cut short his useful service after just two years, when he retired to Londonderry and the money he had banked.

Keith Jarrett and the cerebral haemorrhage which ended his playing days prematurely are a different kettle of fish. The trouble here was that Barrow sold off vital players in order to raise the £15,000 they paid Keith, and even the Welsh 'golden boy' could not compensate for a basic absence of supporting talent. Keith was on trial at Wigan, apparently set to make good, when his breakdown forced him out of the game.

The ironic point is that Wigan had wanted him in the first place, but declined to match Barrow's offer. If only Keith had discussed his future with me before putting pen to paper I would have advised him to accept less cash and join Wigan. Bonus payments would have made up the difference, and more, in the succeeding years.

Stand-off half Tom Brophy, capped eight times by England at Rugby Union was another who found the going hard at Barrow. He was a clever player but lacked the speed necessary in our northern game. Mike Coulman, the England prop who came to Salford, also struggled for a while. Even after a year in the game he still used to play his rugby in bursts, whereas the commitment demanded of a League forward is non-stop.

For example, since our game has no mauls or line out, the immense care before importing star performers from elsewhere. It is simply not as straightforward as it looks. I often dismay my friends at Newport by dismissing some of the great Union players of the seventies as potential League stars.

For example, since our game has no mauls or line out the ideal League forward need stand no more than six feet in height, with his weight and strength packed into thighs and trunk. To be six feet four inches is no advantage at all, indeed such bean-poles are far more vulnerable to non-stop heavy tackling. This rules out men like Geoff Wheel, Allan Martin, Derek Quinnell, Andy Ripley, Gordon Brown,

Roger Uttley and even the great Mervyn Davies himself. Charlie Faulkner — whom I always thought of as the 'ArtooDeetoo' loose-head prop in the Wales pack — never possessed the necessary initiative to play League, and I doubted the willingness of Bobby Windsor to drive himself hard enough. But Graham Price had, and has, all it takes to make good in the other code, as do one or two of Wales's back row forwards of recent years.

A number of clubs used to show interest in Barry John and Phil Bennett, but I have reservations about their ability to have survived the rigours of the north. Barry for instance, was a touch player without a shattering turn of speed or a big appetite for tackling. His genius might have been swiftly stifled by constant bone-shaking collisions with some of our hard men. Mind you, it is possible that the excellent goal-kicking of him and Bennett would have redeemed them.

Gerald Davies, I have no doubt, would have been a wow in League football. He stands out as the best wing I have ever seen in either code. J.P.R. Williams likewise had the physique to succeed and the intelligence to adapt himself to a new game. It is sometimes forgotten that he was a top grade junior tennis player, but put the sport aside because he was not convinced that he could become a world-class player. In rugby he knew that he could. Being a realistic and practical man, he decided that tennis must go.

Close behind these men in the seventies has been the flying Scot, Andy Irvine. After his Lions tour of 1974 he was offered £15,000 by Salford plus £2000 a year for five years. Alas, he could not be tempted away from his homeland. I would love to have had Andy in our back division. We also failed to sign New Zealand's star wing Brian Williams in spite of offering to pay for his university education in Britain.

Which brings me to Gareth Edwards, perhaps the sole genuine superstar thrown up by Rugby Union and one who, in my opinion, could have played successfully in almost any position in Rugby League. Why did he never turn professional? The amazing answer is that, as far as I am aware, no club seriously approached him.

Let me explain. Gareth was, almost literally, a priceless asset to the Union game. Northern clubs feared to approach him lest they should be laughed out of court. For what was his worth? £20,000? £25,000? £50,000? Supposing an offer of that order had been made to Gareth and he had turned it down: the story would speedily have gone on the grapevine that Mr Edwards had thumbed his nose at such and such a club. So, carefully guarding their pride, the northerners left well alone.

Certainly, he had the necessary ability right to the end. In his later years I felt great sympathy for Gareth as he put up with a stream of uninformed criticism. After some International matches folk would comment, 'Edwards didn't do much today,' or 'Gareth is over the top.' Had they troubled to look around at his challengers they must have noticed that, even during an indifferent game by his own high standards, Gareth was still turning in rugby that was streets ahead of the rest.

Let's stop theorizing now, however, and consider how you win a secure place for yourself in League rugby. Before looking back on my own case, let us briefly salute the approach of men such as John Bevan, a disillusioned misfit in Union but one who imported all his native aggression and will to win into the professional game. Maurice Richards was an exception to the general rule in that it was he who made the initial approach to a League club, Salford, rather than vice versa. It took me very much by surprise, and I could not believe it when Brian Snape asked me to accompany him to a meeting with 'a certain Maurice Richards, who says he's a British Lion and wants to join us.' But there was Maurice! He had taken a deliberate career decision — and over the years he has made it work.

Keith Fielding, the fastest thing on two legs that I have ever seen, spent a season or two being a bit selfish before learning the lesson that you must play for the team as well as for yourself. Salford and he are the better for it.

As for myself, I spent a fair time, as you know, suffering doubts and hang-ups about my ability to come to terms with my new code. A major turning-point, after which I never looked back, came in November 1970 when I finally got my domestic life straight and was married at Libanus, Ebbw Vale, to Jane Talbot.

I had actually known Jane before my abortive first marriage, and, soon after it broke up, bumped into her again when she attended Rodney Parade to see a county match in which I was playing. Firm bonds soon developed between us and, more, I soon found that here was a woman with whom one could actually hold an intelligent conversation about rugby! As a teenager her hero had been the hefty Cardiff forward Dannie Harris, but now she settled for a more modestly proportioned partner.

Jane shared my agonizing over the Salford offer of 1967 and, while careful not to influence my final decision, gave it her full backing once it was made. She then endured four difficult years in digs near mine while we strove to secure a divorce from my wife. The moment it came through we went down to Gwent and a wedding day which was really memorable. Many new friends from Salford made the journey to be with us, sharing celebrations that lasted well into the night and delayed the departure of the bride and groom!

The landlord of the Wiltshire hotel which accommodated us was a man from Neath who kept me talking into the early hours; and when I finally joined Jane I nearly blew us both up trying to light an antiquated gas-fire to stop her shivering from the cold. To cap it all, she had to make do with a shortened honeymoon squeezed in between important Salford fixtures!

But she has been a tower of strength, as they say, building and sustaining my confidence in the difficult transitional stage, never allowing self-assurance to overflow into conceit once I had mastered my new craft. She has borne me, first, young Nicholas (he first saw the light of day in Manchester, so if Wales should not need him at stand-off half in 1990 he will be a cert for England!) and later a daughter, Victoria, and is in every way a great partner for living.

However, it is not quite enough to have a wife who roots whole-heartedly for you on the touch-line, and it is through achievement that the newcomer to Rugby League must stake a claim for recognition. Reliability and consistency are great virtues, perhaps the greatest of all, and I have no hesitation in naming these qualities as the ones which mainly endeared me to the fans in the north.

I still look back with amazement at the sequence of matches I played through between April 1971 and April 1974 for Salford. They added up to 140 games on the trot and constitute a world record, leaving the runner-up more than forty appearances behind. Because they prove resilience and dependability I put them first among a number of achievements which give me particular pleasure.

Included in that total are ninety-two successive games in which I scored, another world mark. Not that I let the sequence play on the mind; I was simply happy to be piling up points for Salford. My run came to an end one day against St Helens, after I had missed five shots at goal. We won 5–0 and my spirits were high as we trooped from the field. Only at the tunnel entrance did a spectator deflate me by jeering, 'So there, bloody Watkins — you didn't get any today!'

Luck and determination keep one going in Rugby League. But I also seem to have possessed a gift for making a quick recovery from bumps. More than one physiotherapist has told me, 'You can play tomorrow — but that injury would have kept most players out for another fortnight.'

And so to some bursts of scoring which also pleased the fans. Altogether my League career contains six hat-tricks, including four touch-downs in one meeting with Hull. Against Barrow at the Willows I once ran up three tries and two conversions, that is 13 points, in the space of five minutes. That's another world record. So is the time for the actual tries, four and a half minutes.

A proud day came along in January 1972 when I landed 13 goals against Keighley to equal Gus Risman's club record. That was one of ten occasions when I kicked ten or more goals in a game, and also the day when I notched my best match score, twenty-nine points.

In 1973 I set another world record with 221 goals, contained in an eventual season's bag of 493 points. The second figure is a Salford record, but falls short of Lewis Jones's 496 scored in one year for Leeds. However, if we count charity games I finished with 514 points against his all-games total of 502. Incidentally, if you equate such scoring to Rugby Union you will find that it would come to more than 600 points, bringing me into the realms of wonder-kickers Robin Williams and the late Sam Doble of Moseley.

Looking back at my try-scoring ratio for Salford I see that it approached one in every two appearances. But I would not want you to think that our club was a one-man band. Let me quote you some figures from 1971–2, when I crossed twenty-nine times: that year Keith Fielding got forty-six tries, Maurice Richards and Paul Charlton thirty-three each, and Chris Hesketh twenty-two. Between us we piled up over 1000 points.

Such scoring prompted a Leeds fan to write in the Press, 'Salford's wings seem to get more than their fair share of tries.' Commented Leeds and Great Britain wing John Atkinson in reply, 'No wonder. They're playing outside the best centre three quarter in the game.'

A nice compliment to me. But — centre?

Yes. After four years as Salford's stand-off half I was told by Brian Snape in September 1971 that he wanted to move me out to the midfield. 'It will give you more room for manoeuvre,' he said. 'We're not using your speed and agility enough.'

I left the club-house in a brown study. Stand-off half was the berth I had occupied since schooldays. In Union and League it is the place where the team's field marshal plays, dictating tactics and controlling the tempo of play. It was *my* position. So Brian Snape's words hit me like a thunderbolt. 'Am I being demoted?' I asked myself. 'Is this the beginning of the end?' A week's unrelieved depression followed.

My first outing at centre took place at Whitehaven, where the young and promising Kenny Gill was at stand-off for Salford. However, not for the first time the instinct of Brian Snape proved well founded. Far from feeling rather 'spare' as I had feared, to my relief I seemed to be as involved as ever in calling the shots. It still fell to me to put in the tactical kicks, the touch-finding penalties and the attempts at goal.

In addition I relished the extra space an inside centre gets to operate in, contributing two important tries. Within eighty minutes the gloom had lifted, and I knew that I could cope with the new role. Altogether the adjustment took no more than a month, and soon I was even winning caps for Great Britain as a centre. After that I never had second thoughts.

The Salford fans had watched the experiment closely and sympathetically. They sensed how I felt, probably realizing that a *prima donna* of a rugby player in my boots might have kicked up no end of a fuss. When it all jelled, they were not slow to show their appreciation that the immigrant Welshman had behaved as a good club-man. With that and a spot of record-breaking, I date my final acceptance by northern crowds to autumn 1971. It was a good feeling.

That year our supporters made me their player of the season, presenting me with a commemorative tankard. Letters came from outside our club, including one from Halifax, a team which spent the early seventies in the doldrums. 'Thank you for leaving Wales and coming as a professional to the north,' wrote my correspondent. 'You are now the best and most sporting player I have known in many years spent watching the game. We Thrum Hallers would soon be out of trouble with a couple of blokes like you. In fact, just one would do!'

Even Wigan fans were reluctantly converted. They stopped shouting, 'Fairy, where's your handbag?' at me, and began bellowing, 'Dirty Welsh bastard!' That, we have noted, is a sign of respect!

My confidence was at last restored to its old 1967 level, as a few golden moments on the field of play demonstrate. One day at Bradford Northern I really let rip and ran in a scorcher of a try which began forty yards out with a well-timed pass from Colin Dixon. Stepping inside my centre I trod on the accelerator and covered twenty-five yards as fast as I ever have on a rugby field. That burst took me clear of the Bradford wing, and it remained to jink past the full back and reach the line.

Afterwards I was invited to the home side's board room and taken aside by Albert Fearnley, a coach whom I respected. 'David,' he told me earnestly, 'here at Bradford we have more respect for you than for any other opponent in the game.' That was a compliment to treasure.

Sometimes the recollection is of putting a team-mate in for a great try, as during our Floodlit Trophy Final of 1975 against Warrington. Injury had kept me out of the drawn first encounter, and in the replay I was struggling to find form and fitness. Then, suddenly, it all happened.

A 45-yard penalty attempt by Warrington drifted past our right-hand post and down into my clutch. A split-second decision to run the ball out brought instant dismay when the way ahead was barred by two burly forwards. The only solution was to duck to daisy-top height — after which there suddenly opened up ninety almost empty yards between me and our opponents' goal line. Keith Fielding was coming out of defence on my right and, as I veered towards him, lone defender John Bevan found himself trying to cover two men, both of whom were up to top speed.

A feint to the left drew him fatally in my direction, at which I managed to find Keith with just the pass he needed to send him on the long sprint to the posts. Our effort was voted the 'televised try of the year' — one, I may add, which was worth seven points. For out of sheer frustration one of the Warrington forwards clobbered Keith as he rose to his feet, so that I was able to add a penalty to my simple conversion. With that sort of boost to our morale there was no way Warrington could deny us the victory.

Indiscipline also figured in an exchange I had with Alex Murphy in 1972. This time the score was 4–4 and Warrington looked set for an away point, when I took a high ball close to the right hand touchline. Murphy, who had been urging his team-mates to 'get' the golden boy all afternoon, came in snorting and grunting as the second tackler and gave me a real shaking-up, thereby conceding a penalty for foul play.

As I cracked the leather with all my might I told myself that it was Alex's backside — and the crowd roared as the ball soared between the sticks from 45 yards' range.

Sometimes my place-kicking got me out of some hot spots and placated fans who had just been turning the air blue with anger at me. Four minutes from the end of a Challenge

Cup tie at home to Wakefield we were trailing 8–6 when I managed to break the defence down the left flank. Inexplicably, however, I ignored the shout for a scoring pass on my inside, and was bundled into touch by the sole defender three yards from the corner.

Everyone at The Willows thought I had thrown the game away, so you can imagine my enormous relief when a last-second penalty shot from near half way just cleared the crossbar to get us a replay at Wakefield. There, against the odds, we won by 14 points to 6, largely thanks to a ploy between Maurice Richards and myself which ended with the wing crossing at the flag. Peaks and precipices are never far apart in the rugby game.

Finally on this theme of acceptance let us talk about referees and refereeing. The newcomer to the game stands in awe of officialdom. It was several seasons before I felt equipped to talk on an equal footing with men like Billy Thomson and Fred Lindop, whom I rate the tops. And no doubt it took referees some time to decide that the impudent newcomer from Newport understood League rules and knew what he was doing.

Probably it was the reputation which I won as a clean, fair player which saved me from an early bath on the one occasion in my career when I fully admit that I should have been sent off.

We were at Barrow some years ago for a fixture whose underlying tension was, as usual, heightened by the pre-match exchanges between Bill Oxley, Barrow's national selector, and Brian Snape. 'Jarrett and Brophy are streets ahead of Watkins,' Oxley would say. 'Watkins will never make good in Rugby League. And Barrow will fix him today.'

Among the visitors' strong-arm boys who had been detailed to nail me was Robin Whitfield, who got his paws on me quite early in the game. Several other players piled on top of us, and at the bottom of it all Whitfield suddenly started tearing with his fingers at my eyes and lips. Afraid for my sight and the flesh around my mouth and unable to free a hand to protect myself, I took the only course open to me and bit my tormentor's thumb to the bone, causing him to loose his grip and scream out loud.

Intervening swiftly the referee stood us to attention before him and delivered the longest, angriest dressing-down I have ever known. 'He bloody bit me,' protested Whitfield. 'Look at my mouth,' I retorted hotly — and indeed it was literally spilling blood. Finally, 'Get back and stop the nonsense,' snarled the ref. I am sure that it was only my bloodied appearance which persuaded him not to give me marching orders.

In general I believe that the standard of refereeing has declined since 1967 when I made my League debut. Too many officials these days want to be stars like the players. They strike over-dramatic poses, especially when the television cameras are present. They court popularity with the crowd, often at the expense of the visiting team.

This last fault led to one of the saddest episodes which befell Salford in my time. Let me set the scene by recalling the fracas at Leeds when Mike Shoebottom was badly injured in a heavy but fair tackle by Colin Dixon. He left the field with a fractured jaw, there followed complications in hospital, and shortly the scrum half found himself wheelchair-bound with a temporary paralysis of his limbs.

At Salford we heard of his misfortune, but were nonetheless totally unprepared for the savage reception which greeted our next appearance at Headingley. Before the kick-off the wrath of the crowd was raised to frenzy-point, first by the distribution of blown-up photographs depicting Colin's boot apparently making contact with Shoebottom's jaw (a carefully selected picture can be made to prove any point) and then by the sight of the man himself being wheeled around the touch-line by his wife. 'Look at my maimed husband,' she shouted to the crowd.

This was nothing to what happened during the match. From the start Colin got the 'nigger' cat-call every time he was near the play. Leeds were clearly out to nobble him, and time after time the big fellow was shaken by tackles which were late and unforgivably ferocious.

The referee on this disgraceful day was Dennis Brown, a Preston schoolteacher who was ranked among the top half dozen officials in the land. It lay in his power to afford Colin the complete protection of the laws of the game. I regret to say that, affected in my view by the ugly mood of the crowd, he not only permitted Colin to suffer everything that Leeds threw at him, but also went out of his way to penalize our team-mate for tackles he himself was putting in. No fewer than thirty-six penalties went Leeds's way; Colin was virtually whistled out of the game; and, our spirit broken, Salford went down to a heavy defeat. The crowd relished it all.

Afterwards an invitation to the Leeds board room to have a drink and bury the hatchet specifically excluded Colin Dixon. A white-faced Brian Snape ignored it, ushering us straight to our team bus. We drove away to the sound of breaking glass and missiles landing on the roof.

The incident escalated, I believe, because Mr Brown allowed Leeds to have Colin as a sacrificial offering to make up for Shoebottom's injury. Whether he had feared a rough handling from the crowd had he officiated any other way I cannot say, but I am sure that he found it hard to sleep that night. I hope so — for allowing himself to be pressurized by a home crowd seems to me an inexcusable abdication of responsibility. Like players, our referees are supposed to be professionals.

To their credit Leeds's directors showed common sense and maturity by inviting Salford to a special banquet in 1974 to smoke the pipe of peace. Brian Snape slapped a three-line whip on his players, who all attended. In response to some carefully-expressed sentiments from our hosts I delivered an off-the-cuff speech about friendship and sportsmanship in Rugby League — and thankfully relations between our two clubs are stronger than ever.

As a paid employee it is good to feel accepted by one's peers. And once that happens one is also in a position to tolerate, though not condone, the unacceptable face of Rugby League that sometimes exposes itself.

CHAPTER 17

The World Game

Since in this chapter I am going to discuss Rugby League around the world I cannot avoid beginning in Australia, top nation in my time. The prospect does not please me one bit.

Frankly, I have reservations about Australians in the round. Generally, I suspect that emigrant stock from the United Kingdom is composed of people who down the years have been unable to make good in the land of their birth and have gone off discontentedly and sullenly. Australia in particular contains many descendants of types deported by law courts in bygone days. On a rugby field it is easy to get under their skins with cracks about how hard it is to run fast with a ball and chain around your ankle!

Seriously, however, I find Aussies brash and loud. Often they carry chips on their shoulders. They will demand menacingly of the visitor, 'What do you think about our country? Isn't the sunshine marvellous here? How do you like our beer?' If your reply is less than ecstatic they start to sulk and shout the odds about pommie bastards.

So it goes against the grain to admit straightaway that as dedicated games players they rank second to none. Perhaps because of their complexes they possess a highly developed will to win in International competition at cricket, swimming, tennis — and League rugby. Their 13-a-side he-men are undoubtedly the best-tuned sportsmen in the world outside athletics.

For a start they are full-time professionals, not part-timers like us in northern England. This leads to a strictly imposed discipline in club play. Men who do not train when the coach demands it do not play — and do not earn. In addition they make few mistakes in handling or tackling, and great finesse is needed on the part of opponents to outwit their defensive organization.

The game in their country is strongest along the north and eastern coasts in Queensland and New South Wales, though tourists these days often stop off at Darwin for a match or two in the north west before moving on to the Rugby League heartland. Here are league structures based on Sydney and Brisbane surrounded by strong district associations out in the country which feed stars into the more glamorous city clubs. Mike Cronin of the 1978 Australian party in Britain is a rare example of a man reaching Test level straight from a country team, where he was a big fish in a small pond. But in the end he too proved unable to resist the £60,000 three-year contract offered by Parramatta.

When he signed, Mike knew that the lump sum was only the beginning. He could also look forward to appearance money and match bonuses amounting to over £100 per game. If he played his cards right he would be snapped up for television commercials, like Bobby Fulton who advertizes central heating and air-conditioning systems, Artie Beetson with wines and spirits, or Ron Coote who plugs track suits, sports gear and school uniforms. Australian Test players have recently been wearing the logo of a brewery, reputedly netting them £500 for a televised match.

Compared with our rivals Down Under even those of us who play for big English clubs like Wigan, Leeds and Salford are mere paupers. It is no wonder that Mal Reilly was lured into the Aussie fold, or that having accepted an £8000 signing-on fee from Wigan the promising John Gray went for £30,000 to Northern Sydney — who also bought out his contract with Wigan.

I myself was offered £10,000 for a six-month coaching attachment after my stint as Great Britain player-coach in 1977. It came late in my playing career, by which time uprooting my family and taking long leave of absence from Forward Trust were not attractive propositions. But like others in the north I was sorely tempted, and this potential 'brawn drain' was what persuaded the Rugby League Council to impose a ban in 1976 on registered personnel accepting temporary or close-season appointments outside Britain.

But where does the big money, like the £20,000 paid by Manley in autumn 1978 to Union stand-off Kenny Wright, come from? It is made available by the big-time, big-thinking approach to the sport on the part of clubs. Initially, their promotion and publicity is cleverly thought out, so that cup finals and Test matches may be watched by crowds of 80,000 or more and 12,000 is normal for routine fixtures. Rock-hard bargaining is the practice before any big matches are sold to television companies.

Committees make sure that their membership includes personalities with genuine charisma. These may be anybody from cricketers like Richie Benaud and Keith Miller to top politicians like the former Prime Minister Gough Whitlam, who happily sink pints with the players after the final whistle. To attract and keep such folk the clubs have built headquarters buildings which would dwarf any to be seen in any sport in Great Britain.

Take that of Sydney's Eastern Suburbs club. You have to picture something like the Piccadilly Plaza in Manchester or Cardiff's Hodge Building to get some idea of its size — it needs to be that big, since if all its members decided to turn up on the same evening there would be some 160,000 people clamouring for entry on the same night! That is to say, three stadia the size of Cardiff Arms Park would be needed if they all wanted to see a match!

On the bottom two floors of the 11-storey structure are accommodated some 1200 fruit machines where customers can spend twenty-four hours a day gambling if they so wish (after an hour 'feeding' the bandit they are allowed to lock it off and go for a beer, safe in the knowledge that no hanger-on can arrive to cream off a quick profit).

One floor up is a vast indoor swimming pool the size of Blackpool's Derby Baths. Then comes a games floor with a full-size rink for bowlers as well as snooker tables and darts areas. Higher still are banqueting suites, a cinema and a huge variety of bars and lounges big enough to house all the inhabitants of Blaina and Nantyglo and leave room for more. At the top, almost as an afterthought, are luxurious office suites and reception rooms for VIPs.

Furnishings are invariably lavish, making even Salford's fine facilities seem almost threadbare by comparison. At the West Coast club my eye was caught by the depiction of a sunset measuring thirty feet by twelve covering the whole of one wall. Looking more closely I discovered that the material used was not emulsion paint, or even oil on canvas, but thick carpeting of contract quality! Money attracts money, and it is common for big clubs to report profits of up to one and a half million Australian dollars per year.

Perhaps half of those ploughing in the cash are social members with little interest in playing or watching rugby. But the genuine supporters are complete fanatics who not only understand the game but also keep complex statistical records of its progress. They accost players after a match with notebooks at the open: 'You were called upon to make fifteen tackles,' they will announce accusingly, 'but in four cases you let your man get away.' To a goal-kicker they will say, 'Your success rate is seventy per cent — but that Welshman Watkins is doing better — he's on eighty per cent!'

That, roughly, is the Rugby League background in a country which has dominated the game during my time. Again, I have to make an admission: just as South Africa was the only nation against whom I was never on a winning side at Rugby Union, so Australia were the only League opponents to deny me a victory to remember. For Great Britain, for Wales and for Salford I played against the Aussies seven times — and was always a loser!

Yet I have vivid and pleasurable recollections of these encounters. For example, there was an Arctic occasion in 1973 when I spent forty minutes on the subs' bench watching Australia and Great Britain slogging out a Test match on iron-hard turf. The tackles were so devastating and the thuds so loud as players hit the ground that I felt sheer fright that I might be called into action against these giants from the southern hemisphere.

Immediately after half time, however, Roger Millward came off injured, obliging me to remove my nice warm track-suit and get into the game. Soon the first confrontation came along; I tried not to flinch, and to my great relief brought down my man. Things felt better straightaway, and the next forty minutes simply sped past.

We lost, though, as we did in our first Test of the 1974 tour when the Aussies scored a decisive but controversial try at the posts with two of our side lying on the ground immobilized by injury. But that day brought a memorable personal duel which is still talked about between myself and the brilliant Bobby Fulton.

So closely did we mark each other that at one stage he snarled at me, 'Watkins, you're round my ankles so much you feel like one of my boot-laces!' I got in a couple of forty-yard bursts, but on the whole I suppose you could say that we played each other out of the game. That day a mutual respect and friendship developed between us which is cemented each time one of us crosses the world to the other's country.

League players look forward to tours as a good time to bank some cash. My first major overseas trip since 1966 was that 1974 tour. It included the worst injury of my career, which I shall come to later, but financially all the party did well. For openers, the Rugby League made £350 available to all wives and dependants being left behind, which was realistic for a three-month period.

Our pay on tour was £30 a week. That may not sound much, but was more than enough for casual expenditure—and the important thing was that our contracts included a ten per cent share of the gate money. In the end that came to £2500 for each tourist. Press and television interviews brought more money into the kitty, and as I personally was able to do useful business with the Midland Bank's Australian associates, the Commonwealth Bank of Australia, Forward Trust generously kept me on full pay.

The system was different in 1975 during our World Cup matches and on the 1977 Great Britain tour. This time we were paid a basic £80 a week, plus winning bonuses of £30 for provincial matches and £50 for Tests.

By this time sponsorship was really taking off and our players benefited in different ways. Besides lavishing boots, track-suits and all-weather kit upon us, Adidas chipped in

£1000 on condition that we wore their strip in matches. Coca Cola once paid us £1000 for playing an exhibition match of touch rugby.

More money came in from private enterprise on a smaller scale, as when Roger Millward raffled a jersey for £400 and a couple of autographed balls for £200. Once in 1977 when we had a free Saturday our manager Reg Parker let us accept an up-country challenge match for which each player was paid a special fee of £150.

Yes, life can be very sweet on tour, especially if it is Australia you are visiting, where the sun always seems to shine, beaches are never far distant and the sea feels warm even in the cooler months. Several hundred miles to the south, New Zealand's climate is not nearly so agreeable, and the 1977 British Lions were not the first tour party to experience a 'long, wet winter'.

My first visit there had of course been in 1966 as an amateur, and I was delighted to return in 1974 with Great Britain and see what great strides the League game is making in a country with a particularly strong Union tradition. Eight years earlier I had formed the strong impression that New Zealand's whole sporting aspirations began and ended with the fifteen-a-side game in winter, and some cricket and athletics in the summer. But by the mid-seventies League was drawing big crowds and providing a lucrative outlet for players who wanted to make some cash out of their ability.

Oddly enough, so I was assured, the Union game itself had contributed to this swing. The British Lions had, for the first time ever, defeated the All Blacks on their own soil in 1971, undermining the enthusiasm of marginal followers who attended Test matches simply to cheer New Zealand victories. Some of their loyalty had transferred to up-and-coming League clubs, and was further fortified by the Kiwis' test victories in Britain during 1973–4.

As in northern England the League game is based on ports and industrial areas, and has a working-class character. A lot of the best players come from dockyard backgrounds, meat markets or mining. Auckland, Wellington, Christchurch and Greymouth are the principal centres, running active local leagues, producing district XIIIs to play other cities, and combining to provide North and South teams that play annual inter-Island fixtures.

In my time the Kiwis have shown themselves to be hard, talented opponents. I think back with admiration to Henry Tatana, a teak-hard Maori forward who also slotted goals with the greatest of ease. Bennie Lowther was a centre who must have been in world-class as a midfield player between 1970 and 1975 and would, in my view, have been good enough for an All Black XV at that time.

But it is hard to make direct comparisons, since New Zealand Rugby League players are bred and mature within their own game, and seldom have a prior Union track record to judge from. So it is as impractical to compare Lowther with, say, Bruce Robertson as it is to compare Paul Charlton with J.P.R. Williams. Men like Joey Karam and Kent Lambert, who switch from amateur to professional ranks, have traditionally been the exception rather than the rule.

Partly, I believe, because there is no history of 'poaching' by League scouts, little or no hostility exists between the two codes, rather the reverse. In 1974 our party were invited to the famous Maris club, home of All Black 'greats' like Sam Strahan, Peter Whiting and Brian Williams, where we spent a delightful evening.

The Welsh party of 1975 went one better with an invitation from the exclusive Sporting Club of Auckland. Each member was invited to make a stage appearance, to be greeted by Wilson Whineray whose New Zealand Union side I had helped Newport to defeat a dozen years earlier. Also in the gathering that night were my old friend and foe, flank forward 'Waka' Nathan, and Ron Rangi, an All Black wing of 1966. Our players received sheepskin rugs to remind them of the occasion and were made to feel very welcome. What a contrast to the United Kingdom, where a League man venturing into a Union gathering will be asked in hushed tones, 'Should you be here?' or 'I suppose you've had a special dispensation this evening?'

Ties in two World Cup tournaments have now been played in New Zealand, and one could not fail to be aware of the money which is now flowing into the game. Concerns like New Zealand Airways and a brewery or two are keen to sponsor Rugby League — not surprisingly, since their country has now overtaken France as the world's number three nation in the sport, and now has a Test victory over Australia to its credit.

France, as I have hinted more than once, have been a disappointment in my time, finishing bottom in most major competitions during the seventies. It may be that Rugby Union players are so well looked after there, with jobs, cars and other 'perks', that the top men do not need to move into League for cash; but, whatever the reason, the French seem to produce few men of real Test calibre. The most I can say for them is that they bring some colour into the game and are always kitted out immaculately!

From time to time Great Britain loses representative games across the Channel, but usually because of blatant 'home' refereeing. You really have to run 90 yards with the ball safely in your hands and plant it under the posts before French officials readily award a try against their country.

Britons, like Ellis Devlin and Jimmy Fidler, who have occasionally joined French clubs to seek their fortunes as players or coaches, invariably return disillusioned men. They have enjoyed the travel, the chance to learn a new language, and the broadening of their outlook; but their careers have stood still.

Far more fruitful missionary work is being done on the other side of the world in Papua–New Guinea where the game is rapidly taking root. Perhaps the Rugby League men of Darwin on Australia's north coast can take credit for this transplanting of enthusiasm, just as their countrymen further east willingly visit Tonga and Fiji for long coaching stints. New Rugby League nations in this area now compete in their own Pacific Islands championship.

One caution: head-hunting is no longer commonplace in New Guinea, but European visitors like the British Amateur Rugby League party which toured there early in 1978 sometimes need steady nerves! In one match the first try scored against the local team prompted hordes of spectators to burst the barriers and attack the players. It needed a high-level meeting of tribal chiefs to issue an edict that henceforth such conduct by onlookers would not be tolerated!

In South Africa the game appears to be dormant at the present time, so that the United States is the only other country where opportunity for real expansion by our game could occur. Grid-iron football is the entrenched sport, but one in which it costs some £300 to kit a man out in his full armoury for combat! Americans are realizing that the pattern of Rugby League play can be no less robust and stirring, while the most expensive item of equipment is a pair of boots at £20 or so.

The United States made an approach to English Rugby League in 1977 through their representative, Mick Mayo. He had taken the trouble to travel with Great Britain on their southern hemisphere trip that year, the better to understand and appreciate the game's philosophy and finer points. 'Rugby League is lifting off in our country,' was his message. 'We will prove ourselves quick to learn. Already our television audiences have demonstrated their appetite for showpiece Rugby League entertainment, such as the telerecording of your 1978 Cup Final.'

At the time of writing the Rugby League are playing it cool, as are senior players like myself who have been sounded out as possible 'missionaries'. The Americans' main need is cash for organization and promotion, but the British must do much more market research before committing a great deal of money and effort to this foreign cause. However, if the risk is taken it could yield long-term dividends in terms of spreading our game around the world.

My final word on overseas adventures is a cautionary one, concerning my leg injury during the 1974 Great Britain visit to Australia. It could have left me a cripple for life, and I dwell on it in the hope that some of my younger readers will be somewhat wiser as a result.

The scene was Brisbane, under floodlights, in the seventh match of the tour. After an eight-year gap I was delighted to be abroad again, with a chance to renew memories and friendships dating back to 1966 and my summer with the Lions. Having hit good early form I had won a Test place the previous Saturday alongside Chris Hesketh in a game which we lost 11–6.

On this Tuesday night I ought to have been resting, but was obliged to play in order to cover an injured player. The fateful moment occurred about half an hour into the match when, heavily tackled by a Queenslander, I heard and felt a sharp crack just above the knee. Although the joint was at once terribly painful I waited until half time before confiding in our coach, Jim Challenor.

'Colin Dixon's off and we can't have another substitute,' he replied. 'Let's strap it up and see whether you can manage in the second half.' So I tried; but the pain only got worse, and a subsequent hard tackle in the same area caused my whole limb to feel numb. We left the strapping on afterwards, and I retired to bed for two whole days before our journey down to Sydney, where it was decided that I must see a specialist straightaway.

To cut a long story short, I saw two medical gentlemen. The first gave me the shock of my young life and totally destroyed my morale. Important ligaments behind the knee were severed, he said, meaning that I could never play rugby again and would probably carry a limp for life. He had no constructive or consoling word to offer.

At times of crisis the Rugby League is capable of great concern and compassion. No matter how expensive, our manager Reg Parker ordered that his one-legged Welshman should have a second opinion. Another specialist confirmed the first diagnosis, but added that all was not lost. He prescribed a course of extremely demanding exercises for the injured leg which he said could in time repair the damage. Both men, be it noted, had taken copious X-ray photographs.

Determined to avoid the threat of being sent home I followed his instructions to the letter, doing my daily dozen faithfully each day and going on long training runs while the other boys relaxed and sank a beer or two. I started telling myself that the knee was improving, though I was still puzzled by pain which seemed to centre on my femur, an inch or two higher up the leg. In our final Australian fixture against Grafton I actually took the field as a substitute for the last ten minutes, and so was able to persuade a sceptical management to take me with the party to New Zealand for the last month of our overseas trip.

Here, on our first game against the Maoris at Huntley, I was included at full back. But the first time I played the ball, another tackle on the suspect leg brought all the agony back and sent me hobbling to the side-line — in tears for I knew that the tour was over for me as a player. No real healing seemed to have taken place. There began a period of private torment, when I feared not only for my rugby career but also for my health throughout the rest of my life. Would David Watkins ever walk properly again?

I tried hard not to be a burden upon my companions, acting as an unofficial PRO for them and undertaking Press and TV interviews. The New Zealand television sports department used my spare time to make a documentary film comparing and contrasting my two experiences of their country in 1966 and 1974.

Not until my return home, however, was the mystery cleared up and the spectre of lameness finally banished. Salford sent me to Alan Glass, surgeon to Manchester United, who was determined to get to the root of the trouble. And indeed, it did not take him long to go one better than his Australian counterparts and diagnose a fracture of the thigh — two inches above the knee at the very point where I had been feeling the most pain. By now it had calcified and effectively healed, providentially in the correct position. So I did not need to have the bone broken and re-set, though I was obliged to spend five weeks in plaster during August and September.

Perhaps one moral of the story is that, whatever people may say, British medicine is sounder than that in most other parts of the world. But if my Australian doctors were, to put it mildly, negligent in their diagnosis, I was myself equally culpable in allowing my keenness to stay with the touring party to overrule a sensible judgment about my long-term future. Looking back, it was foolhardy to play while knowing in my own mind that all was not well. My advice to established men and newcomers to the game — indeed, to any game — is never to take the slightest risk where an undiagnosed injury is concerned.

Possibly the management were also at fault in not insisting that I returned to Britain for treatment straightaway. But I had to admit that my protestations about my true state of health must have sounded convincing enough to men who had other problems on their mind. I am a professional rugby player, and such a man ought to be trusted to declare his fitness or the reverse.

At the end of this episode I told Salford that, at the age of thirty-two, I would now be calling it a day and getting out of the game. The club had hád seven years of loyal service, and I felt that an honourable retirement was now my due. Coincidentally Forward Trust promoted me to be manager of their Merthyr Tydfil office, and Jane and I moved down to Wales, settling on the outskirts of Newport. Salford generously conferred an honorary directorship on me. It was a great wrench to leave the north, but my wife and I felt sure that our future lay back at home.

As everyone knows, that was not to be the end of the story. With the arrival of winter I did some light training, finding to my delight that the old speed and nimbleness were still there — so was the pleasure to be had from handling and kicking a rugby ball. So, although people were saying that I must be crazy, I did respond to Salford's emergency call in January 1975 when injury to a key player forced them to request my return for the replayed BBC Floodlit Trophy final. It was to be a 'one-off' appearance, but I obtained the score later voted as 'try of the season' and seemed to play as if there had been no interruption. Somehow it seemed the most natural thing in the world after that to ease myself back into regular rugby. The smell of liniment, the feel of the turf, the lure of competition — all these added up to a disease that was still in the blood!

Since then I have commuted happily and safely (except for the icy morning when I drove across instead of around the roundabout at Ross-on-Wye!) between Gwent and the north. And thus I can claim to have supplied an extra half decade's service to a game that has given me so much.

CHAPTER 18

Nations at Play

Although I have owned up to finding Australians brash and noisy, I also have to admit that the test series of 1978 in which they took part was the best thing to hit Rugby League in Britain for a heck of a long time. And not simply on the field: modern Aussies are great travellers, and hordes of them invaded northern England that autumn in caravans, old bangers and jalopies, having crossed the world to root for their heroes. They brought colour and passion to our streets.

Until 1978 it was fashionable for League followers to boast proudly that the club network was the heart and soul of our game. We had no International occasions comparable to those at Twickenham, Murrayfield or Cardiff nor, said many folk, did we really want that sort of thing in Yorkshire and Lancashire. Then, suddenly along came this cracking trio of Tests, to which national fervour added a special flavour.

And in poured the customers! The Wigan game drew over 20,000; 25,000 were at Odsal to see Great Britain square the series; and another 20,000 packed into Leeds to see the decider. And what entertainment rewarded them, with a no-hope British side pulling itself up by its boot-laces for an unexpected second Test victory before succumbing to the Aussies' power at the third time of asking. And the rivalry is now an on-going business, with Great Britain just having failed to win back the Ashes in 1979 at the time of writing.

I had never known quite such excitement in all my dozen years in the North, and I felt delighted that International encounters in these parts had at last generated the *hwyl* (excitement) and verve with which amateurs in the rest of the UK are so familiar.

Part of the reason, in my view, was the Rugby League's belated realization that it must 'sell' itself properly. The authorities won a £150,000 television fee for coverage of the three matches; and, determined to get their money's-worth the TV people played an unprecedented part in pre-match publicity. This in turn was a factor persuading Forward Chemicals to sponsor the series and part with another £150,000. I suspect that these achievements were the first fruits of behind-the-scenes efforts by David Oxley, who succeeded Bill Fallowfield as RL secretary in 1974. I shall have more to say about both men in due course.

The League game needed these life-giving injections very badly. If they are honest, my friends in Manchester, Leeds, Bradford, Wigan and elsewhere will agree with me that it had been in slow decline since the early sixties. The short-comings of club competition were disguised once a year by the glamorous goings-on at Wembley; but at representative level the situation quite obviously left a lot to be desired.

Partly because the French have down the years been the only regular northern hemisphere opponents for Great Britain or England teams, International matches have enjoyed a low priority. For example, selectors could not always guarantee that players offered International caps would accept them. Except among Packer cricketers, where the circumstances are different, in what other sport could you imagine that happening?

The reason was financial. Match fees were low, and in order to appear for their country men often had to suffer a loss of income. The same consideration meant that, even if they were prepared to turn out in the match, they usually dodged squad training. So coaches were on a hiding to nothing.

Pressure upon their players to decline invitations also came from clubs — in case a star performer should break a leg playing for England. They knew that the fans would rather support a team that was on top of the League than one which contained ten International players. People in the north have always been surprised when I have spoken of the esteem in which capped players are held in the Union game, particularly in Wales where no-one would dream of standing in the way of a man needed by his country. For example, if the Welsh selectors want to run a squad session, then no club commitment on earth must prevent a player's release.

Another sign of the low rating of League International appearances is the fact that caps are sent by post to recipients a few days after the game — sometimes, I am told, they don't even bother to register them! Here again I wish that a leaf could be taken out of the Union approach; they hold a post-match banquet, at which new Internationals receive their caps from the top table and wear them proudly throughout the rest of the evening (even if sometimes they are not a very good fit!). In one or two respects there have been improvements: League players may now keep their match jersies, which until recently had to be handed in after a game to be laundered ready for the next match or the next user! Rugby League International squads now get track-suits and emblazoned sweaters, which amateurs have been gratefully accepting for years. You may call them trimmings, but I consider such things all help to foster that important ingredient, team spirit.

I have heard League officials argue that as our players are professionals, all that is necessary after an International match is the provision of a few convivial drinks before they all split up and go home. Not true: we are human, like all other sportsmen, and would welcome a touch of pomp and ceremony to salute our achievements. A banquet costs money to lay on — agreed: but when you consider the pickings generated for the game at large it seems downright penny-pinching not to accord a little star treatment to the men who pull in the crowds.

Despite all this, the players who have carried England's banner in my time and performed superbly for Great Britain are a great bunch of lads. Naturally I give pride of place to my club-mates Chris Hesketh and Stevie Nash. But my admiration for Roger Millward, so often Steve's partner at representative level, is well known, and his long reign as

England's captain speaks for itself.

John Atkinson of Leeds is a winger whom I've always respected, and likewise the durability of his clubmate Les Dyl, who had chalked up twenty-one caps and three trips 'Down Under' as a centre while still only twenty-five. I'm in good company, too, when I 'rate' that hard man George Nicholls, who besides holding thirty caps ended 1978 as Trumann's 'Man of Steel' and Division One Player of the Year. Hull's loose forward Steve Norton and Bradford Northerner Jimmy Thompson complete my short-list of favourite friends and rivals.

It is a shame that Irishmen and Scots do not come over in sufficient numbers for the formation of national Rugby League XIIIs. True, some border Scots from places like Hawick do venture occasionally into Cumbria, signing for sides like Workington and Whitehaven, but there is never a quorum. How pleasant it would have been to congratulate Wigan's super Scotsman George Fairbairn from Kelso on the cap he must have gained had the opportunity been there.

In contrast, although Wales's participation in International competition has been sporadic down the years, at least it has been possible, thanks to a stream of my fellow countrymen who have been prepared to take money for playing the game. When you think for a moment of post-war signings like Billy Boston, Lewis Jones, John Mantle and Terry Price you can appreciate how proud I feel to be among a band of exiles who have added lustre to the northern scene.

There used to be a regular Welsh team in the early fifties, and again in 1967–8 when remarkable victories were registered over France and England. Alas, each time the initiative lapsed; and although I have higher hopes of the squad that was re-formed during my time I also have some reservations, as I shall explain.

The revival of 1975 was very important, and I am glad to have played a part in it. The Great Britain entity was split into England and Wales, so that for the first time ever the Rugby League World Championship was fought out between five nations, with Australia, France and New Zealand making up the quintet. In a genuine attempt to balance out factors involving seasonal fitness the matches were staged at three different periods during the year; Europe in March, the Antipodes in June, and Europe again for the final stages in the autumn.

Not only did the Welsh entry add extra interest to the tournament — it was also perfectly realistic, as we demonstrated by finishing third. Although no longer a youngster, and busy recovering from my serious thigh injury, I was still capable of making a contribution, albeit from full back. And with performers of the calibre of John Mantle, Kel Coslett, Clive Sullivan, Roy Mathias, Frank Wilson and Jim Mills, Wales made up a side who were not only formidable opponents but also crowd-pullers anywhere in the world.

We were organized and selected by a dedicated group of 'Anglo'-Welshmen. There were Reg Parker, Ronnie Simpson (who was to enjoy a long reign as a popular team manager), Dick Gemmill and Dewsbury's Mike Lumb. They co-opted me, presumably to introduce an element of genuine *hwyl*!

That didn't help much at Toulouse, where we had the honour of opening the tournament against France, only to lose 14–7 in spite of gaining a lot of possession. However, once we got 'Down Under' there followed a tremendous win over England in our 'home' game at Brisbane, and we later scored victories over New Zealand and France to ensure our respectable middle position in the table behind England and top team Australia, who thus regained a title they had lost in 1972.

So — we may have been written off by the critics as veterans, but there was no way in which we would have let the good name of Wales down. And had our fixture schedule not been so crazy we might have fared even better on the field. To give you an example, after our rousing defeat of England we were obliged to travel straight down to Sydney and take on Australia a mere four days later. No team can lift itself twice in one week to deliver rugby of world standard, and it is no wonder the critics complained that the match was a let-down, with Wales unable to raise a head of steam. However, it couldn't have suited the Aussies better if they had planned it that way, and they took advantage of our fatigue to romp away to a 30–13 victory.

Sometimes, though, circumstances worked in our favour. Imagine the delight of our team of exiles when, at the prompting of the Rugby League, I acted as a Welsh undercover agent and managed to book the St Helen's ground at Swansea for our home game against New Zealand on 2 November! This venue is a municipally-owned ground, so although it makes Union die-hards choke over their beer there is nothing to stop professionals playing on its pitch — which is a pretty good one.

The prospect seemed grand. My team-mates and I were dead keen to prove, on our native soil, that we had lost none of the skill which we used to parade in the ranks of Llanelli, Swansea and Newport. And from the pre-match bally-hoo it was clear that the fans would be motivated by nostalgia and sentiment as well as enthusiasm for the spectacle we were determined to provide, and would flock in to shout again for old heroes like Roy Mathias, John Bevan and Stuart Gallacher.

In the event 20,000 fervent Welshmen poured onto the terraces, and we rewarded their loyalty with a cracking game. Wales emerged victors by 25–24 but the Kiwis never gave up, and the excitement before the final whistle was tremendous as they closed the gap to one point with a converted try. Altogether a great occasion, which the Rugby League authorities rated a success.

Only one thing marred it — the dismissal of Jim Mills for cruelly raking an opponent's scalp at the Mumbles end in full view of the crowd, not to mention the television cameras. Now, since many people whose opinion I respect say that they thought it the most horrifying incident they have seen on a rugby field, I must just state that there were extenuating circumstances.

If you don't know Jim like they do up at Widnes let me assure you that besides being immensely skilful at his game he is the most mild-mannered, unruffled fellow you could hope to meet off the field. He is held in great respect by players and fans alike, and he is so tough that I have never known him to be hurt, or at least to admit to it. He can be the life and soul of a party, especially when moved to give his rendering of 'Amazing Grace'.

Possibly, therefore, this outward show of indifference to physical suffering or discomfort leads certain opponents to needle and provoke him. This was true of a Kiwi called Greengrass, who had started a feud out in New Zealand; and, at Swansea that November, big Jim's patience simply ran out. Greengrass had spent a lot of the game insulting our man, putting the boot in from time to time, and generally being a bloody nuisance. Then he scored at the posts; and as he lay getting his breath back the Mills boot descended once, twice upon his unprotected head. Jim had to go, and for once a Welsh crowd had no sympathy.

Having outlined the background, let me now add that in no way do I condone what was in anyone's language an outrage. Nor was the offence an isolated incident, for by the end of 1978 Jim Mills had been dispatched to an early bath no fewer than nineteen times — more than once for butting, which has earned him the nickname 'Lurpak', the 'best butter'!

So I must conclude that somewhere deep inside him is a blind spot which permits him to overstep the mark under provocation, whereas other equally robust players bite their lip and find the presence of mind to unclench their fists and keep their boots under control. I like Jim, but he knows my views — that he has a lot to answer for and has sometimes brought our game into disrepute.

Personally, I deeply regretted this blot on the good name of Rugby League football. I suspect that it may have affected the willingness of Welsh crowds to turn up and root for us. Certainly it is true that we have never subsequently generated quite the enthusiasm in later years that our appearance in Welsh jerseys on Welsh soil evoked in 1975. However, I think that there are other reasons for this too.

If you look back at the Welsh squad of that year you will observe that all of us had respectable Union pedigrees! We were genuine emigrés who had been born and bred in Wales itself. But since the bandwagon was set rolling the most amazing claims to Welsh ancestry have been made by players who include men like Harold Box, Tony Skerrett,

Brian Gregory and Derek Watts, all of whom pay the Welsh a huge compliment by wanting to be one of us but have to dig deep into history to underwrite their claim with the discovery of a Welsh great-grandmother! And since such men never participated on the big South Wales circuit, spectators there are not motivated to come out and watch them play.

However, you can scarcely blame the players for taking any opportunity that presents itself of improving their status. It is the authorities who are at fault for succumbing to the financial temptation to field a 'Wales' XIII full of men who are English in all but remote ancestry. They may get a £75 match fee plus occasional trips to the sunshine of places like Narbonne, where we played our first Test of 1979 in the Jean Galea Trophy tournament. But shams never work for long.

If what I would consider an authentic Welsh side cannot be selected — and my immediate influence upon such decisions is now slim — then for the time being at least I would prefer its place to be taken by an 'other nationalities' team. It could include such men as the South Africans Dave Barends and Green Vigo, of Bradford and Wigan respectively. How exciting it would be to see them teamed with, say, Keighley's French Algerian Bak Diabra! And there will always be half a dozen Welsh, Scots and Irish candidates to make up the numbers and form a side capable of giving England and Australia a real run for their money.

And money — plus glamour — is what a professional game is all about. As an additional International attraction between 1975 and 1978 Wales certainly brought cash and colour to Rugby League, and it seems to me important that this momentum be kept up.

If you doubt that, just consider finally the sums now changing hands between the big clubs for top player transfers. At the beginning of the seventies five figure fees were almost unheard of, and Salford's payment to me was comfortably a record for many years. Mention of an £8000 fee would raise eyebrows, and £4000 was the average price on a man's head.

But by 1978 Hull KR were quite happy to fork out

£35,000 to bring Phil Hogan from Barrow to Craven Park, setting a new United Kingdom record. A Castleford reserve team half back, Clive Pickerill, went to Hull for £22,000, even more than the same club paid for Steve Norton. We at Salford got £15,000 from Wigan for our midfield man John Butler; while a complete newcomer to League, who had scarcely forged a reputation in Union, Waterloo full back Rod Tickell, cost Barrow an £11,000 signing-on fee, plus incentives.

But such figures are only the proof of the pudding. With far less publicity the money generated by League rugby's revival is being put to excellent use by our Council. Thanks to low interest loans smaller clubs can undertake the building of proper grandstands where before there were only seedy terraces. Schools are getting cash aid. Under-24 International matches, to give youngsters a taste of the big-time, are becoming a practical possibility. And the British Amateur Rugby League Association is receiving funds to improve its image and mount missionary tours to far corners of the world.

Good thinking at club level, with many, many improvements on the social side, has contributed to the new buoyancy within the game. But much of it, I argue, has become a reality through the fillip provided by well-staged International occasions. Back in Wales they are fond of describing representative rugby as their game's shop window. I believe that the League authorities, too, have realized that this makes sense. The more you can capture the imagination of your potential customer, the more likely he is to put his hand into his pocket and come inside.

CHAPTER 19

The Men in Charge

Rugby League football is a world game. It has immense crowd appeal, it throws up glittering stars, it is favoured by the media. At its best it is tremendously dramatic, thrilling to play and watch. And today it is run by men who intend that it shall stay that way.

Despite this, there is no doubt in my mind that in the not-too-distant past it was one of the worst administered sports in the land. Rugby Union, people say, is a game for amateurs run by professionals; during my early days in northern England, Rugby League was a game for professionals run by amateurs.

Agreed, there was one dedicated and expert man at the top in secretary Bill Fallowfield, for long thought of as 'Mr Rugby League'— and quite happy he was with the description, too. But strong, determined characters are often content that the power and influence of fellow administrators shall be limited. And this was certainly the case in our game.

Take the example of the Rugby League Council, admittedly a clumsy instrument for shaping policy, comprising thirty members from the leading clubs. During most of Bill Fallowfield's era its chairman was elected for one year only, and spent the whole of that period learning how the system worked. By the time he knew the ropes and felt willing and able to propose some reform or other, his term was finished and he was obliged to stand down. Thus the only continuity of planning lay in the hands of the Secretary. So it was always Mr Fallowfield who took important decisions about the framework of the game, the arranging of fixture-lists and the mounting of competitions such as the Challenge Cup.

In 1973 he bitterly opposed the proposal of Salford's Brian Snape and others to extend the chairman's tenure of office to two years but, perhaps because the days to his retirement were numbered, he lost the day. Those who objected to dictatorships considered the move good for the game.

I think that Bill Fallowfield lived back in a 'golden age' of Rugby League, set somewhere in the nineteen-forties and early fifties. Certainly he never realized that by the mid-sixties all spectator sports needed to promote and sell themselves as never before. The day was fast approaching when even top clubs would be unable to pay their way simply through takings at the turnstile. The leisure explosion had arrived and sports fans were in a buyers' market.

One illustration of what I mean is Australia's success in promoting League, which ensures that whenever Great Britain tours in that country records fall: gate receipts multiply and the crowds pour in. But, as we have seen, until 1978 their teams could visit England and scarcely cover their expenses for the tour. Yet the quality of the entertainment was no less high.

In the game itself there were confusions and anomalies under the Fallowfield régime which made Rugby League football hard for spectators to follow — and, let me add, for players to play! Remember the crazy way the Championship play-off used to be run? — with Lancashire and Yorkshire sorting out their top clubs separately before the lottery of the four trans-Pennine encounters. Then club number one played club number sixteen, number two met number fifteen, and so on. It was a wonder that an eventual winner ever emerged!

Do you remember how, on the field, the laws once dictated a six-tackle limit, then it became four, then six again? How, in International matches, five tackles were once the limit? How club hookers packed underarm with their props, and International hookers overarm? How a dropped goal counted two points for Salford but only one for Great Britain? What a madhouse! Sometimes we players had to check what jersey we were wearing to see what level of game we were in. It was hard enough for regular fans to understand the game, let alone those potential converts which a sport is always trying to attract.

Then there has been the image of our club system, tarnished by numerous unambitious committees who saw no need to improve their grounds and facilities. Hence their teams played on indifferent turf, in front of ever-decreasing crowds lining scruffy terraces, before showering and changing in third-rate accommodation. Financially such clubs were content to be feather-bedded, season after season, by their share of television fees. On the whole my readers will know who these clubs were — and are — but I do not hesitate to say that during my time those dragging their heels included household names like Doncaster, Dewsbury and Halifax.

But I do not blame them entirely, for nobody in a position of influence at the top level sought to spur them to greater things. Rather, the reverse. Mr Fallowfield would visit Salford and be shown the efforts we were making to attract and hold paying customers. Seemingly he would dismiss everything with an airy wave of the hand. 'Social club? Bingo? A five-star restaurant? Sauna baths? Squash courts?' — I can almost hear him saying, "Twouldn't have done when I was a lad.'

My friends at other go-ahead clubs like Hull KR, Leeds and Wigan confirm that the Secretary was capable of delivering, in effect, a snub to enterprise and initiative. He either could not or would not see that, far from indulging ourselves with luxuries, we were engaged in a fight for survival.

Fellow players also confirm a private opinion that I hold about Bill Fallowfield; namely that he bore an almost pathological dislike towards Rugby Union men who came North. In spite of having played Union and rubbed shoulders with Union men (during the war) he made it quite clear that he had no time for the 15-a-side game or products of it like Mike Coulman, Keith Fielding, Maurice Richards and myself. Indeed, after my first League International appearance, he told me, 'Make the most of it, Watkins. There won't be a next time.' Which only goes to fortify my view that towards the end of his full-time administration career his judgment was scarcely infallible!

As I hinted much earlier in this book, it is said that northerners — along with Welshmen, Scots and other 'provincials' — have always felt an inner sense of inferiority towards the smooth, well-groomed Home Counties type commonly associated with the running of the Union game. Certainly I think this is true of the older generation of Rugby League administrators, who are blind to the fact that in many parts of Britain the Union game belongs to the people and is by no means the preserve of the 'upper class', whoever they may be.

However, this has changed with the accession of David Oxley to the Secretarial responsibilities. If it is true that the public school chap bears an extra assurance and polish, then Oxley has it. Imported from a teaching job at an exclusive southern school, he is a well-rounded, truly modern bloke who can hold his own in any company. Already his influence upon Rugby League's life and times has made itself felt, and I believe that in time he may transform the northern scene.

The Oxley era has brought about the appointment of a public relations officer for the game. David Howes, formerly a Hull-based journalist, knows his subject from A to Z, and is proving that the Chapeltown Road office can sell very hard to sponsors and the media. I understand that the excellent bargain struck with Europa, the equipment firm, for kitting out representative sides owed much to his negotiating skill. And it cannot be a mere coincidence that, since he and Mr Oxley took the helm, players are more contented and feel better treated. There are more 'perks' around for genuine professionals to bid for. Far better accommodation is provided for men obliged to travel to appear in representative matches.

I trust that this civilized attitude towards the employees of the game will soon penetrate clubs whose directors still live back in Victorian times. As late as 1979 I travelled with Salford to Bramley for an important match. It was a terrible winter, and after disembarking from our coach and gingerly testing the pitch we decided that it was far too hard and frosty to play on. We told the referee so.

But one of the home side's directors heard us. '*Prima*

donnas,' was his expert comment. 'I remember playing on this ground in 1947 when it was far harder than it is tonight.' Which only showed how totally insensitive the man was to the players' point of view. Why should we risk breaking a leg or snapping a collar bone simply to please the astrakhan-coat brigade in the grandstand? I understand the anxiety of committee-men for their free whisky in the boardroom afterwards but they completely overlook the man who may be lying in hospital, robbed of the chance to earn his match fees for a month or two.

I know that some older Board members also resent the high earnings of modern players, which I consider are well deserved. Such men will reply to requests for an extra bonus or gratuity for a good result, 'No chance. You've already made enough lolly to be going on with for one week.' I also find it embarrassing and downright offensive to hear directors during their post-match booze-up publicly lambasting one of their players who may have had a bad game.

However, such tactless denunciations do not stop at directorial level. There are players, too, with big mouths whose ourbursts the Press are only too happy to print. You cannot really blame the journalists for recording and publishing such material; though I do wish that they would take less notice of the hot-heads and pay more attention to more thoughtful people.

To give an example, let's recall Alex Murphy's castigation of young Kenny Gill when the Salford man was picked for the Great Britain tour of 1974. The then Warrington coach went into print with the comment that Gill was 'not good enough' to represent his country. What a thing to say about an up-and-coming youngster! Can you imagine Brian Clough, for all his outspokenness, or Tommy Docherty, allowing themselves to undermine the confidence of a player from another club in such a way? I wrote an outraged letter to the *Manchester Evening News* condemning Alex for his lack of tact and common sense — but the smear had already been applied.

All right, I agree: players cannot be gagged. But surely we need some kind of screening process to ensure that what is said will not damage the game or the men who play it. Maybe each club should appoint a Press officer to give guidance on the subject. We need the media, and the majority of reporters are responsible men, who can be trusted. But some of them are skilful at trapping youngsters into allegations and admissions which they will bitterly regret on seeing them in print. A little greasing of the palm, obviously, can also loosen the tongues of older men who ought to know better.

An odd post-script to the short-tempered exchange between Mr Murphy and me was his challenge to take him on in a one-to-one match under Rugby League rules. He went round telling people what he would do to me when he caught me in possession, and forecast that a huge crowd would turn out to see the Welshman put in his place. I had heard of single-wicket cricket, but the Murphy proposal seemed crazy to me, and I rejected it out of hand.

But on reflection I wish that I had accepted! There is no way that he could have laid a hand on me without the other twelve to help him. And as for my marking of him — why, I'd have had Alex on the deck before he had trundled a yard or two! No problem.

But let us get back finally to the running of our game. Although I have spoken harshly about some referees elsewhere, I consider that they have contributed to a cleaning-up of the game since I came into it. Back in 1967 the cloggers were still with us; but the refs have generally proved themselves ready to root them out.

I also think that our system of fines and suspensions is about right. You do hear players grumbling about £30 fines, four-match suspensions and the yellow card 'totting-up' system — but, once bitten, offenders are usually twice shy. I must add that I believe our game has speeded up since 1967: that means that the cloggers — usually the less nimble-minded men on the field — have had less time in which to think up novel ways of crippling opponents.

Linesmen, too, play a valuable role in the identification of bad men, and it was interesting to read early in 1979 that the Union administrators were tagging along behind Rugby League (as usual!) and experimenting with ways in which touch-judges (as they call them) could assist referees. About time, I say. To expect one man to spot all the 'aggro' — and who started it — in a highly physical game involving thirty players seems an impossible requirement to me.

One idea which they did decide to try out was the 'sin-bin', a device which apparently works well in ice-hockey. Players committing a hot-headed offence not quite meriting a sending-off are dispatched to the side-lines for a cooling-off period of up to twenty minutes. They are then supposed to re-enter the fray sadder but wiser.

I hope that the 'sin-bin' never comes into Rugby League. My view is that for all offences which go beyond the spirit of the game, like punching, kicking or trampling, players deserve the maximum sentence. It is right that the guilty one's team should have to complete the match a man short. A 'sin-bin' seems to me a licence for the unruly to calculate just what degree of dirty play they can get away with, thus contributing to an increase in niggling offences.

Furthermore, the belief that a short spell on the bench would convert an evil-doer into a knight in shining armour strikes me as naive. And, finally, his return to the field of play might invite retribution from opponents who have had time to plan it coldly.

Such innovations seem to me to be mere gimmickry, unlikely to be brought into our game by administrators who are now beginning to run it along the right lines. The ruling body has a sensibly open-minded approach to genuine reform and innovation. And my belief — and my hope — is that as we move into the eighties men in posts of responsibility are aware that, however important cash and sponsorship may be, the most important qualities they need are a deep love of Rugby League football and a fanatical dedication to its survival in their part of the world.

CHAPTER 20

The Shamateurs

The one thing that has constantly bugged me since I turned professional in 1967 is the bogus piety of many of the folk I left behind — those members of the head-in-the-sand Rugby Union brigade who pretend that while their game is white as snow, men like me who have taken money to play are second-class citizens. And they let you know it in all kinds of snide ways.

They could hardly be more wrong. While I know Union players who live in constant fear of being found out for accepting a few 'green-backs' — or more likely 'blue-backs' — and whose consciences are not exactly clear, I have an untroubled mind. All the cash I have banked in the dozen years up to 1979 is above-board. And as a result I feel commercially clean, like professional golfers and tennis players. But the difference is that they can stand happily rubbing shoulders with amateurs in their sports. I cannot.

Let me first underline my own position by highlighting the Benefit I was granted in 1978 by Salford. Between us my co-beneficiary Chris Hesketh and I netted around £15,000, a more than satisfactory tax-free sum to share even though, as individuals, we did not approach Tony Karelius's record £9800. People suggested that we would have been better advised to take separate Benefits, but we are satisfied. We knew that Mike Coulman and Colin Dixon were due to follow hard on our heels, and even top performers cannot expect the fans to keep dipping into their pockets over a period of three or four years. Anyway, Chris never complained to me about his half of the 'take'.

The point is that the cash, in addition to my match fees and the £1500 retainer Salford forked out each September was legitimately mine. Nobody whispered behind my back that I was money-mad. As a professional, it was thought natural that I should seek to exploit my status and the years of good service given to my club.

Many thanks are due to people who worked extremely hard on my behalf. By 1978, of course, my base was back in Wales, so I could not have done without my on-the-spot Benefit committee. Graham Atkinson was treasurer, aided and abetted by Tom Burgin of the *Salford Reporter*, Keith Snape and my good friend, Ray Ratcliffe. The others will forgive a special acknowledgement to that ace fund-raiser Peter Scholes. In him Salford have a marvellous pools promoter, who applied a great deal of his expertize on my behalf. My advice to every beneficiary is to work as hard as his committee to repay all the hard work they do.

But the list does not stop there. A glossy brochure was put together for Chris and me by John Maddock, sports editor of the *Sunday People*, who had done a similarly fine job for cricketer Farouk Engineer. Besides securing most readable contributions from Brian Batty of the *Daily Mail*, Paul Harrison of the *Sun*, Jack McNamara of the *Manchester Evening News*, Jack Bentley of the *Daily Express* and Ron Marler of Radio Manchester, he had persuaded that fine actor Windsor Davies to put pen to paper. Articles arrived, too, from top Rugby Union writers Brian Wall and Vivian Jenkins.

Perhaps its price, 50 pence, was a little high for the market, and we might have settled for a more modest publication selling for the normal 20 pence. But then Chris Hesketh and I would have forfeited a fine production that will grace our bookshelves for the rest of our lives. It makes a wonderful souvenir.

Generous as ever, the Salford club allocated to us the proceeds from their Rugby League draw. That, too, was a gesture worth nearly four figures after the prizes had been paid out to holders of tickets bearing the names of the clubs involved in the Challenge Cup competition.

There were also shows given for us by singers Peters and Lee and comedian Bernard Manning for which we shall always be grateful. Stars from soccer like Jack Charlton supported us with personal appearances, as did cricketer Peter Parfitt. And many of our great playing contemporaries, Welsh and English alike made the long journey to South Wales one Sunday to lay on an exhibition match at Cwmbran Stadium which drew 6000 spectators. We made sure that the boys had a four-course dinner and a night-club visit in recompense for putting themselves out. And this is a good point at which to record our thanks to Torfaen Council and sports officer, Geoff Whitson for making the Stadium available for a nominal rent. Besides some excellent rugby, the crowd also enjoyed the snacks and beer provided free by Peters Savoury Products and breweries like Welsh Brewers, Whitbreads, Courage and Scottish & Newcastle of Caerphilly. These firms contributed generously to a grand occasion.

Such organization involves a great deal of hard work to make the most of every chance offered, as first-class cricketers will agree. The latter have a shorter playing season to exploit, and therefore I do not blame them for the practice of taking collections at certain games, when a few colleagues take a blanket around the boundary to catch coins tossed in by their admirers.

However, I drew the line at this: if people wanted to salute my contribution with a gift of their own free will, that was fine — but I wanted no-one to think that I was parading a begging-bowl in front of them, or that I was trying to squeeze the last pips out of their generosity.

In one way or another, I was better off after my Benefit by over £7000, none of which was coveted by the Income Tax inspector. Some tasty icing on the cake for a businessman like me with what I hope is an assured future with Forward Trust. You can say that I cashed in if you like; that does not bother me one whit. As a professional, it is the done thing.

The most outstanding of my amateur friends have done so, too, and let me say straightaway that I do not blame them.

Wilfred Wooler, Clem Thomas and Bleddyn Williams are three of the older generation who have augmented their incomes very satisfactorily by writing about

Rugby Union for the Fleet Street newspapers. I read their views and admirable reports avidly, even though I suspect that it is their status as former Rugby Union — that is, amateur — Internationals rather than any outstanding skill with words that has made them big-name journalists.

The same goes for my successor in the Wales XV, Barry John. Soon after his enormously memorable tour of New Zealand in 1971, when the Lions beat the All Blacks for the first time ever and he earned the nickname 'King' John, Barry declared that the pressures involved in playing the game at top level were too much for him and that, at twenty-seven, it was time to run his own life rather than have it run by others. I am sure that there was more to it than that: he knew that the time had come to make a 'killing' out of his fame as a Rugby Union superstar. So — out came his memoirs in the *Sunday Mirror*, some best-selling books followed, and soon he was taken on by the *Daily Express* as a critic. And very readable he is, too.

These men, and others like Peter Robbins, Bryn Meredith and latterly John Taylor, made clear-cut decisions to exploit their names professionally. As one who made a similar decision, I respect them. We are all 'commercials', though my breadth of sporting experience is now considerably greater than theirs.

Because the stringent amateur laws prohibit anyone from taking part-time cash as a direct or indirect result of having played Rugby Union while continuing to play or administrate the game, such people know that they can never coach a team, sit on a club committee or bid for a place on the various Rugby Unions. However, it seems to me that the position has changed subtly in the last few years, especially in Wales.

One of the most famous of our 'outside half factory', Phil Bennett, opened a sports business in Llanelli while still a player with that club. A team-mate, Barry Llewelyn, had quit teaching to embark on a similar enterprise some years earlier. My old partner, Clive Rowlands, also has a shop selling all manner of sports goods, even though he has been a member of the Welsh Rugby Union's general Committee and a national selector for some seasons.

By now my friends in the north will be asking themselves wide-eyed, 'So what? Why all the fuss?' It is because business activities of that particular kind seem to many people to contravene the amateur principle forbidding the gaining of material benefit from playing or having played the game.

This was the subject of a tremendous brou-haha when it became known in the spring of 1979 that Dr J.P.R. Williams had sold his memoirs to a publisher. In order to continue representing Wales and Bridgend — whom he was in the process of leading to a Triple Crown and a Challenge Cup victory respectively — Dr John had to say that his royalties would be used to set up a sporting clinic, from which persons injured playing rugby and other games would benefit. But what is the difference between putting your famous name on a shop front in the hope of attracting customers and putting it on a book in the hope of winning readers?

The late seventies also saw firms who numbered well-known rugby players among their employees using their names and pictures in company advertisements. Sometimes it was beer that was being promoted, sometimes industrial protective clothing, sometimes financial advice and assistance. Instinctively all this seems to me to be at odds with the spirit of pure amateurism.

It all adds up to a vast grey area, in which players do not know where they stand and where the book of laws is made to look an ass. Gareth Edwards, while still Wales's top scrum half, received a big fee for participating in a TV 'superstars' programme — as a direct result of his fame as a player. Gravely debating the issue the Welsh Rugby Union ruled that he could keep the cash, but that nobody else would subsequently be allowed to do so! Colin Meads, the great New Zealand forward, put the receipts from his best-selling life story into a trust fund for his family, and continued happily coaching his provincial XV.

Top people, apparently, can get away with gently bending the rules. Therefore who can blame lesser lights for deciding that an evening of their company will cost their hosts £100, discreetly provided in a brown envelope? Or that three-figure expense accounts may be submitted for travelling a couple of hundred miles to star in a charity game? Or that their post-match beer-money should not be £2 but £22?

Rugby Union seems to have got itself into this pickle because of an horrendous fear of cash for cash's sake dating back to 1895, when the northern clubs severed relationships over the broken-time payment issue and set up a professional Rugby League. But because sponsors have rushed to jump onto a bandwagon which television has made increasingly glamorous, money is now gushing into the game in unprecedented amounts. It is not surprising, rather inevitable, that some of it finds its way into the pockets of individuals, leading to the situation distastefully described as 'shamateurism'. Up north it simply makes people snigger — and not just the League buffs in the heart of Salford and Wigan but also the soccer fraternity at Manchester United and Manchester City.

Is there a way out? Let us be blunt: at any one time in Rugby Union football there are unlikely to be more than a score of players with the charisma to make sponsors and admirers pay them large sums of money for personal appearances. Barry John's name may help to sell pairs of boots, but that of J. Jones, third XV prop for Blaina, would not. Only top men's opinions are worth paying to read in a book or hear on the air.

I would alter the laws to let such entrepreneurs — who show the courage to go into business or the energy to write a book — keep what they can get. Since the problem is limited to a few cases I cannot see what harm it can do. I would however, draw the line at personalities being paid for advertisements, since I think that money laid out for strictly commercial purposes ought to contribute to the general good of the game, not to an individual hired because his face looks good on a hoarding.

The Rugby Union hierarchy must move on these issues if they do not wish the situation to become even more tangled and dangerous. Because the game in New Zealand and Wales commands such huge public interest and enthusiasm, the problem is a genuine one and other nations less troubled by quasi-professional squabbles must realize that it cannot just be brushed under the table. Some Englishmen got on their high horse when they heard about J.P.R.'s publishing deal; well, they really ought to appreciate that their country has simply not produced players in recent years who can command five figure payments for a book. On the other hand, if the trend towards cashing in continues, one can envisage the day when an England XV will decline to take the field against Wales or New Zealand through suspicions of professionalism. Things badly need to be regularized.

However, paid man though I have been, I would not advocate match fees for Rugby Union players. Such payments would create a two-tier society on the field and demolish team spirit. For instance, can you imagine J. Jones, on £5 a match, being willing to put in a suicidal tackle to save a try if team-mate G. Edwards, on £100, is also at hand to do the job? Moreover, I accept the insistence by most Union men that they wish to play basically for fun, not for chances to line their pockets.

But there is a better reason: simply my doubt that there is a big enough cash-flow, even in Welsh rugby, to permit a professional circuit to flourish. When they hear of northerners buying up Union stars for £10,000 and £15,000 folk down south imagine that the League game is awash with money. True, some clubs are wealthy. But on the other hand, the continued survival of smaller ones like Whitehaven, Doncaster, Batley and that off-shoot of Liverpool, Huyton, is a constant source of amazement. The secret is TV fees, for certainly the 500 or so hard-core supporters of such clubs do not pay nearly enough at the gate for the upkeep of a professional squad.

Indeed, I would go as far as to say that the administrators in such places would view a long winning run as a financial catastrophe, through having to fork out a series of £25 bonuses rather than simple £8 match fees! Smaller clubs in Wales like Abertillery, Newbridge and Maesteg would swiftly find themselves in equally deep water if pro rugby came to Wales. Even big clubs like Cardiff and Newport could find themselves in trouble, since their viability depends even now upon behind-the-scenes profit-making by their athletic clubs rather than gate-taking alone.

This brings me to the point with which I began this chapter, the hostility between the two rugby codes. For it seems to me to arise out of the fear of Rugby League's financial power and popularity. It is a fear that has obsessed Union folk for over three quarters of a century and has contributed to the cold-shouldering of League professionals down the years amounting to a kind of white apartheid.

Let me say immediately that I have experienced only kindness from my old club Newport, where I am still a member. Other Gwent clubs like Pontypool and Ebbw Vale have always made me welcome. But now and then something happens which underlines the fact that many folk still think of me — and others who went north — as aliens and undesirables.

At Cardiff Arms Park in 1977 the BBC were about to interview me on my forthcoming trip to the Antipodes as Great Britain coach. They wished to bracket me and John Dawes, Lions coach-elect, as two Welshmen who had major responsibilities on the year's summer tours. So, after watching a Cup semi-final there, I stepped onto the Cardiff pitch before the cameras.

No sooner had I done so than white-faced club official came hurrying along to tell the flabbergasted camera team that under no circumstances could they interview me on the famous turf. It might embarrass Cardiff RFC, he said.

What about my own embarrassment? — both then and a few months later when the same club forbade my entry to the Press box to broadcast comments on one of their matches! See what I mean about apartheid? When the late Hubert Johnson, as club President, subsequently invited me into the committee room for a post-match drink I decided that this was simply the manifestation of a guilty conscience.

I was allowed to broadcast from the Talbot Athletic Ground — but only after Aberavon had carefully checked that their lily-white amateur status would not be compromised by having me as a guest on their premises. Other men have been less lucky. Salford's former England International Mike Coulman has been refused entry to his old clubhouse at Moseley. John Anderson is not, I am told, welcome at Newport. Don Devereux was pressured into relinquishing his post as coach to a Wales schools squad. On the other hand, that former great loose forward Russell Robins is not only welcomed with open arms to his old club, Pontypridd, but may also teach cadets at Beachley to play Union since he and they are all in the Army!

Again, since 1967 Welsh Rugby Union secretary Bill Clement has been forbidden by the rules to allocate me my International player's ticket to see Wales play at Cardiff. Yet on a personal level he is always the soul of friendship to me when we meet, as is the WRU treasurer Ken Harris. What anomalies!

Yet, to explain them all away I have to come back to this deep-seated and quite irrational fear of the rival code. It is not confined, incidentally, to the rugby fraternity as such. At the beginning of the seventies a British Lions wing, who had been eking out a living as a junior member of the teaching profession, negotiated a contract with one of our top northern clubs. The news got around, and he received a communication from his local education authority which said, in effect, 'If you ever come back to Wales, you needn't bother to look for a teaching post in this area.' That, I suggest, is not far removed from blackmail.

It is true, I suppose, that once upon a time, when Rugby Union men in Wales were closer to the bread-line than is ever the case today, any Rugby League pro coming into contact with the amateur scene was rated an interloper, a potential secret agent bent on luring top performers away from the land of their fathers with large bundles of ten pound notes. And of course it used to happen.

But few of the new generation of top Union players any longer find it an attractive proposition to give up the glamour, travel opportunities and glittering career prospects now offered by the game in exchange for short-term cash rewards. Some still answer the call north for peanut payments, but they are usually second-rank performers who feel that they can go no further in the unpaid ranks. Like Clive Griffiths, who won one cap as a replacement for J.P.R. Williams in 1979, they are briefly missed, but their departure has a pruning effect which brings virile young successors into their vacated berths.

So I say that the time has come to bury the hatchet. By now Rugby Union ought to be sure enough of itself to cast the old hostility away. It is a world game whose portfolio of popularity and funds has increased manifold while Rugby League has had to battle its way through a period of hard times and falling gates. The money is no longer there to pick off stars like Terry Holmes, Gareth Davies, David Richards or Tony Ward.

There is one gesture the Rugby Unions could make. It bitterly disappoints those of us who have returned to our homeland that we are unable to contribute experience and know-how to a game that we are so familiar with. I myself would dearly love the chance to apply my coaching ability, such as it is, in the 15-a-side context, if only at youth or junior level.

So I would argue for re-instatement of retired professionals once they have completed a term of, say, five years in the League game (the time limit would prevent hustlers going north just to make a quick buck and see how it suited them). The Union game in the north country and the Midlands as well as in Wales surely has much to gain from our skill and, dare I say it, professional approach.

This is probably the boldest stand I have taken on the issue. The past 'incidents' that I have described have drawn no retort from me; although they hurt inside, outwardly I have always pretended that they were beneath my notice. However, now is the time to say that I simply want League professionals to be treated with the respect they deserve when they move in amateur circles, or when they return south. I want people to stop saying, 'Of course, the money was good but you couldn't have enjoyed it much up north.' Or: 'You can't coach our kids — your hands are dirty.' Or, at a pre-International gathering, 'Who let you in here?'

And I want Rugby Union people to understand that 'up North' is a sporting scene which rivals theirs for friendship, fraternization and fun. Cash is not everything. At its best the dedication of the players is as intense, and the atmosphere in the clubs as warm, as in any amateur club that I know. I just cannot accept that the lawful passage of a few pound notes from one hand to another should be allowed to sour relationships between the codes from here to eternity.

The Joe Erskines of this world are welcome in the Union clubs. So are the Geoffrey Boycotts, the Brian Huggetts and the Roger Taylors. Will someone please explain to me what is the difference between such star professionals and the great exponents of Rugby League football?

To end on a mischievous note: sometimes, as I have said earlier, the administrative machinery of that pillar of amateur rugby, the Barbarians FC, breaks down. Two years after turning pro I received an invitation to attend the club's annual dinner. It was a mistake, since I am now in a separate category of untouchables as far as the Ba-Baas are concerned.

I often wonder what would have happened had I turned up. Would I have been kicked out? Ostracized? Condemned to sit at a separate table?

It would be nice to think that the civilities of British hospitality would have taken over and that I would have been greeted like any other member of the club — as a professional gent.

If they slip up again, I think I'll put them to the test!

CHAPTER 21

Leading from the Rear

A good recovery from the leg injury of 1974, plus the resumption of my Salford career, led people to comment that old Rugby League stars never die. But to many, my move to full back in early 1975 must have suggested that I was fast fading away.

During my four month lay-off circumstances had naturally been changing at the Willows. Firstly Paul Charlton, the finest full back I ever saw in the League game and certainly in J.P.R. Williams's class as the best of the lot, had been allowed to re-join his home team Workington. With his world record of tries during a season from full back and other tremendous feats he had more than repaid the £13,000 spent on him by Salford. And now, a little way into his thirties he invoked the clause in his contract permitting Workington to 'rent' him back from us for a nominal sum each year. A sure defender and an attacker of great originality, he is still active in the game as I write.

Although his berth was now vacant Salford had strengthened the midfield by importing John Butler from Rochdale to play alongside Chris Hesketh. Kenny Gill was doing all that was asked of him and more at stand-off. Since we were well served on the wings by Keith Fielding and Maurice Richards there was only one way I could go for the evening of my career — backwards to full back!

This change of position, however, brought none of the trauma I experienced when transferring from stand-off to centre. By 1975 I had become a maturer person who could tell himself confidently that he had little left to prove about his basic ability. More importantly, I had for some time been keen to seize the opportunities full back play seemed to hold out to a player of flair and ability. Could I use them to bring novelty and new ideas to the game?

The first answer was given in a home game against Wigan. The men from Central Park began in storming mood, camping on Salford's line for fully fifteen minutes. Then suddenly Kenny Gill, an expert at drawing defenders and creating gaps for team-mates, came bursting away from the danger-zone. The ghost of an opening tempted me forward and I managed to time my arrival on the ball perfectly. Rapid acceleration and a bit of fancy footwork allowed me to send Keith Fielding off on a long sprint to the posts. We pulled off the manoeuvre not once but twice, to go 10–nil up and lay the foundations of a satisfying victory. I like to think that it was the result of a little applied brain-power — yes there is room for it in Rugby League, whatever the diehards may say!

Before long we were outwitting our bogy side of the day, Castleford, whom we had to meet on two successive Saturdays in League and Cup fixtures. In the first clash, somewhat to the chagrin of many Salford traditionalists, I hit on the new tactic of collecting kicks ahead after our opponents' final tackle and, while Cas' anticipated an upfield run, putting the ball over their heads into unguarded territory. This gained 40 or 50 yards for our forwards, and relieved them of the need to graft for possession while moving ahead. Mal Reilly, Gary Stephens and the others — not to mention one or two men on my own side! — were pretty puzzled by this curious innovation.

A week later our Challenge Cup tie found Cas' hanging back in readiness for these deep kicks of mine. Hence there was a lack of commitment about their plan allowing us to employ more orthodox moves and cruise to a 25–3 win.

I told myself with glee that I was right! Maybe I could not exercise the old constant control of tactics from full back, but there was no doubt in my mind that sudden, devastating interventions were always 'on'. Tracking along just behind the three quarters you can see the pattern of the play much more clearly and are ready for gaps in the defence to open up. Men like Widnes' Dave Eckersley, George Fairbairn of Wigan and Workington's Great Britain star Paul Charlton consistently bear out my point.

The Salford fans were finally convinced that Watkins had not been 'relegated' in the last game of the 1975 season, when I recall beating five Dewsbury opponents near our line before handing on to Gordon Graham who hared 60 yards for a try that was hailed as the best of the year. They also seemed to approve of the diagonal kicks that I began putting in, a throw-back to Union days which, when properly executed, would sit up obligingly for our speedy wings to gather.

Full back play, of course, is not all about attack. When the opposition has the ball you spend most of your time covering, covering, covering, and trying to anticipate where they will put in their main thrust. Then, when the time comes to put in a tackle it is usually a last-ditch effort which must not fail.

Right through my final three or four seasons I retained enough speed to take most opponents from the side. This was fine out in the midfield with plenty of space available but in a head-on tackle close to the line my frail 11 stones could not be guaranteed to check a big, determined forward. So there were several occasions when opponents crashed over for scores that a heftier full back might have prevented. But I think my team-mates forgave me since, if I conceded two tries in that way, I often compensated by creating three!

At any rate, when I finally bade farewell to them in May 1979, I had enjoyed four seasons in which my club were always happy to have me as their last line of defence. Growing business commitments with Forward Trust, added to the sheer dreariness of trekking up and down the motorways between Newport and Manchester, more or less made up my mind for me that it was time to finish; and the same factors meant that in the last two years I did not train as hard as in earlier days.

Not that I ever reached the slowcoach level, mind you. Before big games I used to sit in the dressing room, stretch my arms and legs, and announce, 'There you are, boys. I've done my training!' A few minutes later, to their chagrin, speed merchants like Keith Fielding and John Knighton would be forced to admit that the old gentleman could still turn on the pace when he wanted to!

But why should that be surprising? Consider some of the other 'geriatrics' still in business. Who will deny that Neil Fox, John Mantle and Kel Coslett have remained formidable opponents well into their thirties? I have indicated my admiration for Paul Charlton, and even at thirty-eight I still rated him our game's outstanding performer in his position. And in the Union game remember how Gareth Edwards, Gerald Davies and John Williams (the Llanelli wing) could show the under-thirties a clean pair of heels.

It is my view that the figure thirty represents an unnecessary mental barrier in rugby players' minds. At that juncture in their lives many of them surrender to Father Time. True, to keep at it demands extra discipline and keen resistance to social pressures linked with rich food and alcohol. But it can be done. And let me remind the faint-hearts that premature retirement swells the number of seasons they will have to spend on the touch-line, itching to get onto the pitch and show how things ought to be done.

Reaching thirty-seven is a different matter. All good things must come to an end sometime. However, I must admit at this point that although I stayed long enough to help stave off relegation for Salford in 1979 — and how narrowly we avoided it! — I am deeply concerned about the club's future. In spite of his record at Leigh and Warrington Alex Murphy always seemed to me to be a disruptive influence at the Willows. The hard-line, bullying methods he used of old never worked at Salford. The club had too many sensitive, intelligent men who did not react well to bluster.

Whether Alex will have survived by the time these words are in print in anyone's guess. Certainly my meeting with Brian Snape at Wembley in May 1979 underlined his great anxiety about the course Salford had taken. For personal reasons connected with the arrangement of his business affairs Mr Snape has lived in the Isle of Man for some years and spends only a limited time each year on the mainland. The club seems to me to have suffered from his remoteness.

Anyway, that day at the Challenge Cup Final he told me

again of his wish that I had become Salford's coach. Certainly the post could have been mine, for following the resignation of Les Bettinson both Colin Dixon and Chris Hesketh found it too demanding for their liking. But my commitment to a future in South Wales proved narrowly too strong for my loyalty to Salford, which remains complete in every other respect. And there is no way that I could have coached a club from a range of nearly 200 miles!

The fact is, too, that I have never attended a formal coaching course. Yet that did not prevent my appointment as player-coach to the 1977 Great Britain party which went Down Under to compete in the World Cup. Totally unexpected by me and most other people, it was nonetheless an honour that moved me greatly. It came late in my career, but I truly consider it to have been one of the pinnacles.

Now, it is my view that at representative level you do not have to teach the game or its basic skills. What you can do is inspire and lift your players, or motivate them, to use the current vogue word. And under my guidance, the 1977 Welsh XIII, put together with nuts and bolts, had registered a notable victory over the might of England. Only 12–7 — but we had done it! This, I imagine, sowed the first seeds of an idea in the minds of the Rugby League Council.

It began to grow once Reg Parker was appointed manager of the World Cup party, a man with whom I had worked smoothly and happily on Wales's 1974 tour. But when the Chapeltown Road office advertised for a coach I did not at first respond. The field seemed too strong, with Alex Murphy, Peter Fox, David Cox, Mal Reilly and Ike Southwood all in the running. A mere Welsh convert to Rugby League would surely be a non-starter.

Then Reg Parker intervened. 'Don't hang back, David,' he counselled me. 'Have a go. I know that you've got what it takes.'

To cut a long story short the names were whittled down to four: Murphy, Fox, Cox and myself. But I was still astonished when Paul Harrison of the *Sun* rang me at Merthyr Tydfil to tell me of my appointment and offer congratulations. I contacted Jane straightaway to test her reaction. Loyal as ever she said that of course she would miss me but that I should accept the job.

In the Salford board room before long it was fascinating to attend as adviser to the tour selectors, in spite of not having a vote. My opinion was called on a number of times, though I am not sure how much notice was taken of it. Besides Reg the group comprised Sumner Baxendale, a Wigan director, Harry Womersley of Bradford Northern, Colin Hutton of Hull KR, and our own Brian Snape. Barrow's Bill Oxley ought to have been present, but an extraordinary administrative slip-up meant that he got the date of this vitally important meeting wrong. We did without him!

In a way I'm glad that Oxley was absent, since I think that five selectors is the right number to pick a team or a tour party. You need an odd number to get a clear-cut vote; but a three-man committee gives insufficient breadth of vision, while seven men are likely to over-indulge in argument and discussion.

Although it was my first experience of selection from the inside I was not surprised at the partisan approach of the various clubs' representatives. It is liable to happen, and does, in most team games. The Welsh Rugby Union's 'Big Five' deserve credit for having put it behind them — though the eyebrows of other nations were certainly raised in 1977 when coach John Dawes made sure that more than half his Lions side were Welsh!

In Manchester Colin Hutton, for instance, was pushing Len Casey for all he was worth, while Brian Snape rooted consistently for Stevie Nash. But there were also unpredictable, imaginative choices such as that of Phil Hogan, the loose forward from Barrow in Division Two. His claims were championed by Reg Parker (whose judgment was vindicated two years later when Phil changed clubs for a record £35,000 fee). I can recall, too, long arguments over the hooking position, for which Keith Bridges of Featherstone must have been favourite. In the end we picked two men, and Keith was squeezed out by fine all-round players in David Ward of Leeds and Widnes's Keith Elwell.

Our overall balance was later affected by the withdrawals of Jim Mills (with a hernia, which probably averted diplomatic squabbles in New Zealand), Eddie Cunningham (for personal reasons), Phil Lowe (because of contract complications between Hull KR and his Australian club Manley), and finally Tommy Martin who, after receiving his tour invitation, suffered a badly pulled hamstring. But the selectors still managed to provide Reg and me with a good side with lots of potential and a sound captain in Roger Millward.

I would still advocate, however, in order that justice may be seen to be done to all candidates, the introduction of a five-man panel of specialist selectors to do the job in future, uninhibited by club loyalties and the expectations of their own players.

Another reform I commend to the authorities is the provision of full cover for all overseas expeditions, including World Championship tournaments such as awaited our side in 1977. On the 1979 tour there were thirty men; we were allocated only twenty, presumably because our trip was to last only seven weeks, and they were not enough. I got some stick for over-playing myself on the early New Zealand stage, but with two Tests among the four games scheduled for our first fortnight, my presence at full back was needed to give first choice George Fairbairn a rest.

So an extra half dozen men on strength would have been welcome. Fortunately we did have with us Salford physiotherapist Dennis Wright who prevented our injury list becoming too large.

Both my players and myself were stung by the 'no-hopers' tag conferred on us by the British Press before our departure and by the Kiwi and Australian critics in the Antipodes. So, in our early New Zealand team talks, we decided that we would show these clever dicks a thing or two. There is nothing like a hostile climate to knit team personnel together. And in due course, France, cock-a-hoop after victories that winter over England and Wales, were defeated at Auckland, after which we dealt with New Zealand, the unknown quantities, at Christchurch. We had demonstrated that we possessed guts and determination.

But it was after these early successes that I really began earning my keep as a coach. My experience with Wales stood me in good stead, for I had already learned the vital lesson that on the bench it is imperative to stay calm and think straight. I suppose that coaches are leading candidates for heart attacks; although your adrenalin runs as urgently as any player's, unlike him you cannot release it into physical action. Nor is it any use bawling and shouting, for in the heat of combat your men will be unable to hear you. Better to assess the team's performance quietly and coldly, retaining the capacity for good judgments about tactics and substitutions.

Sometimes rockets have to be fired, of course. A few were necessary towards the end of our visit to Australia, by which time we had nothing left to prove but still a reputation to guard. Against North Queensland the boys gave a disgraceful first half performance to trail 17–8 at the break. At which point I gave full vent to my fiery Celtic temper, took advantage of the unlimited substitutes dispensation to remove three of the slackers from the pitch, got into the action myself, and goaded the team into a second-half display that left us losers by just 21–20.

A good coach needs to keep training interesting, and I put a lot of thought into varying my routines. In return I demanded discipline and scrupulous attendance from the boys. Once only did I impose a curfew, on the eve of our final fixture, against Northern League at Grafton. I wanted us to leave Australia on the crest of a wave. The team got the message and came up with a masterly display which even the Aussie critics hailed.

My relationship with skipper Roger Millward was important, and it worked. I have always been a big fan of the man from Hull KR — though not as big, it often struck me, as many Australians. Previous tours had made the captain a favourite there and he was lionized like Muhammad Ali or Georgie Best.

The test of our bond came when I had to drop a hint that his play in Australia had become a little selfish. Maybe crowd pressure had something to do with it, prompting the feeling that unless he showed his brilliance every time he took the field he would lose his 'Roger the Dodger' nickname. The fact was that more than once he failed to get the best out of the talented men in his three quarter line. In selection sessions, where Roger joined Reg and myself, I pointedly speculated whether he should be tried at scrum half, with Francis or Holmes outside him. I think he got the message. And certainly his loyalty to me never wavered.

Other psychological teasers which had to be worked out included the balancing of George Nicholls's view of himself as the senior professional with that of the temperamental Eddie Bowman. Ever eager to be the ball-player and director-in-chief of forward tactics, Eddie always feared that he was about to be dropped if he got left out of a 'move' in training. So, 'Everybody play off Eddie for five minutes,' I would call out, savouring the gratified look on his face. Behind the scenes, too, I kept assuring him that his presence was every bit as vital to the team as that of George. It seemed to work!

One also had to mend the 'us' and 'them' split which inevitably emerged between the Test men and their deputies. In particular Keith Ellwell and Alan Hodkinson took it hard when David Ward and Steve Pitchford relegated them to second team status. In mid-tour they had fits of sulking, and affected loss of interest. Again, long, emotionally-demanding heart-to-heart talks had to be undertaken to regain their confidence and acceptance of the situation.

All these things had to be combined with TV and radio appearances several times a week, Press conferences, the writing of articles and the delivering of speeches. Most of the latter, however, were given by Reg Parker, who also underwrote my authority as a disciplinarian.

Not that the 1977 party needed much of the big stick. The nearest we came to a diplomatic incident was when the manager, coach and captain took their tee-shirts off in the sweltering heat while playing at a toffee-nosed golf club. A busy-bodied official dashed half a mile from the club-house to the fifth green to order us to cover up our hairy chests!

For the rest, I can assure the British public that our men were superb ambassadors for their country. I have known rugby tourists in both codes who behaved like louts at their hotel and pigs at the dinner table. The Great Britain side of

1977 never let itself down. I consider that the unbelievably lavish eve-of-departure dinner thrown for them at Rugby League headquarters in Sydney proved that our players were regarded by their hosts as a bunch of gentlemen.

Mind you, they could let their hair down too. During a couple of days' break from training on a small off-shore island near Townsville the boys hired the local fleet of 'mini-moke' run-arounds. Apparently they treated them like dodgem cars, and were finally recalled to base after reports of burst tyres, dented bodywork and shattered windscreens. A few deposits were lost that day!

Such a grand crowd of men deserved to finish on top of the world, and to my dying day I shall feel bitter about the refereeing error which cost us both victory over Australia in the Final and the title of champions. For once, 'home' refereeing cannot take the blame, since the name of England's Billy Thompson had come out of the hat to do the game.

The crucial moment came comparatively early in the match. A Pitchford try goaled by George Fairbairn, had overhauled Australia's early lead through McMahon's try. Now, near our 25 Stuart Wright cleverly read our opponents' attempt at a scissors move, intercepted, and set off for the line with a ten-yard start over defenders who were in any case committed to going forward.

A try was certain — but to our horror the whistle went as Stuart gathered speed. The reason was obstruction by an Aussie, giving us the penalty. But Australia got the chance to re-group, and our chance of points had vanished.

Billy Thompson later said his blast on the whistle came the moment he spotted the Aussie infringement. Had he held his breath for a split second to look for advantage, as all top referees should, then I know we would have scored at the posts. The conversion would have made it 10–3 and swung the match our way. As the world knows, we eventually lost by just 13–12.

You can't win 'em all. But the World Championship of 1977 was a title that Great Britain could and should have gained.

Afterwards, however, I had to put aside my private chagrin and find words to cheer up poor George Fairbairn. Not only had a misunderstanding between him and Francis let Australia in for a decisive try; our normally dependable full back had missed a 30-yard penalty shortly before full time that could have given us victory. There was a big job to be done rebuilding George's shattered morale, and even at a time of mourning the coach was still earning his pay!

So it was that Reg, myself and the boys returned to Britain as gallant also-rans rather than triumphant world-beaters. But we had done far, far better than expected and could not be branded as failures. A most touching personal moment came when on behalf of all the players Roger Millward presented manager, coach and physiotherapist with silver trays by which to remember our expedition. In their hard, professional judgment at least, management had done its best.

And my reaction to it all? Well, let's be frank, there is no thrill like total involvement in the play: beating a man, scoring a great try or putting in an effective tackle. But the inspiring and manipulation of men, which is what coaching is all about at the top level, rates a close second.

The greatest challenge — and here comes my advice, for what it is worth, to all aspiring coaches — is to forge a team that can dictate the pattern. Too many sides in which I have played, including British Lions, Welsh and Great Britain teams, have said to themselves, 'How can we stop the opposition?' My slogan would always be, 'We'll do it our way. Let the other team do all the worrying.'

In 1977 I was an untried Welshman whom the warm-hearted folk of Lancashire and Yorkshire trusted to make the attempt to put their handling game on top of the world. We did not quite succeed, but I shall always be grateful for that accolade paid to me by the North. It was the final, great proof that they had taken me to their hearts.

It is ironic, and it saddens me to know, that in my own country, wedded to a different code, I shall never get a similar opportunity.

CHAPTER 22

Which Game?

And finally — the sixty-four dollar question: the one people have asked me constantly throughout my career, and which equally regularly I have tried to dodge. Now, I suppose that I really ought to give my answer after six years at the top in Union and another dozen in League: which is the more enjoyable to play? It is time to come off the fence.

Anyone brought up like me in Union, amid all the verve, glamour and intensity of the big Welsh circuit, is in its thrall for ever. There is no experience that quite compares with an International match in Cardiff, Paris or Auckland. Nor at a different level can there by anything more rewarding than one's debut for proud little clubs like Blaina. A man's sporting first love never relinquishes its hold on him.

But view Rugby Union with an unprejudiced eye, and see what happens then. On a visit to Wales my friend Aidan Breen once attended a big club match with me. All he could talk of afterwards were the fifty-three lines out and thirty-two scrums that he had counted — all clearly boring and fruitless in his estimation.

'Why do people pay good money to watch that sort of stop-start rugby, David?' he demanded of me.

It was no good telling him of the craft and strength at maul and ruck of stars like Geoff Wheel and Graham Price, the line out agility of Allan Martin, or the precision of a Gareth Edwards line kick. To his eyes, Rugby Union even at that level was no more than all-in wrestling on the move!

However, Union adherents who see a League game can be equally irritated by our players' dying with the ball, those inevitable moments when the handling game ends up ingloriously on the deck after a runner has made no attempt to avoid a tackle or flip a shrewd pass to a team-mate. Such observers become frustrated by this different kind of 'stop-start' rhythm, especially since they see thirteen, not fifteen, men on the field and, apparently, more space.

So the beauty of each code is undoubtedly in the eye of the beholder. The only way to answer our question — which is the more enjoyable to play? — is to imagine a man from Mars landing on this planet and deciding that he feels like a fling with the oval ball. He notes that one set of rules are used at Salford, another at Swansea. He cannot play both. Which does he choose?

If he has any sense he will ask me to advise him. With twenty-one caps for Wales and the captaincy of the Lions in my career portfolio I have tasted the best the amateur game has to offer. Thus my six League caps for Great Britain, on top of nineteen for Wales, make me probably the best-equipped man in these islands to pass judgment.

I would tell the Martian to play League.

Spectators must choose for themselves, but for total player involvement the northern game narrowly takes the palm. The thirteen men in a League side need all the virtues: stamina, speed, finesse, good handling, good tackling, plus the nimbleness to beat a defender.

And these skills are constantly in use. In League, wingers do not take the field on a cold November afternoon wondering if they will get a chance to warm up. Nor are our forwards taught that the back division are handlers-in-chief. Men like Colin Dixon and John Mantle could tell our Martian of the unbeatable — and *regular* — thrill of thundering thirty yards with the ball under an arm, handing off all and sundry and creating alarm and despondency among defenders!

No, in whatever position our spaceman chose to play, he would know that he had been in a game. Whereas if he got involved in a Union match he might find himself required to scrummage in a front row all afternoon with as many glimpses of daylight as a miner in winter. He could be a wing outside a selfish pair of centres. He could even have been the Welsh stand-off half at Murrayfield that day in 1963 when D.C.T. Rowlands kicked endlessly to touch.

Of course, my advice to the visitor would be to fit in a game of Rugby Union if he had time. But I would warn him that fun cannot be guaranteed. In League it almost always is.

All that is splitting hairs. Unlike our man from Mars I have literally been able to enjoy the best of both worlds (and am only sorry that in the foreseeable future they can never be one). I know, too, that they are good worlds, inhabited by fine races of men.

If you set out to read this book expecting its theme to be 'boy wonder makes good', I hope it will have dawned on you by now that even for so-called top players life is seldom a bed of roses. Remember how they once said that I was too immature for a first International cap. Remember how Wales once decided that they could do without me. Remember my Cup Final disaster with Salford, the disbelief on the part of many that I could make good at the northern game, the threat in 1974 that I would hobble my way through the rest of my life. But the great lesson about life that rugby teaches you is that after the hardest and most painful tackles you must get up and continue the game.

The last tackle, I suppose, is retirement from active participation. It took me a long time to accept that my days at Salford were finally over, and I thank them for the farewell match they set up for me against Swinton, when I took my leave of the Willows with nine goals.

But now I look ahead with a big appetite to furthering my career with Forward Trust, to another relationship I am fostering with the State Express tobacco people to promote Rugby League and other games, and to writing and broadcasting as often as I can on rugby in the eighties and hopefully the nineties.

Sometimes I feel my age. On other days, after an hour spent sprinting on the meadow beside my house, I feel as fit as when I was twenty-one. And frequently, when I sit watching big rugby on television, the thought enters my head that I would love to be at stand-off half for one of the teams.

I'm sure that I could still show Gareth Davies, Ollie Campbell, Steve Evans and John Woods a trick or two!

Epilogue

And finally — surprise, surprise! — a last fling for me during 1979–80 in the colours of Swinton.

I made myself available for the Lions mainly to help my good friend Roy Fisk, a man cast in the mould of Brian Snape. The arrangement was that I would appear in matches when it was convenient for me to travel north — and the cause seemed a good one, if only because Roy had got the club out of the red for the first time in its history. And since Swinton were in Division Two, there was no question of my compromising my loyalty to Salford in my rugby dotage.

The players appeared to welcome me as a sort of a father figure! Certainly in the company of great triers like Gary Fletcher, joker Bobby Bruin and the former Wigan star Kevin O'Loughlin I immediately began enjoying the change to a less demanding level of rugby. Old mates Gordon Graham and Alan Grice soon came on strength too — possibly influenced by my presence at Swinton.

The club, of course, paid me generously for my services. But — truly — I joined them simply for another season's fun, and to meet the challenge of rallying a club that was experiencing hard times.

You may conclude that I must be some kind of 'Rugbyholic'.

And, perfectly frankly, I admit that I am!

Index